The Owl of Minerva

A Memoir

Mary Midgley

LONDON AND NEW YORK

First published 2005
by Routledge
2 Park Square, Milton Park, Abingdon, Oxon, OX14 4RN

Simultaneously published in the USA and Canada
by Routledge
711 Third Ave, New York, NY 10017

First published in paperback in 2007

Routledge is an imprint of the Taylor & Francis Group, an informa business

Typeset in Perpetua by RefineCatch Limited, Bungay, Suffolk

British Library Cataloguing in Publication Data
A catalogue record for this book is available from the British Library

Library of Congress Cataloging in Publication Data
Midgley, Mary, 1919–
The owl of Minerva : a memoir / Mary Midgley.
p. cm.
1. Midgley, Mary, 1919–. 2. Philosophers—England—Biography. I. Title.
B1647 .M474A 2005
192—dc22 2004026169

ISBN10: 0–415–36788–3 (hbk)
ISBN10: 0–415–37139–2 (pbk)
ISBN10: 0–203–02739–6 (ebk)

ISBN13: 978–0–415–36788–2 (hbk)
ISBN13: 978–0–415–37139–1 (pbk)
ISBN13: 978–0–203–02739–4 (ebk)

The Owl of Minerva

For John and Maureen, who shared such a lot of it

Contents

Illustrations

Acknowledgements

The only piece of this book which has appeared before is part of 'Gender queries' from Chapter 24. This was printed in the *Journal of the Oxford Society* for May 1999 under the title 'Trouble with the Zeitgeist', and was reprinted in *Changing English*, Vol. 7, no. 1, 2000 with the title 'Sorting out the Zeitgeist'.

I am grateful to John Bayley for allowing me to quote five lines from a poem by Iris Murdoch in Chapter 4.

I have, as usual, had endless help from my family and friends, and particularly in the tracing of particular details from my three sons and from Ian and Jenny Ground, Claire Lamont, John and Maureen King, Willie Charlton, Judith Hughes, Alexander Murray, Roy Holland and Peter Conradi.

My sons, along with Ian Ground, have also done a wonderful job in helping me to control my word-processor and to thwart its occasional efforts to destroy the whole text.

Foreword

Light, darkness and owls

I have borrowed the owl for my title from Hegel, who is well known to have remarked that, 'the owl of Minerva spreads its wings only with the falling of the dusk'.[1] This is a potent and mysterious symbol that might have various meanings. But the thought for which I want to use it is that wisdom, and therefore philosophy, comes into its own when things become dark and difficult rather than when they are clear and straightforward. That – it seems to me – is why it is so important. And this may help to explain why people like me want to spend so much of their lives on it.

The imagery of the Enlightenment, which centres on the metaphor of seeking light, can, I think, mislead us here. It may seem to demand that we should attend only to what is already clear, turning our backs on everything dark and doubtful. That is surely why many people have supposed that physical science – because it deals with an already defined and limited subject matter – sets us the ideal for all enquiries. The wonderful successes of this science lie in areas that are now brightly lit. The thought of turning away from them to the vast range of other mysteries that surround them can be daunting. So it can seem that all studies ought to imitate these sciences by being brightly lit already, or that these other studies ought to be abandoned.

That same distaste for exploring the darkness also sometimes gives philosophers themselves the impression that they are professionally obliged to stick to familiar problems – ones which already occupy their colleagues – rather than trying to deal with new confusions that are arising around them all the time in the world. This thought struck me lately when I read, in *The Times* for 13 January

[1] It comes at the end of the Preface to his book *The Philosophy of Right*.

2004, an interview with that very bright analytic philosopher Colin McGinn. The interviewer mildly asked McGinn why he and his colleagues never discuss 'the metaphysical questions that most of us ask'. McGinn replied, 'The trouble with *the meaning of life topic* is that people would love to say something about it, but *what can you say that is new, interesting or worth while?*' (emphasis mine). Similarly, in his delightful autobiography *The Making of a Philosopher*, McGinn explains that 'readers in search of a book about eastern philosophy, or Continental philosophy, or "post-modern" philosophy, will not be rewarded by this one. This is a book about philosophy as it is practised today in the university departments of the world and which is now largely the "analytic" kind of philosophy' (p. xi).

The world, however, is surely quite a big place and is often held to include even Europe and the East. Certainly it is true that analytic philosophy is widely taught in it, just as American is spoken all over the world, and probably for rather similar reasons. But that doesn't mean that it's the only kind needed or available. Even in the West itself, departments of philosophy often run courses on other kinds, simply because students want to know about them.

From where McGinn stands, on the linguistic plateau to which Bertrand Russell and G. E. Moore moved English-speaking philosophy a hundred years ago, this whole landscape of wider speculation can hardly be seen at all. I, by contrast, have always lived in this landscape. I have had no difficulty in finding plenty of occupation in various parts of the landscape of meaning – the meaning of life, not just the meaning of words – for most of my working life. I would like to say to McGinn that there is a lot of that landscape left unexplored, waiting for the attention of sharp and benign people like him. From where I now am, I can, of course, see the plateau where he and his colleagues are busy and I can well understand why people might want to go there. I have visited it myself, and I try to keep a telescope trained on it to watch what is happening there. But I don't know of any reason why people should want to stay there for ever.

It seems to me that we have here the old story of the man who keeps on looking for his car keys under the same lamp-post. Someone asks him, 'Is that where you dropped them?' 'No', he replies, 'but it's much the easiest place to look.'

To return, however, to that owl. Owls, being associated with night, are used in many cultures as symbols for two things – first for death, and second, rather differently, for wisdom. Going out in the dark brings danger of death. But, if you have to go out, then it is surely a good thing to have with you a creature that can penetrate the darkness.

On top of this, the bird's binocular gaze and general resemblance to a thoughtful human has probably led people to consider it as a thinker. Thus in many mythologies sages are accompanied by an owl. Minerva – or, to give her her Greek name, Athene – always had this companion, which was why it appeared on her coinage. Indeed, it is possible that she herself was originally an owl-headed goddess. She may have been so partly because crowds of small, ordinary, real owls had always lived on the hill of the Acropolis. Indeed, the proverbial phrase in Greek for doing something unnecessary was 'bringing owls to Athens' as we used to say 'bringing coals to Newcastle'.

I hope I am not infringing Hegel's patent by using his haunting image. The point I am making was certainly an important part of his meaning, though it may not have been the whole of it. I don't think he can have meant (as people sometimes say) that philosophy has no effect at all, that it always comes too late to change anything. He can't have meant that because he has just been describing the appalling effects that *bad* philosophy – philosophy unlike his own – has actually been having on the world, and he wants to offset this damage by his own better doctrines. When he talks of having to wait till night, I think he is pointing out that philosophy has to work indirectly, by changing people's outlook as it makes certain things clearer, not by immediately ordering particular actions.

These are matters for Hegel scholars. But the point is anyway a different one from the one that chiefly interests me, which is that philosophy, in spite of all its tiresome features, is not a luxury but a necessity, because we always have to use it when things get difficult. That is why I have spent such a lot of my life on it, and I hope the story I tell will explain how this has worked.

1

Early Days, 1924–33

Greenford Rectory

I think it is best to begin a story with something that one particularly likes and wants to share. So I shall leave my ancestors aside for the moment and skip hastily over my own early life so as to start real business with our discovery of the garden at Greenford Rectory, the house we moved to in 1924 when I was five.

I have only vague impressions of our life before that move. I was born in Dulwich, in the east of London in 1919, when my father was a curate there. But I remember nothing from that time and I have only faint memories of our life in Cambridge between the ages of one and five, memories so faint that they are now just echoes of echoes. I remember a benign old lodger called Commander Weatherhead who lived on the top floor of our Cambridge house and who sometimes called me and my brother up to show us beautiful little Indian figures and other treasures that he kept in a glass-fronted cabinet. I remember the Pem and the Pot, those elegant little gutters – named after Pembroke and Peterhouse colleges (Peterhouse is Pothouse) – that flow along Trumpington Street. And I remember once being outside King's College Chapel, where my father, Tom Scrutton, was chaplain, in the evening with a number of people, and being told that the others were all going to church there, but that I must go home because I was too small to come in. I remember the height of the chapel soaring over us – twice as high then as now. It seemed very important and I was cross at being shut out from something so serious. If my family had kept up this policy of exclusion, perhaps my religious career might have been different. But the scene stands alone.

I have also some vague memories of our Cambridge house at 3 St Paul's Road. But one of these memories is certainly false, since in it the dark back-hall in which I am talking to Kate the cook – also remarkably tall – seems to be a rocky cave with a distant cavernous ceiling. And I remember, much more clearly, seeing my brother Hugh's small overcoat hanging on the line to dry after he had managed to fall in the water during a children's party which some rash person had held on a motor launch on the Cam. Hugh explained that he had only been trying to show how he could climb up a brass pole that held up the awning, but he had fallen in and apparently a whole squad of fathers had dived in to save him, each thinking that he was their own child, so that there was widespread confusion. I was too small to go to this party, so the overcoat was my only link with that event.

Another incident from Cambridge has left me no memory, but it must have had an effect later. Apparently an acquaintance who met us in the street presented a brace of dead rabbits to the family by dumping them on my pram – something which seemed to him quite normal. On this I am said to have screamed the place down and refused to be comforted. This incident quite likely does account for my lasting dislike of fur, and for a lasting uneasiness about the question of where it comes from, which has played a part in my later concern about the way we treat animals.

So not much remains clearly with me from Cambridge. But it must have got deep into my psyche, because when I go there in later years the place always seems slightly strange and magical, in spite of the threatening traffic. Particularly I am charmed by the way in which street-names are put up in Cambridge. When I see 'Silver Street' in those small, blocky white letters with big serifs on a black background I know that things are all right.

It is in Greenford, however, a little place in Middlesex to the west of Ealing and Southall that the light suddenly comes on in my memory and things become real. Here we have no longer a terrace house in a street, but a red-brick, gabled country rectory, a comfortable house built in the early 1900s, in a big garden with a lot of out-buildings. The demesne is absurdly large and – this is the beauty of it – has been systematically neglected for years. Except for the house, the buildings are out of repair and, since the farming has ceased, nobody is ever going to bother to repair most of them again. So, essentially, we can have them as a playground. There are lots of trees and bushes in the garden, including intriguing ones like a chestnut and an ilex and an enormous Austrian pine, and there is pampas grass, which is excellent both for darts and for plumes. Beyond the garden wall, to the south, is the churchyard, which we can also explore if we want to, containing a lot of tombstones, some of which, unusually, are wooden, and the small but beautiful Early English church with three bells – dingle, dongle, dingle, dongle, dong, dong, dong . . . (Or, for funerals, just Dong. Dong. Dong . . .)

I don't know why it was that the earlier rectors of Greenford, like Fielding's Parson Trulliber, had aspired to be farmers. They had got themselves several fields and a big farmyard on the north side of the house, containing not just a stable, harness room and coach-house which any gentleman might want, but a large woodshed, two small barns, a potting-shed and an unmistakable pigsty. All this was there for us to explore. But Mr Swain, my father's predecessor, had been a more contemplative type and had let it all fall gently into decay. His policy seems to have included the house, where for a long time he did no repairs, merely moving his bed when the rain came through on top of him. (The problem which habits like this set to incoming parsons is known in clerical circles as Dilapidations. It made trouble in *Mansfield Park*. 'Dr Grant and Mrs Norris were seldom good friends; their acquaintance had begun in dilapidations, and their habits were totally dissimilar . . .') My parents, however, must have dealt with these difficulties fairly calmly before we moved in, since, to their credit, I remember no lasting worries or recriminations. It probably helped that Mr Swain, unlike Mrs Norris, was by then tactfully dead.

He had, however, one other effect on my own view of life by his connection with an extraordinary object which stood on the south side of the house, in the rough grass outside the study window. This was a tall narrow hump, perhaps seven feet high, entirely smothered in creepers and rambler roses. It was, we were told, the root of a huge elm tree which had formerly stood near to the house. The rector, it seems, had been writing one day at his study window when he had seen this elm begin to sway gently to and fro, 'So' (said my father) 'being a philosopher, he sat still and waited to see what would happen. And it fell the other way . . .'

I thought, 'This seems to be strong magic – I must find out more about it some day'. That thought was strengthened when, slightly later, I was at school and was being told off, as usual, for not eating my greens. 'You really ought to be more philosophical about these things', said my headmistress crossly. 'What's philosophical?' I asked. 'It's eating up your cabbage and not making a fuss about it', she replied tartly. Strong magic, thought I again. One day I'll have to look into this . . .

Meanwhile my parents, very sensibly, bothered only with the parts of this odd estate that they could use and left us to make what we liked of the rest of it. They civilized the near parts of the garden – which were quite big enough for any reasonable person – and the large kitchen garden, which produced lots of fruit and vegetables – peas, peaches, currants, raspberries, the lot. They also installed a swing and seesaw and later on a hammock, which was strong enough to serve very well as a boat in a terrible storm. But all the rest they left as rough grass, trees and bushes, for our territory. The same went for the most of the outhouses, especially the pigsty. These continued to decay gently to that admirable state where wood doesn't actually fall down, but proves soft enough to be carved on the surface by the creative penknife. The only parts taken over for adult use were the two barns, which were salvaged and joined to form a parish room, and the coach-house, which became a garage in about 1925 when my father, greatly daring, bought a car.

At first this was a solid-tyred Leyland Trojan, but it was soon followed by an even more excitingly up-to-date Trojan with pneumatic tyres. The chief reason for getting this splendid machine was to take me and my brother Hugh the three miles into Ealing when we went to school there. (Before this, some neighbours drove us there for a time in a pony-trap along with their own children, but that turned out to be too slow.) The Trojan had many merits. It was reliable on the whole, and it had one great speciality – a starting-handle that was not in front of the bonnet but down to the right of the driver's seat. Thus my father, unlike most drivers of the day, did not have to run hastily round to the side in the rain and leap in when the engine finally started. He also wouldn't be run over if he happened to leave it in gear. The car was, of course, open, which meant that one got properly blown about and thus fully appreciated the dizzy speed at which it could run, often reaching thirty or even thirty-five miles per hour on good days. It had, however, a hood and talc windows that you could put up if conditions got too frightening.

We travelled to school in the Trojan until, when I was about eight, buses arrived and made this effort unnecessary. (Later still I used a bike.) Here the wider world impinges on the private drama of the rectory. Anyone who has heard the name of Greenford, which is now an unnoticed region of Greater London, must be puzzled to hear it called a country place. That, however, was what it was in 1924. It was then a village with 1400 inhabitants, though ten years later, when we left, it had (I think) 18,000.

In fact, we had moved in just before the flood of semis, mixed with outbreaks of what my parents called bungalitis, rose up and engulfed the plain round the little river Brent. That plain was then just a patch of rural Middlesex, gradually sloping up to Horsenden Hill and Harrow Hill to the north, dotted with small farms and clumps of cottages. It was rather flat, but green and fertile and particularly rich in ponds – indeed parts of it were often flooded. Greenford, however, soon acquired its own railway station on the main Paddington line, so that its inhabitants could go shopping in Ealing and, almost as easily, in London. This connection was probably one reason why so many people soon moved there. It was probably also the reason why its half-dozen big houses no longer housed traditional gentry, who might have acknowledged some responsibility for the village, but contained instead fairly rich people who frequently moved on and took little interest in their neighbours.

At first, then, we lived in a fairly timeless style in a world with very little traffic. I remember how, on Hugh's enterprising suggestion, we climbed one day into one of the row of pollard elms outside the front gate, provided with a store of conkers. Our plan was to throw these at anybody who passed, and then, when they said 'Did you throw that stone?' to reply 'No' because it hadn't been a stone, it was a conker. The beauty of this logic was irresistible, but the scheme proved disappointing because, during what seemed like a long afternoon, nobody actually did pass. I think this may have been the road's normal condition.

Mostly, however, we played in the garden, climbed the trees (especially the walnut, but avoiding the wych elms because we took them to belong to witches), ferociously attacked the nettles by the back fence and built clay fortifications by the muddy stream that ran from the nearest pond. Correctly dressed as Red Indians (for Indians were still red then and wore feathered headdresses, skilfully made by their mothers) we carved passages through the dense thickets of snowberry to ambush invading hordes.

We also spent a lot of time fishing in more remote ponds for newts and other creatures. This occupation fascinated us. With nets and jam-jars, we stalked cautiously round the ponds, peering into the clear, sunlit water to search for movement on the brown land beneath, detecting there the subtle movements of the little Palmate newts or their larger and more exciting cousins the Great Crested ones with orange bellies. Usually they darted away, but quite often we did catch them and put them in our jars. The trouble was, what to do with them then? The whole thing was far less fruitful than it should have been because the adults round us, though sympathetic, were quite ignorant about these creatures and couldn't direct us. We never learnt that newts don't actually live in water all the time and should not be put in an aquarium, even if it has rocks sticking out of the water. We did notice that they often escaped and would be found wandering downstairs or over the sewing-machine, but we never drew the moral that it would actually have been better to leave them where we found them.

Still, the ponds were endlessly interesting. In spring some of them were covered with lovely white flowers of frogbit, and in one of them we found a huge assembly of mating toads whose carnival we watched with awe. From another, more distant, pond we once fished out a drowned book called *The Spiritual Exercises of St Ignatius*. (I still wonder who threw it in.) We took this home and dried it out delightedly in the airing-cupboard, only to discover that the find upset my father, who apparently considered the book to be actively dangerous. This still seems odd, since in general he was ecumenically tolerant, but I think remnants of Romophobia lingered in the background thoughts of most Anglicans at that time.

I once managed to fall into another, and much grander, pond in Kew Gardens, when we made an expedition there. This was due to my chasing a frog and I thought it was going to be a fearful disaster, but it actually didn't turn out badly at all. My parents luckily knew the Director, A. V. Hill, who had been their friend in Cambridge, so I was taken to his house and dried out comfortably in the sun on the leads there while the grown-ups talked in the garden below. But it didn't put an end to my interest in amphibians.

Besides the newts we kept mice in home-made wooden cages and followed their doings with breathless interest, even though I am ashamed to say that, not having space for an infinite number, we usually sold their children back to the pet shop. In fact, in early life we were very zoophilic. But since nobody taught us anything about animals or connected them with other things that seemed to matter, we largely dropped this interest, as many people do, after we were about twelve.

*

For me, the topic suddenly surfaced again when I read Konrad Lorenz's book about animal behaviour, *King Solomon's Ring*, in the early 1950s. Lorenz throws a flood of light on that connection. He shows how close to us the lives of other animals actually are. He dissolves the strange unrealistic stereotype of 'an animal' – something abstract that might just as well be a flea as a gorilla – which our culture has invented to protect mistaken ideas of human dignity by making us seem remote from our whole animal nature. This revelation gave me enormous relief and refreshment, bringing together parts of life which had seemed to be hopelessly separated. I went on to read everything I could get on the subject and it became a central element in my thought.

I suppose this zoophily has some connection with the fact that, when small, I always greatly preferred stuffed animals – bears and dogs for choice – to dolls. In fact I couldn't stand dolls, which seemed to me creepily dead and frozen. People gave me four or five of them, but I hardly ever played with them and I can't even remember their names. With the animals on the other hand I played a lot, building houses for them in corners of the nursery and inventing their complicated life-stories. When I was about eight, I was advised that the time had now come for me to pass on my large teddy-bear to my small cousin Daphne. I saw the force of this reasoning, but I did have to explain it pretty carefully to the bear himself.

We started our education in Greenford – still in traditional style – by sharing a governess with some children who lived at the big cream-coloured Regency house up the hill, by the War Memorial. They were Twink (really Mary) Lawrence and her cousin Teddy Hobson. I think this is where I learnt to read, since I vaguely recollect an alphabet book there, and certainly we did a great deal of copying of rather mysterious proverbs – 'Fair and softly catches the pony', 'It's a long road that has no turning'. (*What* long road? These points were never explained.) The house was beautiful, and it still provides the scenery that I see when I read Jane Austen. We had lessons in the dining-room, which faced out through a big bow-window and a curved veranda onto sloping lawns dominated by a cedar and a large hickory tree. These lawns were big enough for games like French and English and the shrubberies beyond were ideal for Hide-and-seek.

Twink was a brisk and usually amiable blonde who did most of the talking. Teddy, rather quieter, was an impressive figure because his parents were in India (as happened to many children at that time) and also because he had only one eye, having lost the other through careless use of scissors – something which our nurses did not fail to impress on us. I remember Hugh's saying to Teddy, in a rather awestruck voice, something like 'Well you are peculiar. You've got one eye, you're Irish, and you were born in India . . .' He didn't mean any harm and nothing particular followed, but it has stuck in my mind as an instance of the difficulties that beset friendship among children. The idea of asking oneself what a remark is going to sound like to the person who hears it simply doesn't occur to one until a good deal later in life, and, even when it begins to, it takes time to learn what to do about it.

At this point our life may begin to sound rather grand, and it does give me an insight into a slightly alien grandeur, but it didn't stay that way for long. We did have a nanny of our own, a country girl from near Cambridge who had come to Greenford with us and stayed until we went to school. She was a sweetie who was called Hepzibah May Hart, though she tried to keep quiet about the Hepzibah part, which she thought was old-fashioned. I see her like some benign Fate figure, usually occupied with textiles, not actually spinning but sitting at the big table in the nursery placidly turning the handle of the Jones sewing-machine (which was later passed on to me and still serves my son's family) or sometimes washing and ironing. There were, of course, no washing-machines and most of our clothes were made at home. Also we had the church washing to do – vestments and lots of little things called Purificators, with which the priest used to wipe the chalice. (No doubt he now uses Kleenex.) These things needed a lot of ironing. Both my mother and Hepzibah May spent a good deal of time on these matters.

We all got on well with the Lawrences' nanny, who was, however, a rather sterner and more professional figure than ours, since she had full charge of the children all the time. In upper-class style, Twink's parents – quite unlike ours – often weren't in the house at all, and rarely visited the nursery, where a baby, Nona, was looked after as well as Twink and Teddy. Twink's mother, a mysterious fragrant presence in a fur coat, did sometimes appear, but I don't remember ever seeing her father, Lord Lawrence. Teddy, Twink and Nona shared a large but cosy night-nursery with their nanny, who had a huge bed with brass knobs on the corners – a bed so big that several of us would be put to rest on it after lunch, where we took a great interest in unscrewing the knobs.

Nona's pram gave us all a great experience once when we were overtaken by heavy rain while out for a walk. The nannies packed several of us into the pram, put up the hoods at both ends and raced home with it, so that we bounced all the way there in the dark, shrieking with delight. I suppose we didn't squash Nona, or something would have been said about it. Twink also had a much older brother called John, who occasionally appeared and impressed us deeply by taking eight lumps of sugar in his tea. The absence of adults in this family was rather soothing and allowed us to explore many parts of the house that would otherwise have been out of bounds. I remember an excellent game of Shipwrecks – climbing round the room without ever touching the floor – carried out in what must surely have been the billiard-room, without any apparent awful consequences.

Besides Nanny we always had some servants – a housemaid, a cook and a charlady – as well as a gardener for our big garden. Thus all my life I have been cosseted in this regard, which obviously distorts my notions of reality to some extent. The large staff may sound absurd today, but since there were no microwaves or washing-machines or ready-made convenience foods they all had plenty to do, and my mother would not have been able to do a lot of useful work in the parish without them.

My family's relations with the maids always seemed natural and amicable enough but they weren't particularly close. This may have been partly because though the rectory was big it was divided in a way that gave both parties some privacy. Instead of the attics and cellars between which servants in typical tall London houses oscillated so exhaustingly it was a two-storey house with a distinct wing at the side housing the kitchens, pantries, storerooms, etc., and the maids' bedrooms above, behind baize doors with a separate staircase. This wasn't a complete separation – we came into the kitchens often and games like Hide-and-seek, for instance, went on up and down both staircases – but it made for two distinct social centres.

In the early days I spent quite a bit of time with the maids, sometimes having tea with them in the big comfortable kitchen, and later I was often there helping my mother with jobs such as making jam or bottling fruit. I do clearly remember our first two maids, Florrie and Eva, whom I liked. They were both local girls. But of the various other pairs who succeeded them in turn, and who mostly came from a distance, I can only recollect one – a pair of Welsh sisters called Winifred and Eveline who were memorable because of their dazzling red hair. They had come to us because times were hard in the Rhondda coalfield, and after being with us quite cheerfully for a time they found other jobs which they preferred to domestic service. I think that, like them, most of the other pairs lasted only a few years. This indeed was the normal course of things during the 1920s and 1930s. Women drifted steadily away to kinds of work that had been opened to them during the First World War, and those who remained would no longer put up with conditions that had prevailed in domestic life for centuries. This led many middle-class women to grumble obsessively about their discontented servants in a way that my mother thought was fairly silly. What (she asked) did they expect?

After we moved to Kingston when I was fifteen we had only one maid, and eventually, during the war, my parents ended up with just a charlady, an admirable Mrs Hall who became a dear friend. After my marriage I had a succession of charladies, ending up with wonderful Rachel, a local lady who remained with me for nearly thirty years till she lately retired. Now I have girls from an agency, usually different ones each time – two of them who appear weekly for an hour like a flight of exotic birds and work like whirlwinds for an hour, babbling cheerfully the while in a succession of languages. I have had to give up trying to find out whether this week the language is Bulgarian, Colombian or Portuguese, and even whether this lot are students or asylum seekers, because I'm getting too deaf to be sure of hearing the answers. Maybe these girls shouldn't be there, but I'm very grateful to have them.

Starting school

When lessons with the governess ended, we both went to school in Ealing. Mine was called St Leonard's, 109 Uxbridge Road. It had about seventy pupils, mostly girls but with some small boys. This place was also something out of a past age, but from a quite different social stratum. Two middle-aged ladies in reduced circumstances, the Misses Bowden, ran it in their own house, carefully stacking their more fragile furniture in corners early every Monday and bringing it out again at the weekends. Coming for a piano lesson on a Saturday, one saw the drawing-room restored to its full Victorian glory of little tables and knick-knacks and had to be careful not to knock anything over.

Miss Annie, who wore a green overall and had her hair done up in a cottage-loaf on top of her head, was the very capable headmistress and did much of the teaching. Miss Helen, with her hair scragged back in a bun, kept house and did the cooking. This was unfortunate because she hated cooking and didn't think much of children. Most of the time she was in a simmering state of bad temper.

I don't think Miss Annie or most of her staff had ever seen the inside of a college, but they were mainly excellent teachers. As long as I stayed at that school, I got on well with Mathematics and Latin, both of which were taught by letting us work through examples on our own, only going up to the teacher if we had a difficulty. I suppose this can only have succeeded because discipline was actually very good, so that we got on with our work and didn't disturb each other. But the remarkable thing about it was that one seemed to keep two strands of attention going at once – hearing the explanations that were given to other people at the same time as getting on with our own problems.

This raises thoughts about how schools used to be kept in the days when several classes were taught at once in a single big classroom. At one time Miss Annie taught my class Latin at the same time that she taught some bigger girls about mythology. She set us going with our Latin exercises at the back of the room and then talked to the ones at the front about Demeter and Persephone and the rest. I took in both things at once quite comfortably. I don't think I could do it now, but it's interesting that it was possible.

This rather individual way of teaching probably fitted in well with another feature of the place which made it quite different from today's schools. There was absolutely no sense of competition. We had no exams, no lists of ranking order in class, and I don't think we ever thought about our position there. This meant that people could be moved from one class to another easily without causing comment. Thus, when I was about ten, I and a girl called Leah Levy were shifted to a class containing girls who were about two years older than we were. Nobody suggested that this was done because we were particularly clever or hard-working – it just seemed to be a matter of convenience. I suppose that in fact we had got ahead with our work to the point where the move seemed sensible. Our new companions showed neither admiration nor resentment when we joined them; they just thought that we were rather funny – we looked alike, both having straight dark hair and glasses. But their amusement was not unkind, and as there were two of us this did us no harm. Incidentally, nobody took any special interest in Leah's being Jewish either – in fact it took me some time to notice that she was so.

A much more important thing that did happen to me at this stage was falling in love for the first time, which I did with proper suddenness – right off a cliff and without the slightest warning. This is the experience that Cherubino tries to describe in *The Marriage of Figaro*. People who haven't had it tend not to believe in it, but I can assure them that it is real. There was I, sitting at one side of a long table, quietly listening to a Geography lesson and doing (as they say) nobody any harm, when suddenly the world was filled with a wonderful and quite unaccountable light and warmth. Trying to make out where this radiance came from, I gradually realised that it centred on Daphne, who was sitting opposite. We beamed at each other and the Geography lesson went on. Further experience showed that she carried this light and warmth about with her so that it followed her when she went away, leaving behind a kind of cold and darkness that had not been known before.

I don't think that the physics of this strange phenomenon has ever been fully explained, but it makes a lot of trouble for people like me and Cherubino. Regardless of fashion, I have gone on doing it for much of my life – and, since you ask, after leaving school, always with men. I wish I understood it better. There is probably something to be said for starting on it early in life, as I did, so that you do at least get used to it rather than suddenly being hit by it in adult life, as some people apparently are, without any warning.

Among the advantages of this school was that we were taught grammar – grammar of the invaluable traditional kind which linguists now despise but which is actually indispensable when you are trying to learn an inflected language. We learnt it by a game which involved becoming a particular word and having to find your proper slot quickly among the various parts of speech. This is easy if you are something straightforward like *bucket* or *slowly*, but much trickier if you are an awkward word like *always* or *neither* or *between*. But we got very good at it, and my goodness was I grateful for it later when I was struggling with Latin and Greek.

Another good feature was fairly frequent visits to Sights, such as the Tower and St Paul's Cathedral, and to various museums. It was when they took us to the Natural History Museum that I had the experience of seeing that evolution was real. Strangely, this didn't happen when we saw the big dinosaurs near the entrance, but upstairs, in a smaller room, when we got to the Megatherium – the Giant Sloth who still stands there, reaching hungrily up to munch his tree. Perhaps because he was of a more manageable size than the dinosaurs, it suddenly came through to me on that dark winter afternoon, with the light failing, that these bones had indeed actually done then just what they were doing now – that they were the very bones of a sloth who had gone about his business among distant trees so long ago. I began to glimpse the endless panorama of history. (Miss Annie, incidentally, didn't seize this opportunity to make sure that we were orthodox on the subject of Creation. Perhaps she didn't think this was necessary.)

Yet another experience that was very important to me was being taught about perspective. Our drawing teacher showed us how, from the front window of number 109, you could look straight up the street that ran away opposite and see people getting smaller and smaller at an astonishing rate. Holding a pencil out in front of us at arm's length, we measured how incredibly small these pedestrians managed to get before they fortunately vanished over the hill, and also how the road itself got narrower. On another occasion, too, she set a chair on the table and showed us how cleverly its various parallel lines all converged until they met, neatly and reliably, exactly on the eye-level. She also asked us to look what colour the white paint on the window-frame was when you saw it next to the sky, and we found to our surprise that it was purplish-grey.

This lesson was one of the things which made life begin to become slightly more comprehensible to me, sorting out some of the extreme confusion that surrounds one in early childhood. Its value went far beyond its usefulness for drawing and painting, though I have always loved doing that. Grasping how perspective worked made it clear that things really do look different according to where you stand – yet they are still really the same things. It showed how amazingly large these differences sometimes are – a point which is not easily grasped until you take your pencil and actually measure them. It showed that this difference of individual perspectives is not just baffling and random, not just a hopelessly confusing fact of life, a destructive spanner in the works of comprehension, but something that you can, if you work at it, actually understand. This connection between drawing and thinking is not just a literary fancy but something central to my thought.

I think this is probably why I find that I often find that I prefer to put landscapes, and ones that show vistas to remote horizons, on the walls of my rooms. This isn't at all a deliberate policy, but I have ended up with a lot of them, including a reproduction of Bruegel's *Hunters in the Snow*, which lately arrived above my bed.

The catch about this singular school lay in its background ideology, which was very different from that of my parents. St Leonard's was intensely bourgeois, conservative, fundamentalist and much occupied with sin. Miss Annie's Scripture lessons took us carefully through the Book of Judges and other fierce parts of the Old Testament, noting with regret – but also with a certain satisfaction – how incessantly the Israelites, and most others involved, had made it necessary for the Lord to punish them. I specially remember her slight apology about the case of the man who was struck dead for accidentally touching the Ark of the Covenant. She explained that this might seem a bit hard, but, if you have a rule, it never does to start making exceptions.

The Bowdens were an Anglo-Indian family, the father having probably been in the Indian Army. They were making out with some difficulty on a small income and (my parents said) were also supporting several ne'er-do-well brothers. Like the people in Cranford, they made a virtue of genteel poverty, considering economy to be good taste and extravagance – such as putting the gas-light on when you didn't actually need it or eating butter as well as jam on your bread – to be vulgarity, which they denounced sharply. (I have to say that – though I now eat butter as well as jam – I have always kept this thrifty bias, which was intensified later by the war. Waste, when it isn't even fun, does annoy me.)

However, they had other ideas which had less point than thrift. They considered a lot of rather surprising things to be vulgar, such as looking out of the window in such a way that you could be seen to be doing so from the street, so that we often found ourselves in trouble even when we didn't know we had done anything wrong. Altogether I think they sustained their hard life by a good deal of denunciation. The General Strike in 1926 made them furious. And I well remember, at the time of the Jarrow hunger marches, Miss Helen's declaring that the whole thing was a fraud, exclaiming fiercely, 'No man is ever unemployed if he's willing to work'.

Their mother, who did not teach but pervaded the place, was surely a witch. Small and virulent, she was usually occupied in reading the Bible or pamphlets from the British Israelites or the Protestant Truth Society. She came down on me once out of the blue when I had just accidentally knocked a hat off a peg and was bending down to pick it up. 'I saw you!' she shrilled, pointing a trembling finger at me. 'You deliberately knocked that hat down. You did it on purpose and you were just going to kick it!' Denial seemed hopeless so I let things ride, but it all added to a slight general sense of bewilderment and apocalyptic danger. My parents explained to me that the Bowdens held rather peculiar views on some subjects, so I tried not to worry too much about such things.

On much more reasonable grounds, I was constantly being told off, both then and throughout my school life, for being disorganized – clumsy, muddled, ill-equipped, untidy and late. When scolded for these faults I often grew upset and cried, but at this Miss Annie would say sadly, 'Crocodile's tears, Mary, crocodile's tears'. She had noticed – as I had myself – that, despite the tears, I seldom became reformed afterwards. Later, when my sons went to school, I found that they too seemed to produce much the same astonished indignation in their teachers about faults of this kind. There was the same sense that this was a grave psychological emergency, that nothing like it had ever been seen before, and that, if something wasn't done about it immediately, final disaster would strike.

In the end, all of us became more or less tidied up, and I am not sure what effect the scolding had on the process. The trouble about it is that it tends to make one think of order as an alien standard which it would be hopeless even to try to reach. Untidiness and carelessness are a real nuisance, and of course scolding children for them does make their exasperated elders feel better. But I don't know if it makes any difference to the speed at which a child learns to control its possessions. One difficulty is that schoolchildren have an extraordinary number of these possessions to deal with. If grown-ups had to manage this constant stream of gym-shoes, hats, gumboots, homework books, sports equipment, paint-boxes and all the rest of it, I doubt whether many of them would escape punishment. I get the impression that this problem has, if anything, got worse rather than better during my lifetime because even more occupations, needing their own equipment, seem now to be provided for children. Perhaps they should just be supplied with a simple loincloth and begging-bowl during this stage of their lives. Then things might be easier.

Since I lived so far away, I had lunch at school, along with a dozen other children and teachers. Here the conversation was quite good, but the food was desperate. Miss Helen took out her depressed outlook on life in savage curries, burnt pastry, tasteless tapioca, peppery beef sausages and – once – in some memorably awful cold boiled cod and beetroot. On that occasion I managed to be sick, thus saving myself from having to eat it again.

But we played good word-games, usually started by Miss Annie, and discussed the meaning of life in ways that often had nothing to do with sin or Creationism. It was, of course, at lunch that she told me to be more philosophical. I also remember something striking that she said when I had complained that I knew the answer to some question but I just couldn't say it clearly. 'If you can't say a thing clearly', she replied, 'then you don't actually know what it is, do you?' This is a deep thought which I have often come back to, and it is in general a useful one. It lies at the heart of British empiricism. Though it is not by any means always true, I am glad to have had it put before me so early in life. It's a good thought to have when you are trying to clarify your own ideas, but a bad one when you are supposed to be understanding other people's. Philosophers are always complaining that other people's remarks are *not clear* when what they mean is that they are unwelcome. So they often cultivate the art of *not* understanding things – something which British analytic philosophers are particularly good at.

Moving on

Meanwhile, at home, the cast of my drama was dwindling. When we went to school, Nanny left us. Then Hugh, aged about eight, went to boarding school, duly equipped with a trunk, an iron-bound play-box and a small bowler hat. It now seems to me fairly daft to send children away at this age, when they obviously still need their parents and other familiar people. However in later life he maintained that it was all right, indeed much better than the school he had been at in Ealing. This may only say something about the Ealing school, but I think that St Edmund's School in Hindhead, where he went, may have been more humane than some others. He certainly didn't complain at the time. But he was now absent except in the holidays, and soon after he went the Lawrences moved away. I had plenty of school friends, especially Leah, but since they lived in Ealing they were not neighbours and there were few other children nearby. Altogether I was now left a good deal on my own and I drifted into doing a good deal of reading.

This must, I think, have been the time when I became a fiction addict, always absorbed in some story or other to an extent that mystifies people who don't share the weakness. I remember noticing how far this involvement went once at boarding school when I was about fourteen. During the morning break between lessons, I had rushed up to get my bun and hurried back with it to the library to catch up on *Pride and Prejudice*, where I had just got to the crisis about Lydia's elopement. Devouring the story, I found it quite impossible to abandon that crisis for what is laughingly called the real world. I knew the time for the next lesson was coming, but I couldn't stop for it. I ended up being shockingly late.

Afterwards I took myself to task, saying, 'Dammit, the end of this story is settled already. And anyway it is only a book . . . How can it matter so much?' But somehow it continued to. And I remember two occasions – both, I think, when I was about fifteen – when I started on a novel at bedtime and was literally unable to stop reading it until, bleary-eyed and desperate, some time in the small hours I reached the end. One of these books was Robert Graves's *I, Claudius*, the other was Axel Munthe's *Story of San Michele* – a novel which was a wow at that time, though I'm told it has become quite unreadable today.

It is only in late middle age that a slight change has come on, namely that I now prefer true stories – biographies and memoirs – to most new fiction. Many of my contemporaries seem to find this happens to them too. There may well be various reasons for it but one reason is probably a diminishing willingness to go through so much agony again. After a certain number of novels, one does, after all, know roughly what is going to happen. Thus, on looking at the first pages of Tom Wolfe's obviously admirable novel *Bonfire of the Vanities*, a veteran like me quickly spots the fearsome pile of boulders ready to roll down on the head of that miserable young speculator in financial futures. There isn't much suspense about it. The question then is: are you prepared to stand by this character, to go through with experiencing his catastrophe? And, as life goes on, you somehow get less inclined to answer YES! YES! More agony please!

Of course this reluctance has something to do with whether you take to the particular character in the first place. I didn't like that speculator much, nor indeed does Tom Wolfe. But I think it also has something to do with simply having had enough of misfortunes – at least, of familiar kinds of misfortunes. Disasters tend to look more seductive and exciting in one's youth than they do later on. Anyway the result was that, though I love Tom Wolfe's journalism, I still don't know just how that particular Nemesis got the speculator. I never bothered to finish that story, nor a lot of others that have also been praised to the skies.

Yet this change doesn't stop me incessantly reading biographies and histories, and there are some new novels, even alarming ones, that I still rush through eagerly. These are often ones that display strange ways of life convincingly, rather than concentrating on familiar kinds of personal troubles. One of these was Tracy Chevalier's book *Girl with the Pearl Earring*, about goings-on in the family of Vermeer. Another was Barbara Kingsolver's story *The Poisonwood Bible*, which is about a family of American fundamentalist missionaries set down in a remote village in the Congo. Somehow she shows the two remote cultures that clash here as solid and real – not just worked up to make a book. And the characters are ones that you really want to stay with. Thus the reader is transported to a new place, and previous reading doesn't get in the way at all.

A crucial point in these novels is that we get to see things from other people's points of view as well as that of the central character. The author isn't simply retelling his or her own story but trying to look at the whole situation. David Lodge is particularly good at this – indeed, his central interest seems to be in understanding the bizarre gaps between the ways in which different people see the world. So long as novelists like these keep on writing, I probably shan't have to give up reading fiction.

At this same time, I also read a lot of poetry – mostly narrative poetry. My parents' bookshelf, which I raided freely, contained, along with Kipling and Stevenson and Poe and Dumas and Charlotte Yonge and the Brontës and Mark Twain and Wodehouse and Sherlock Holmes and M. R. James, two fat red volumes of verse by Longfellow and Scott. I went straight through *Hiawatha* and – still better – *The Saga of King Olaf*:

> . . . That was Norway breaking
> From thy hand, O king!

I even read *Evangeline*

> This is the forest primeval. The murmuring pines and the hemlocks . . .

though I didn't think much of it. (Why are hexameters no good in English though apparently they work quite well in German?) In Scott I liked *Marmion* and, still more, *The Lay of the Last Minstrel*, with the mysterious Elfin Page who creates general mayhem by falling down out of nowhere crying, 'Lost! Lost! Lost!' Then there were the *Lays of Ancient Rome*, and Lewis Carroll on *Hiawatha's Photographing*, and Hilaire Belloc and the *Ingoldsby Legends*, with the bit about the curse that caught the unlucky Jackdaw of Rheims:

Never was heard such a terrible curse!
  But – what gave rise
  To no little surprise –
Nobody seemed one penny the worse.

It was these narrative poems that got me into the habit of poetry. I also had a book that contained other, non-narrative ones, such as *The Burial of Sir John Moore*, which I liked as well. But something quite different happened when, aged about eleven, I was sitting under the ilex tree in the garden and read Keats's 'Ode to a Nightingale'. The passage that startled me then was the same one that has had this effect on a lot of other people, and it isn't clear what it is that is so extraordinary about it. It was:

. . . The same that oft-times hath
Charmed magic casements, opening on the foam
Of perilous seas, in faery-lands forlorn.

I think the point probably centres on the sense of real danger – *perilous* and *forlorn* are seriously meant. They mark the issues at stake. Anyway, that moment, like the moments involving Daphne and the Megatherium, somehow shook the world open for me and started quite new possibilities. I think it was probably about the same time that my brother Hugh discovered pictures, which went on to take the same kind of place in his life that poetry did in mine.

Both of us were partial to history, and later on, when we were both students, my mother was exasperated to find that we had loaded the family luggage, on a holiday at Weymouth, by packing, separately, two distinct copies of Gibbon's *Decline and Fall*. I doubt if either of us read very much of it, but I think that was when Hugh did a very good drawing of 'Gibbon Entertaining a Doubt' – 'I have always entertained some doubts . . . '. The doubt was a question-mark sitting on the edge of its chair and nervously sipping tea.

Greenford growing

In the supposedly real world, meanwhile, the main thing happening in our childhood at Greenford was the steady onset of the speculative builder. First, two houses appeared to the south, between us and the Lawrences. At first these were always known as the New Houses. Then suddenly, in the other direction, there was a whole new row next to the station. Next again, opposite the first New Houses a complete new road called Eastmead Avenue boldly branched away from ours. This road was intriguing because it was lined with a most varied population of bungalows. It was also alarming because it was so badly surfaced. Indeed it could scarcely be said to be surfaced at all since there was little substance between the puddles, and bicycling there became a demanding art. Evidently the advertisement for this project had laid great stress on the offer of charming, individually crafted homes and had forgotten crude practicalities.

After this start, road after road branched out at all angles, rather in the way that needles of ice spread across a pond when it is freezing quickly. My parents, in trying to help the new arrivals, were constantly having to add new territory to their map. To save time, they often asked Hugh and me to bicycle over with messages to these pioneers, who seldom had telephones. We did this, carefully skirting the puddles, and often got lost. I remember Hugh's coming back from an exploration to report that he had accidentally found a whole new road which was called Uneeda Drive. 'Ah,' said my father, 'I expect they'll call the next one Butulavta Walk.'

We were often accompanied on these journeys by the family dog – a benign, tough, old-fashioned terrier called Scotty. He was supposed to be a Cairn, but no one at Cruft's would have recognized him as belonging to that or any other particular breed. He was twice the size of our grandmother's cross little Cairn Donald and far, far nicer – in fact a most affable and thoughtful dog. For some time the lack of traffic allowed him to accompany us when we went bicycling, to the satisfaction of all parties. Scotty did, however, have one unfortunate vice. He loved chasing motorbikes, objects which came onto his horizon after we had been for some little time at Greenford. He clearly saw them as a heaven-sent new life-form, filling a long-felt need in his soul for a prey really worth chasing. Though he was small, he ran so fast and barked so threateningly that occasionally the unlucky riders did fall off their machines. When this happened he didn't eat them – indeed he never ate anybody – but we realized that the practice wouldn't do and we did our best to put a stop to it.

When Scotty died, we tried to replace him but found that this was impossible. Such dogs were no longer to be found. An alleged Scotch terrier, bought from an approved kennels and provided with a long pedigree, looked much more like what they have at Cruft's, but he had poor health and had only a short life. So did a second one whom we bought to replace him. My mother then turned to a Dachshund, who did much better but – of course – always had troubles with his unduly long back. What breeders have done to dogs seems to me quite horrible and I have never tried to own one since. But I still think that dogs and other companion animals play a central part in human social life, which is seriously impoverished without them.

To return to the human scene. It soon became clear that most of the people who bought this crop of new houses had not read the small print on their agreements, if indeed they had been given any. The builders quickly sold the houses, often before they were built, but they took much less interest in making them habitable.

Roads, drains, lighting, electricity, gas, telephones and the rest of what we now call infrastructure limped helplessly behind the upcoming stream of semis. I remember a big board that advertised houses to be built, priced from £600 upwards, the deposit being only £5. Naturally they sold like hot cakes, though their proposed site was a field that often flooded in winter. And even when the houses stood up, the people who moved into them had no place where they could easily meet. At first there were seldom even any shops. 'For goodness sake', groaned my father, 'couldn't they at least build a pub or two?'

My parents responded by doing all the visiting and advising that they could, trying always to put people in touch with each other. At first there was hardly anybody else around trying to do this work, so I think that perhaps even people with a deep general distrust of Christianity would allow that they were doing a necessary job. This was the time when our barns were made into a parish room and my mother started a Women's Fellowship there. (She carefully avoided making it a Mothers' Union, since that institution was then still occupied in denouncing birth-control.) From that time on a fairly steady stream of tea, lemonade, buns and other provisions crossed the yard from our kitchen for all sorts of functions there, and we got used to running errands for these as well.

In summer, too, the stream of nourishment flowed out of the house the other way, southwards down the little path to the churchyard where lively parties assembled to clear and tidy the long grass round the graves. This needed a lot of hands and a lot of shears, as well as other tools when awkward corners had to be turned or fences mended. (A lawn-mower cannot steer round graves, nor will it clean the stone or pull out saplings.) All the year round, too, there were flowers to be put in the church and there was decoration to be done for occasions such as Christmas and Harvest Festival – a delightful art at which my mother was skilled, and where she found good helpers.

I get annoyed by novels like Barbara Pym's, where parish life appears as a pattern of ancient stereotypes revolving round a ghostly vicar. The people who came in to help my parents were very various and, since most of them were newcomers to the place, they were not particularly old. None of them was there just from habit.

I can't say anything useful in this story about the mysterious topic of Christianity itself. I think it is an extraordinary feature of the world that people's spiritual experiences differ so much – that it is so hard to bring them into alignment. My father was someone who had been brought up with no real religion going on around him at all. But, as a young man, he was suddenly roused by profound, spontaneous, spiritual experiences which determined his whole life, making him enter the church, quite contrary to his upbringing, and keeping him well-satisfied there till his death. Similarly, my headmistress at Downe House, Olive Willis, came from a totally non-religious background and was suddenly shaken into Christianity by spontaneous experience, which again proved central to her life.

These were two very impressive people. They were not neurotic. They were both conspicuously sane, lively, effective and (on the whole, though of course not always) a pleasure to know. Moreover, the kind of Christianity that they offered was imaginative, humane and liberal. I was very happy with it when I was young and I still think that the sense of being part of a vast spiritual world which it provides is an essential dimension of human experience. Attempts to carry on human life without that wider horizon seem to me much like attempts to do without music or laughter.

There is trouble, however, about the details of what goes on in that space. Both my father and Olive Willis thought in terms of a direct personal encounter with God and this was something I did not have. I was worried about this when quite small when saying my prayers, and as time went on it became more and more of an obstacle to the whole conception. Some Dominican nuns once told me that it is not uncommon for women to have this particular trouble about personal encounter, and they may well be right. Indeed Karen Armstrong, in her fascinating autobiography *The Spiral Staircase*, says that she had immense difficulty of this kind about God's not being there. Of course she must have had much stronger motives than I did for persevering in looking for him, since she worked hard at being a nun for five years before giving up. She didn't succeed, yet some people experience this without trying to at all. The mystical tradition in Christianity does make room for a less personal approach, but it's a long way away from the creeds and most people don't get to hear about it. Certainly today I find it much easier to make sense of this tradition, and of Buddhism.

Geoffrey, my husband, had a tremendous experience in his early twenties to which he gave a Christian interpretation, and he became for some years a devout Anglican. But as time went on the Christian doctrines spelt out to him seemed to him to become stranger and the whole framework less usable. Eventually, one day when he was looking at the rule he was supposed to follow (which he had written out himself) he noticed that it started, '7.30. Rise.' '*Rise*?' he thought. Why not 'Get up'? And the whole thing seemed false; he saw that he could not use it.

This sense of falsity – of being cut off from reality, acting in a play that one cannot get out of – was just what used to trouble me too when I tried to get inside that framework. Indeed it has bothered me on other occasions when I have tried to behave better in ways that other people suggested, especially when I tried to do this by making good resolutions. It is an almost physical sense of wrongness – a slight nausea, a feeling of being cut off from solid earth. It's not that it's impossible to make such changes, but you have somehow to find the right place to start.

Besides this temperamental difficulty, however, it has surely been a great misfortune for the Christian churches that they have become so centred on the creeds. This emphasis on certain compulsory doctrines came about in early times for political reasons, when various bishops were contending for power and needed clear slogans to distinguish their parties, and it then formed part of the general politicization that followed on Constantine's acceptance of Christianity as the official religion of the Roman Empire – which was perhaps a real disaster for it. Where religion is used to produce political accord, governments naturally want it to be unanimous, so they are drawn towards heresy-hunting. But besides that, in the past two centuries the whole notion of belief that we use has been profoundly changed. It has increasingly been narrowed to a limited meaning appropriate for science, as if we ought never to accept anything except propositions that have that have been proved in a laboratory.

If we seriously tried to think like this about the rest of life it is not only the creeds that would be in trouble. We are surrounded all the time by matters that are of the first importance to us – for instance the attitudes of those around us – which we know a good deal about, but where we cannot fully explain our knowledge. And what explicit knowledge we do have about them depends greatly on what we choose to attend to. We have to cultivate the art of deciding things sensibly on very patchy evidence. And when we try to talk about things that are greater than ordinary human life we naturally have to speak about them indirectly, using inadequate images drawn from things that are familiar. The ability to handle such images – to understand symbolic meaning clearly – is essential for our inner life all the time, not just in religion.

Certainly we do right to look for the best evidence available, and to check our insights where we see reason for doubt. But the kind of thinking that is involved in doing this on everyday matters is very different from the kind that is used in physical science. We can never get the kind of absolute certainty in these areas that Descartes supposed we ought to aim at. Trying to get it only distorts our thought.

After we came to Kingston, which we did in 1934, my father engaged in a kind of work that related quite closely to these philosophical questions. He then became vicar of Kingston parish church, which stood in the market place, and he took to standing on a chair in the market place after evening service and asking for questions about Christianity. He would get quite a crowd and the results were often interesting. As he said, the two most common questions were, 'Why has the Archbishop of Canterbury got £15,000 a year?' and 'Is everything in the Bible true?', neither of which was hard to answer. Having replied 'no' to the second question, he would explain the history and the meaning of the traditions, and things would go on in all sorts of directions from there. If he found something puzzling he'd say so, and sometimes bring it up again next week. Sometimes he got hostile hecklers, but mostly the questioners were genuinely puzzled. Later on he often used to do these sessions in London, on Tower Hill or at Speaker's

Corner in Hyde Park, where he alternated with other speakers. This work was important to him and I think he did it well.

My mother took to dealing with parish affairs readily and, being basically practical, she was good at it. But the move from Cambridge to Greenford and then to Kingston had been hard on her. In Cambridge she had, for the first time, after a rather narrow upbringing, enjoyed a lot of lively conversation. She had made friends who were interested in all sorts of things, notably in the arts. It was now hard for her to reach these friends, and not too many people in Greenford were interested in much beyond their immediate difficulties or the work that needed to be done locally. The political theorist Ernest Barker had been one such Cambridge friend whom we still saw sometimes. A number of others did sometimes visit, but on the whole the social scene had narrowed.

I would like to say more about my mother. I remember her well enough and I wish I didn't find it hard to think of notable things to say about her. She doesn't generate so many funny stories as my father, but that doesn't mean that she was less important or less fun. When I think about her, I keep getting the impression that often she simply got things right without friction, so there are not so many striking issues to remember. When we were little she used to read a lot of poetry to us, which we loved. I remember only Robert Browning's *Pheidippides* and Elizabeth Barrett Browning's 'A Musical Instrument':

> What was he doing, the great god Pan
> Down in the reeds by the river?

But there was lots more and it must have laid the foundation for what we liked later. She was powerfully moved by poetry. On one occasion, when the Women's Fellowship had a poetry-reading and somebody read Matthew Arnold's poem 'The Forsaken Merman', she was furious with herself because she had simply had to go out and cry. She couldn't stop herself crying, which she would never normally have done at such a time.

In appearance she was tall, willowy and rather graceful, though sometimes shy. Her hair had gone white early; it was white as long as I can remember. She dressed well, in colours that always fascinated me, often blues and greens. I remember, from very early, a dress of hers in Liberty wool voile with a William Morrisish pattern of dark blue, green and purple grapes. And when we all went to watch some grand procession – I think the celebration of George V's Silver Jubilee in 1935 – from the grandparents' flat in Piccadilly, she and I both had new dresses in which I delighted. Both were made of crêpe de Chine patterned in white, mine cherry-coloured, with a pattern of sprigs and tiny Chinamen, hers turquoise, covered with white leaves and butterflies. She took equal trouble about both of them, and I think she was able, that day, to deal effectively with the awkward grandparents and enjoy being there. I felt quite grown-up myself. Thus, with dazzling weather and other harmless guests whom I don't remember, this seemed somehow a landmark day, even though the procession itself – like other such processions – was a bit disappointing because much of it was just marching soldiers.

When we went to Cambridge from time to time my parents had many friends to visit, but my mother also found time to go to Cambridge market, where she got flowers such as stattis and everlastings to dry for winter, and also to a shop in Kings Parade called the Artificers' Guild which sold things like craft jewellery. She never bought much but what she bought was lovely. I still have a silver, crystal and opal pendant of hers which is probably now a significant relic of the Arts and Crafts movement, but which she bought just because she really liked it. I suppose she could probably have done with a good deal more of this kind of thing. She told us once that she had had a bizarre dream in which she had extravagantly paid eight pounds – *eight pounds!* – for an expensive beauty treatment, which had somehow not succeeded and had damaged her pearls. 'The awful thing was', she said 'that Tom was so good about it! He seemed to take it just as a matter of course . . .' She did have an ambition, she said, to be able, one day, to pat a duck. She thought it was such a pity that ducks would get upset if one tried to feel their lovely roundness. And I remember one time in Kingston market when she asked the stallholder, who had (as usual) just sold her some apples taken from the back of the stall, what he was actually going to do with the lovely ones that were on the front of it? This went down surprisingly well.

To counter the limitations of Greenford, we quite often we went to London to meet friends or go to plays. Theatres must surely have been cheaper then, because they were a central part of our life. We used those handy trains to visit them constantly, from matinées in the early days of *Peter Pan* and *Where the Rainbow Ends*, on through Shakespeares and Chekhovs without number at the Old Vic and outdoor productions in the London parks (sometimes rainy) to Aldwych farces, whodunnits, Gilbert and Sullivans and all sorts of new productions. Some of these plays were experimental shows at small theatres, such as the first production of Eliot's *Murder in the Cathedral*, but many were simply West End shows – *Night Must Fall*, *The Corn Is Green*, *French without Tears*. Apart from Gilbert and Sullivan we never went to opera, which I think at that time was pretty expensive. This meant that when I started to do so later it took me some time to get used to the conventions – not to mind people shouting on their death-beds or wasting time singing long arias in emergencies. Now however, I have got quite used to that. I have come to understand that time works differently in these regions and I really love it – including Wagner. Since those wonderful subtitles now resolve one's worries about what the people are on about, I have become a shameless addict of watching opera on television.

We began to visit cinemas too as time went on, though I think this was more gradual. We missed the lush emotional education that many kids enjoyed from Saturday morning shows, no doubt to our lasting disadvantage. I remember seeing some Charlie Chaplin film quite early on and hating him – which I still do, though I love Buster Keaton and Harold Lloyd. Otherwise I don't recollect many films before we started to go enthusiastically to the Academy in Oxford Street for French films in the 1930s – *Carnet du bal*, *La Femme du boulanger*, *Les Enfants du paradis* and the rest. At that time we also discovered the Marx Brothers, Edward G. Robinson and other parts of the current universe. My father, essentially a theatre man, did not, I think, ever get the hang of films, but the rest of us did. And increasingly, as time went on, my mother went to art galleries and exhibitions, to which she also took us. Pictures became her passion and she even took to occasionally buying them – including a haunting Duncan Grant, which I still have, of some lemons on a sunny wall with the sea behind them.

Parental activities

My father's most notable response to the state of Greenford was to stand for the local council in Ealing, where he campaigned savagely – and I think in the end successfully – to get decent facilities extended to the district, despite the usual obstruction from building contractors and their friends on the council. I remember the impressive robes and cocked hat that he acquired as a councillor. The Trojan, too, was kept particularly busy for a while as he constantly attended meetings in Ealing.

I am not sure whether it was at this time that my father became an active Labour Party supporter and an internationalist. He was one as long as I knew him, though he was always moderate and practical and was never in the least attracted to Marxism. I can't remember a time when the household did not take the *New Statesman*, indeed we took Massingham's *Nation* as well before they were merged. Political interests of this kind were a normal background of our lives, taken for granted as unavoidable like the weather. As a result, I still find it hard to remember that many people aren't actually interested in politics at all and regard the occasional intrusion of political events into real life as an unfortunate mistake.

We supported the League of Nations and worried like mad about things like the war-guilt clause in the Treaty of Versailles and the Allies' misguided attempt to extort payment of reparations from Germany to compensate for the expense of the war. Indeed, when I went to boarding school in 1932 I promptly wrote an awful poem about the iniquity of reparations which was put in the school magazine. These worries were actually quite reasonable because the deliberate humiliation and impoverishment of Germany after the First World War was a central cause of the rise of Nazism.

My parents also belonged to various organizations, I think centring on Quaker Relief, which operated abroad. This caused a stream of foreigners to flow through the house. I can't now distinguish what kind of work they were concerned with – I think some of them were missionaries – but they certainly made for variety. I remember a friendly Polish girl called Miss Kotaska who stayed for quite a long time, a number of Africans and an amiable Indian who brought me a pink silk sari – a kind of visitor not often seen at that time.

My father may well have developed these political interests earlier, when he was a curate in Dulwich at the beginning of the war, which was the time when my parents became engaged. He told me how, in 1914, crowds of people in south London were thrown out of work by firms panicking at the declaration of war, and he was overwhelmed with work in running youth clubs and other forms of help for them. So he drew in helpers from Blackheath, where he had been brought up, and these included my mother Lesley Hay and her sister Maud, who also lived there. He and Lesley married in 1916, when he was already an army chaplain.

Early in 1918 he was sent to the Front and spent a couple of months there before he was wounded and sent home. This brief experience changed his life profoundly. It made him a pacifist. As chaplain, he had to try to give the men some explanation of why they were dying and he found no explanation which seemed bearable. His conviction about this only deepened with experience. He always went on campaigning on the matter, resisting warlike bishops, and becoming chairman of the Anglican Pacifist Fellowship, where he worked with Canon Dick Sheppard and Vera Brittain.

On the whole, I still think that my parents' political views were sensible, even though – as they well knew – the political parties that were supposed to be implementing them were often unsatisfactory My father's absolute pacifism, is, of course, rather a special case because pacifism is so peculiarly negative that people often manage to ignore it. If it is to be effective, it has to be combined with convincing alternative proposals for curing the evils that war is intended to redress. And often, by the time the prospect of war arises, things have gone so far that it is hard to see what these would be. However – as my father and his friends used to point out – in the first place war, especially modern war, is so incredibly destructive and makes things worse in so many ways that it often cannot be said to have solved the problems that are supposed to call for it. If making war were not already seen as a normal option – a regular, respectable way of resolving disputes – it is not something that any sensible person would now think of inventing for that purpose. Disputes would be otherwise dealt with. Moreover it is often used on occasions when the disputes themselves are trivial and unnecessary in the first place, as was surely the case with the First World War.

Campaigning against war is like campaigning against torture in that it is negative. But opposition to torture does not get ignored quite so easily because defenders of torture – as such – are rarer than defenders of war. This, however, is a point about the tactics of campaigning, not about the ethics of the matter. And even at a tactical level, politics needs straightforward talk about distant ideals as well as pragmatic talk about means. As Kant pointed out in his book *Perpetual Peace*, avoiding war is not just an optional aim. It is a necessary one which should never be forgotten.

So in general I thought then, as I do now, that he was talking sense in his work. This, however, did not always make him an easy father to live with. It is a real advantage to be able to respect one's father, but there is usually some sort of price to be paid for it. Scrutton family life was by no means awful – on the whole it was quite cheerful. But it was often difficult in a way that, I think, centres on a wide age gap between parents and children – something that is probably commoner today than it was then.

My parents had married late, and so had both my sets of grandparents. Older parents are good because they have more experience of life, and they have often reached a stage where they positively want their children rather than merely finding, with surprise, that they have got them. I think this was true of mine. But the down side of this extra interest is that their expectations tend to be higher, often unrealistically high. So they are more anxious – especially if they have not been used to living with children before.

My mother must, I think, have been reasonably used to children. At any rate she adapted to them well and showed no great surprise at our tiresome ways of behaving. We felt at home with her. My father, however, certainly was not used to them. On top of this, I think he had inherited a bad pattern of negative fathering which seems to have prevailed in the upper classes around the end of the nineteenth century – largely due, no doubt, to boys' being sent to boarding schools. It is said that when George V was told that his sons were terrified of him, and was asked to do something about it, he replied, 'Well of course they are frightened of me. I was frightened of my father and he was frightened of his father before him. It's normal.'

Many small customs, too, tended to keep the generations apart. My mother told me that, when we were in Cambridge, the local ladies were scandalized to see the distinguished philosopher G. E. Moore actually wheeling his children about in a pram. They thought it quite wrong of his wife to make him do this undignified work – 'Not at all right for a man . . .' they said. My own parents and their friends thought this kind of attitude silly, so I was never in the position of having to take it seriously. But they were decidedly ahead of their times in doing so.

My father's father does not really come into this story till we reach the ancestors, but it should be said at once that he was a distinguished lawyer, devoted to his profession and not given to spending much time talking to his sons. Thus it happened that my father, when at school, once bought a fountain-pen on credit, putting it down on his bill. Nothing was said at the time, but when next Christmas came round, his present turned out to be an envelope containing a neat piece of paper on which was written, 'To Tom, from Father, one fountain-pen – With love'.

My father told many such stories, and I am sure that he meant to break entirely with this tradition. But it isn't easy to build up a better pattern. When we were small, he often seemed to be simply embarrassed by us – stiff, puzzled, sometimes disapproving of us and sometimes – what was equally annoying – facetious, teasing us for what we were doing rather than trying to understand it. I think also that, because I was a girl, he found me still more puzzling, and indeed somehow more threatening, than Hugh. His vagueness about girls emerged once on a later occasion, when I was about fourteen, when he told me that my petticoat was showing beneath my skirt. This evidently worried him and he went on to explain that the matter was serious. 'They may do things like that in Paris', he said, 'but we don't do them here . . .'

A thing that particularly infuriated me when we were small was the custom by which, whenever we had done something particularly noxious, we were sent to Daddy in the study, given a talking-to and then solemnly smacked on the hand – not particularly hard, but very formally. I'm sure this ritual seemed like a matter of course to our parents, and it may well have been true (as people often said) that the parents did not enjoy doing it. But the claim that 'this hurts me more than it hurts you' doesn't help. No doubt these parents thought they were doing their duty. But those occasions simply made me incandescent with rage. (I can see just what Bernard Shaw meant by saying that you should never strike a child except in anger – though that too naturally has its drawbacks.) At that time, too he hardly ever touched us except on these occasions – certainly didn't kiss us or come to say goodnight. I was much annoyed on one occasion when some visitor who wanted to photograph us put me beside my father, who then linked his arm with mine. 'You'd never do that normally', I thought crossly.

These patches of mutual incomprehension got rarer as time went on, but in early days I found them quite intolerable. I remember Hugh's once asking me, 'Do you like Mummy or Daddy best?' I was amazed at the question and said at once, 'Mummy of course'. I wish I could recall more of this conversation. I have no idea what had made him raise the matter. At the time I simply found the question absurd. But my intense exasperation and hostility faded away gradually as time went on. No doubt the merely ritual interactions ended and it became easier for the generations to understand each other.

The excessive expectations, however, still sometimes gave trouble. I remember when I was about ten wandering into the sitting-room after supper and starting to read *Punch*, which had just arrived. My father, who was following me, said, 'You know, you shouldn't be doing that sort of thing all the time. It's not a good idea, it's like eating too many chocolates'. Totally enraged, I threw *Punch* down on the floor, shot off upstairs and, still seething, began to go to bed. My mother shortly followed and asked what was wrong. I boiled over at her, shouting, 'I'm not like that; he knows I'm not'. I was only aware of my injured dignity. It didn't occur to me to point out that *I* wasn't the person who had ordered *Punch* to be delivered to the house every Wednesday.

He was being absurd and he should have been told so. I don't know if my mother did manage to tell him this. Perhaps she did. Anyway he never did it again. But he didn't come upstairs and sort the matter out with me. On such occasions the gap between us remained wide. I think I can see now what made him do it when I recollect the sort of vague anxiety which makes one respond with alarm to a child, particularly a teenager, who does not seem to be doing anything particular. There is a mad tendency to say something wild like, 'Why aren't you learning Russian?' This usually passes off with time, but it can make a lot of trouble before it goes.

Other Scrutton relatives

On the whole, I think that Hugh probably suffered more from the age gap than I did. Elder children always tend to get more of this kind of misunderstanding since more is expected of them and they often have to be responsible for younger ones. Besides, Hugh, though he grew quite strong later, had been a delicate baby. He was born in 1917, when the food situation was very bad and for a long time he seems to have been weak. My mother told me that people who saw him in his pram would say to her, 'Ah, Mrs Scrutton, you'll never rear that one'.

In fact he grew to be six foot five and had quite a happy life. He lived into his seventies and had a satisfactory career as an art gallery director, first, after the war, at the Whitechapel Gallery (which he put on the map) then at the Walker Gallery at Liverpool, then in Edinburgh at the National Art Collections of Scotland. But I think he always did have to fight against a certain tendency to despair, a sense that everything was too much for him, which probably came from these early difficulties. As a child, for quite a long time he used to find the arrival of visitors – especially adult visitors – almost unbearable ('Oh *God* – Not *again!*'). Similarly, when I did anything which didn't meet his exacting standards, despair would descend on him ('Oh *God – Mary!*').

This meant that, though in general we got on well and spent a lot of time giggling together, he too contributed – as elder brothers no doubt often do – to my sense of incompetence. I think that a lasting effect of this was to give me a strong sense of the conflict that can arise between criticism and creation – more widely, between thought and feeling – and an even stronger sense of the need to bring them together. This has been a central theme in my approach to philosophy and it still is.

*

In both of us, this sense of incompetence was further increased by our distance in age from our grandparents. As I have mentioned, both these couples had themselves married late, so that they were in their sixties before we came on the scene. In both cases, I think the late marriage was due to the time that was needed for the husbands to establish themselves in exacting careers. My father's parents were engaged for ten years while he made his way at the Bar. (It will be clear by now that this is a thoroughly bourgeois story, containing many Industrious Apprentices.)

By the time we arrived, then, this senior Scrutton household was pretty set in its ways and could not easily accommodate children. We used to be taken to tea at our grandparents' flat, high up in Piccadilly overlooking the Green Park and the Quadriga Monument, where they were looked after by an ancient parlourmaid called – rather confusingly – Young. (There were no other staff – I think meals were sent up from a central kitchen and I don't remember ever having any meal there except tea.) It was a nice flat, lined with blue Morris wallpaper, but it was not very welcoming. 'Oh, you *are* early . . .' exclaimed my Aunt Jane sharply on one occasion as we arrived. No doubt my mother had taken special pains to avoid being late, but no pains ever enabled us to get things right there. Perhaps indeed, whatever we might have done, we could never have done so. This was partly for reasons that will emerge later and partly because the senior Scruttons had apparently frequented a rather grander circle in Blackheath than my mother's family did.

No doubt in principle they wanted to know their grandchildren. Their theory was that they would begin to do this when each of us became sixteen, by inviting us, from that age, to stay with them on their annual holiday at Sheringham. My eldest cousin Pen did indeed get this visit for a couple of years and Hugh got it for one. But by his account it didn't amount to much, and at that point our grandfather died and the whole project lapsed. It now seems to me remarkable that we didn't share more of our theatrical expeditions with them, and particularly that none of us was ever invited to share the box at the opera that my grandfather regularly had both for Wagner seasons and for Gilbert and Sullivan. I think this must have been one more sign of the unacknowledged coolness that divided the generations.

In general the only time when they seemed to find us digestible was during a festivity which occurred every year at Christmas, when they always dined with us, along with my aunt and my uncles and cousins, and afterwards played all sorts of games – Charades, Dumb Crambo, Up Jenkins and an uproarious card game called Racing Demon. Surprisingly enough, this was always a great success. A splendid vein of dramatic talent emerged – a talent which is, I think, often found in families that are otherwise distinguished in the law and in the church, since drama plays a central, and quite legitimate, role in both occupations.

All Scruttons were great in Charades and Dumb Crambo, but the stars were my grandfather and my otherwise unapproachable Aunt Jane. I wish we could have tapped this vein at other times, but we somehow never seemed to get the chance. At the tea-parties, similarly, my grandfather would sometimes be very funny and would then get into a double-act with Granny who would sit giggling and saying, 'Oh, Ted . . . don't be so ridiculous'. But this somehow never led to anything further.

Aunt Jane had, in her youth, been a student at Girton where she read history, and during the First World War she had been a volunteer nurse. After that, however, she simply lived at home, and I think it is clear that this didn't agree with her. After her parents' death she blossomed out surprisingly and acquired a considerable social life. She had always had theatrical friends, including Bernard Shaw and Barry Jackson, and she now became a member of the Council of the British Drama League and also Churchwarden of St James's Church in Piccadilly. This was the time when she researched the family history and put it in a book – thus kindly giving me material that I shall use on the important topic of Ancestors. I wish I had talked to her more about it then.

One thing that I do remember her mentioning is that, in her grandparents' generation, all the family had talked broad cockney. I wish I knew whether their children's shift to BBC English resulted from a deliberate effort or was just an unconscious part of a wider change at the time.

More relatives: the Hays

My mother's parents, the Hays, were quite a different matter. They were very friendly and we visited them often, both at first when they lived in St John's Wood and later, for much longer stays, after they bought a country house called Flimwell Grange, near Hawkhurst in Kent. The St John's Wood house was a tall cream-coloured villa which delighted us by having, in its upstairs bathroom, a ceiling papered in black with a pattern of stars, really looking quite like the night sky. It also had a double drawing-room which was interesting because one could hide in the curtains which divided the back from the front half – and indeed in the window-curtains, which were voluminous.

Flimwell Grange however played a much larger part in our lives. We went there constantly and loved it. It was a big white Edwardian house with twiddly bargeboards on the gables, large grounds, a rather bumpy tennis court, a big garden, ponds – again, but this time fringed by bamboos – and mysterious surrounding woods. It stood in the Kent countryside which was full of orchards and hop gardens, with their oast-houses still in use and half the population of east London coming down to pick the hops each August.

Whenever I read a standard detective story, this is the house that I still see. It perfectly supplies the scenery against which I watch the crowd of incompatible guests assembling as the clouds gather and the snow begins to fall in the first chapter. (I should probably apologize for keeping on mentioning my limited mental imagery like this, but when I cast my mind back to these days I can't help noticing it.) I'm afraid that the Flimwell house fell short of those in the stories because it didn't actually have a library, though it had plenty of books. But it did have a morning-room, a billiard-room – where we actually played billiards – a lot of comfortable bedrooms, three maids, many attics and a large conservatory. For a time, it even had a butler.

More important than these things from our point of view, however, it had a couple of dogs – Donald, the cross little Cairn, and Jerry the big tolerant Cocker Spaniel – with whom we could walk for ever through the Bedgebury woods. I remember one splendid walk in the snow when we kept having to stop and break off the neat round snowballs that formed on Jerry's long hair, creating an almost perfect ball-fringe. These dogs were quite friendly on walks, but indoors Donald's sense of dignity forced him to stand stiffly on tiptoe several times a day emitting deep lion-like growls, which Jerry never bothered to notice. At dinner time another ritual emerged. Each dog was always so intent on getting some of his partner's food that he was forced to bolt his own helping even faster than dogs usually do, in order to rush across to the other plate. Neither of them ever found anything left when they did this, but this never stopped them.

It will be noticed that I have started to describe the dogs before saying anything about the humans. I'm sorry to say that I think this does represent our attitude at the time. Dogs – being the only non-human creatures in which the grown-ups were also interested – continued to be central to our lives when newts and mice gradually dropped out of the scene. (We did have cats as well, but, as often happens when they are kept as well as dogs, they were retiring and took a back seat.) I have lately seen a diary that Hugh kept for some months when he was about fourteen, in which he only seems to get excited about two topics – dogs (along with a few other animals around at the time) and swimming. It was not exactly that nothing else interested us. Perhaps it was rather that nothing else was quite so easy to grasp – nothing else made sense quite so easily. And often the dogs seemed to understand us when the grown-ups signally failed to do so.

Swimming was a passion with both of us. It is the only sport that I have ever really enjoyed and I owe a deep debt to Miss Bowden's niece Yvonne for teaching me to do it so early and getting me over the terror of putting my head down to dive. Other sports usually baffled me because so many of them revolve round the ability to see a small ball clearly and react quickly to what it is doing. If one is short-sighted and a bit slow one fails to do these things, and if one is also tall one's failures cannot be concealed. I didn't get on so badly at netball, where the ball was larger and my height was an advantage, but at cricket and lacrosse I was abysmal. All this causes games teachers to denounce one sternly and it is easy then to get put off. Actually both Hugh and I could play tennis – not particularly well but quite adequately – and we did enjoy doing so. That we could do this must, I suppose, have been due to the fact that there were no games teachers in the background interfering with us while we picked up the skill; it was simply something that one could do casually with one's contemporaries. We liked tennis, but it never competed with swimming.

At Flimwell, we swam in the big, clear lake in Bedgebury woods, which was wonderful –

> . . . On russet floors, by waters idle,
> The pine lets fall her cone . . .

At home we were almost as lucky because we had friends whose father was a music master at Harrow and – apart from other baths – we were allowed to use the school swimming-bath with them in the holidays. When I see how, today, no child may ever do anything unsupervised I am startled to think how the four of us, all under fourteen, used just to collect the key, bicycle off and have that idyllic spot to ourselves for the afternoon. This bath, called Ducker, was quite a long way from the school. It was a very long L-shaped pool surrounded by trees. The water was a beautiful dark olive-green, fed by a stream which trickled gently in at one end and out at the other. It was doubtless full of germs, but we never got typhoid and neither (I suppose) did the boys of Harrow School. Ducker contained logs that you could play with and we also took our own duck there – a large and very tough inflatable called Jemima Puddleduck who was most useful there and on many holidays.

We bicycled to Ruislip Reservoir, too, but only to swim there. I did not know then that this was the historic spot where, in 1914, the young Julian Huxley had launched the modern study of animal behaviour by making his ground-breaking observations on the courtship habits of the Great Crested Grebe (*Podiceps cristatus*). When swimming there, I never even noticed Podiceps. I never paid the slightest attention to the amazing performances that he and his many relatives – ducks, geese, swans and the rest – do indeed put on in ponds everywhere. Later, when I read what Huxley and Konrad Lorenz and a dozen other people have to say about it, I looked and saw that indeed it was all true. I then found it extraordinary that such things should have been going on before me all these years and I hadn't seen them. But I'm not the only one to whom that happens.

We bicycled, too, to a lot of other places without any special enquiry being needed about what we were doing. People celebrate the new freedoms conferred by the car and the Internet but of course other freedoms like this have been lost. We did not have television, and I don't think there were any cinemas in Greenford while we lived there. But we did not miss these things, any more than people now miss the next load of doubtful blessings that are about to be showered upon them. We did have radio, and we very much enjoyed *Children's Hour*, which had the genuine original Toytown featuring Larry the Lamb, Dennis the Dachshund and Ernest the Policeman – far better than Enid Blyton's soppy travesty. When an aeroplane came over it was prodigiously exciting, and on one occasion Hugh managed to photograph the thing, as his record still shows. But the main point was that, for much of the time, we could do what we pleased and nobody asked us about it.

At Flimwell we did not have Ducker or our bicycles, but we had long and varied walks and we enjoyed the whole place very much. My grandparents used to invite my cousin Pen, who was actually my father's niece, to stay there with us and this made things still more lively, My mother's sister Maud liked Pen and threw herself fully into these activities, walking as far as anybody. My grandparents also enjoyed it though less actively. They were more prone to expeditions by car. (This, in fact, was the time when I came to hate cars, something that I have never quite got over. Cars always made me feel sick, and I much resented being taken away from a place where I could play as I liked for a long drive to something cultural that I did not want to see.)

The grandparents, however, were friendly and they were certainly pleased to see us enjoy the place. I think they were also enjoying it themselves in a way that was not clear to me at the time. To them, this country house was surely the crowning symbol of my grandfather's success. It was the end product of the long and grinding struggles by which David Hay had gradually raised himself from an unknown Scottish engineering student through a long succession of tunnels and bridges to end up as partner in a distinguished engineering firm and co-designer of the Mersey Tunnel.

I have so little information about my mother's family that it is probably best to put the rest of it here rather than saving it for the next chapter. I know nothing at all about my great-grandfather Hay except that he was a small-time railway engineer living somewhere on the Scottish border and speaking (as I'm told) very broad Scots. He must have had the familiar Scotch enthusiasm for education, since he even educated his daughters. Three of these Hay girls – Jeanie, Nan and Sarah – got themselves qualifications from various institutions during the 1880s which enabled them to teach, so that they all made themselves independent. I still have three of the impressive diplomas that marked this feat, all belonging to my Great Aunt Jeanie, who was as independent as they come and very good company.

We were all very fond of her and we used often to visit her in her bungalow at Great Missenden where she grew excellent vegetables, kept bees, studied Greek, theosophy (a high-minded belief system invented by Annie Besant, based on Hinduism), science and Esperanto, supported herself by a bit of governessing and had a wonderful Old English sheepdog who could undo latches and turn taps on and off. She and her two sisters used to exasperate their brother David by having firm ideas of their own about how to run their financial affairs which he was sure that they ought to leave to him. Aunt Jeanie left this bungalow to me in her will. I still possess some of her furniture and several of her excellent saucepans, besides many books – notably a fine copy of Darwin's book on *The Expression of the Emotions in Man and Animals* dating from 1872.

Aunt Jeanie was, of course, a vegetarian. We all accepted her being so, just as we accepted her being a theosophist, without ever thinking that perhaps she was right in this or that we ought to join her. My parents certainly objected strongly to cruel treatment of animals and hated things like hunting, but I think they assumed – as most people then did till the matter was forcibly raised – that animals reared for food were properly treated and had a decent life. I vaguely and unthinkingly assumed this myself until I read Peter Singer's *Animal Liberation* some time in the early 1970s.

By then, of course, the technological revolution that accompanied the rise of factory farming after the war was in full swing and the facts that Singer had carefully collected were unmistakably hideous. All my sons became vegetarian some time in that decade, leading to endless confusion in the housekeeping, and eventually I joined them, though Geoff remained stoutly carnivorous to the end. I don't, however, actually attach half so much importance to the negative aspect of vegetarianism as to its positive correlates. I think it is much more important to campaign to get better conditions for animals than to abstain absolutely from eating them.

To return to the Hay family. David Hay himself was sent to study engineering at the Armstrong College in Newcastle, an admirable institution that was the seed out of which Newcastle University later grew. While he was there, he met my grandmother, Beatrice McCallum, at a concert given by the Literary and Philosophical Society – a centre of local fashionable life that still survives, though it is now not so much of a centre. It occupies an impressive classical building which you can easily see if you look to your right as you come out of Newcastle Central Station.

Unfortunately I know nothing about the rest of the McCallums except that they lived in Jesmond – the pleasant Newcastle suburb where I am now writing. They were said to be a large, harum-scarum family and (according to my Aunt Maud) it was widely agreed that 'all McCallums were either bad or mad'. This is tantalizing. They must have been distinctive in some way, but there is no clue now to what they got up to. (It is mere chance, by the way, that later brought me to live in Newcastle. No connection exists with these earlier happenings. If this was a novel, I would find a deep significance for it, but, as it is, I must just say that my husband Geoffrey got a job here just before we married and that we liked the place too much to leave it.)

David and Beatrice Hay moved to London in 1888 and my mother was born in that year. He then began his employment on the construction of the City and South London Railway – now the Waterloo and City Line – along with Basil Mott, who later became his partner. Since this was the first underground railway it was pioneering work. J. H. Greathead, the eminent tunnelling engineer who was in charge of it, noted that the treatment of certain sharp curves there was 'interesting as indicating what can be done with good instruments in careful and competent hands, and credit is due to Mr Basil Mott and Mr David Hay for the good results obtained'.

In 1890 Hay became resident engineer for the construction of the Blackwall Tunnel under the Thames. He joined Mott again in 1896 to work under Sir Benjamin Baker – the designer of the Forth Railway Bridge – on the Central London Railway, which was opened in 1900, to widespread applause, under the name of the Twopenny Tube. The two young engineers formally became partners in 1902 and worked together on various tunnels and bridges, but chiefly on extensions of the Underground Railway. (We are still using their tunnels today.) In 1912, Hay visited Australia to advise the New South Wales government about proposed underground electric railways in the city of Sydney and also about proposals to build a tunnel across the harbour. Since he advised against this the Sydney Bridge was built instead. He thus altered history and became a great deal less famous than he might otherwise have been.

In 1928 the firm of Mott, Hay and Anderson built the Tyne Bridge between Newcastle and Gateshead – the well-known one that you can see from the train, which was the largest steel arch in Britain when it was opened. And from 1922 to 1934 they were engaged on the Mersey Tunnel. From 1929 onwards they were also holding consultations about building a Forth Road Bridge. That project was interrupted by the war, but in 1964 their successors in the firm eventually carried it out. By then, however, both Basil Mott and David Hay had died – both of them in 1938.

My grandfather Hay very seldom talked about his work. After his death, my mother told me that this was not just because we were children, for he never had talked about it at home. She was distressed about this, because, as time went on, she had seen how important that work must have been and she wished that she knew more about it. There seems to have been a convention that wives and daughters couldn't be expected to understand these things. We did hear something about it of course, particularly when he was engaged on the Mersey Tunnel. And I remember seeing, in his office, a fascinating drawing of St Paul's Cathedral with a slice cut out of it like a cake. I think this probably meant that he was employed as a consultant (perhaps about the crypt) when a lot of engineering work was done on the Cathedral in the 1920s. Mostly, however, he talked about things other than his work. Just as with our other grandpa, serious thought had been carefully cut off from everyday life. Hugh and I were, however, devoted to the Tube, on which we were often taken shopping, and we sometimes used the names of its stations as a magical incantation ('Queensway – Lancaster Gate – Mar-ble Arch – BOND Street'), but we didn't particularly connect it with our grandpa.

I do remember that when Basil Mott or other engineers who were his friends visited, they would sometimes tell funny stories about their work. For instance one of them (I think it was the one delightfully named Marmaduke Tudsbury) had been responsible for designing the deep cellars for Broadcasting House and he described how he had tried to find out where the Underground ran so as to avoid hitting it. He asked the directors of the Bakerloo where they thought it was, and they replied that they were sorry but they couldn't exactly tell him. So he said, 'All right, if we find your tube we'll let you know'.

This is a typical engineer's story and we could have done with more of them, but it was only when several engineers were present that they ever came out. At Flimwell, where we saw most of him, I think David Hay really liked the idea of being a country gentleman better and he didn't want to talk about his work.

When he finally retired, he and his wife and daughter took a long and leisurely voyage round the world, sending or bringing home with them a great selection of presents for everybody – I got some splendid scarlet Japanese pyjamas – and also many exotic objects with which to furnish the house. These were added to an earlier layer of Chinese items which, it seems, had been brought home by my grandmother's brother Alec McCallum, a China merchant who had bought them cheap as loot from the sack of the Winter Palace at Beijing after the Boxer Rising. The effect of these objets d'art in the house was sometimes strange but never grotesque or excessive. I still have some of Great Uncle Alec's spoils, notably some china bowls and a long narrow wooden dragon with a trough down his back in which one is meant to grow flowers. I don't think that it would be any good sending this dragon back to China now, but I certainly sometimes feel uneasy about him.

My Aunt Maud was very lively and intelligent; on the whole she was excellent company. Like my Aunt Jane, she had been at college, reading English at Lady Margaret Hall, and, also like her, she had not worked afterwards, except (I think) for some office work during the war. Both these aunts seem to me to have suffered from a frustrating sense of being half-liberated and this may have made them sharper with us than they would otherwise have been. They belonged to the generation of girls who were always assumed to have lost their men in the war and indeed often had done so. The story that Vera Brittain tells about this in *Testament of Youth* was undoubtedly typical. During the war they all worked, and after it many of them went on to various kinds of career, which must surely have been the best way of getting over the bereavement. If we ask why others, such as my two aunts, did not do this, I think the answer is largely that there was still considerable pressure to live at home and look after your parents if you did not actually have to earn your living.

Ladies and non-ladies

Though I was fond of my aunt Maud, she certainly stood for the element in grown-up female life that I found upsetting and couldn't see how to accept. The kind of elegant dressing expected of ladies at that time, centring on stiff perms and gloves and pink silk underwear, seemed so alien that I didn't see how I could ever get to like it. This naturally cast confusion over the whole idea of growing up. My mother herself was a far less extreme example. She managed to be quite elegant without seeming to be alien. But I always felt too awkward to be capable of becoming like her in this.

She didn't put excessive pressure on me, but she naturally did make suggestions, which I tended to reject with alarm. I think she knew that things were changing, and wanted to help me find new pastures, but neither of us quite saw how to do this. In the end, of course, like others of my generation, I discovered that different kinds of chic were available, centring more on things like chunky Norwegian sweaters and slacks and occasional dramatic long skirts, and I gradually found my way to joining the rest of the tribe. It wasn't that I really objected to being female but I just couldn't see any way of becoming dainty. I don't think that today, when many styles are available and grown-ups themselves are often busy trying to dress like teenagers, this particular difficulty in crossing an apparently fixed barrier arises with the same force, though there is still room for all sorts of other conflicts.

It will be noticed that both my grandfathers had sent their daughters to college, which was not too common in the early years of the century. Conveniently for me, neither side of my family seems to have had any objection to educating girls. Indeed, as I have explained, in the Hay family this willingness had begun even earlier, with my mother's aunts. My godmother, Bessie Callendar, was also a career woman, in fact she was one of the first set of girls who took degrees at Durham University in 1894. She later became headmistress of Fulham High School. She used quite often to take me to plays at the Old Vic and to stay the night at her flat, looking over the Thames on Cheyne Walk in Chelsea, which I much enjoyed. In fact, I don't remember any of those around me in my early years expressing the kind of oafish prejudice on the matter of women's work or women's careers that other girls apparently still had to contend with at this time, and indeed still later.

On the whole I think that these early professional women's attitude was admirable, but it had one slight drawback. They were deeply convinced – no doubt with reason – that it was fatal for a woman to acquire any practical skills outside those belonging to her profession because, if she once admitted to having such skills, she would find herself condemned to do nothing else. This applied particularly to typing, which is why I have never learnt to touch-type properly, something that I've often had cause to regret. The same thing of course held for making the coffee, and again certainly with good reason. It also extended, however, to cooking, and here I think it was a grave mistake. It led to some splendid old ladies retiring, after spending their lives in schools or colleges, without being able to boil an egg. One that I knew in Newcastle was reduced to living on frozen peas, which someone has shown her how to prepare.

I think it was probably this sense of career-danger that prevented my mother from teaching me to cook as a child. She could do it perfectly well herself, but she had heard from Maud and others that it could be dangerous. As I have explained, while we were at Greenford we always had two servants and there was still one maid when we first went to Kingston. At this time my mother herself sometimes cooked, but she didn't involve me much. Then, when we stopped having a live-in maid, she did do the cooking herself and at that time I learnt to do quite a lot of it. But I didn't take a serious interest in it and have never grown half as expert at it as many of my friends are. In later life I grew quite to like it when it was actually needed, especially in an emergency, just because there are a lot of people around and it seems to be time to feed them. In these cases you don't have to worry about planning and you always get a lot of credit for the result.

The cheerful professional ladies that I have been describing were a happy feature of my life from its earliest times. So when, in the 1960s, feminists such as Jill Tweedie began to shout about male chauvinism and female frustration in the *Guardian* Women's Page, I found their degree of excitement slightly puzzling. I could see the point of the political issues about equal pay and equal opportunities all right. These things followed naturally from the earlier campaigns for things like the suffrage. But I was rather mystified by some writers' frenzy of exasperation towards men, by their indignation at men's treating women politely and by their willingness to get involved in fantasies such as Californian separatism. I was still more puzzled by their rejoicings that Britain had at last elected a woman prime minister, namely Margaret Thatcher . . . When, however, I read Jill Tweedie's autobiography *Eating Children* I begin to understand all this rather better. Sarcastic, contemptuous, misogynist fathers such as hers clearly do have a poisonous effect that will take a long time to get out of the communal psyche.

To return to my aunt Maud. She had wide interests and you could talk to her about all sorts of matters. The catch about her was, however, that, being extremely elegant herself, she was fastidious. There were things that she simply could not *stand*, for instance, the smell of oranges eaten at breakfast and certain kinds of everyday muddle and untidiness. This meant that I was often in trouble with her and also, to some extent, with my grandparents.

My mother told me in later life that I was not mistaken in thinking that they were all a little unreasonable about this. She had noticed that they were unfair – that they were always much less satisfied with me than they were with Hugh – and she had tried to talk to them about it, but had got nowhere. I think the trouble was simply that they recognized that boys will be boys but they had no similar beliefs about girls. They may well have expected that little girls would play properly with dolls instead of chasing frogs and would at least manage to keep their clothes tidy. As I've said, I couldn't stand dolls, which seemed to me dead and frozen. I kept company with woolly animals instead, which doesn't have the same ambience.

About clothes, the trouble is that, though I am quite interested in them, I have always been lazy about them and I cannot stand clothes that make me uncomfortable. This often made me quietly undo buttons on skirts and kick off tight shoes. Indeed, even in later life I never found a way to endure high-heeled shoes and I soon gave up trying to wear them altogether. I am impressed at the heroism with which many girls approach these ordeals, but I couldn't imitate it. This meant that, though life at Flimwell was mostly lively and nutritious, it didn't do a lot to remove my sense of incompetence.

This discussion of grandparents brings us round to the point where it seems right to introduce my father's ancestors, thus explaining the background which made them what they were. So – allowing those readers who don't care for the past to take a little time out – perhaps the rest of us can go back a few centuries in the next chapter.

2

The Ancestors

Thomas Urquhart and the universal language

I shall begin this chapter with my best-known forebear, Sir Thomas Urquhart of Cromarty. He was a man who, in the year 1660, 'died suddenly in a fit of excessive laughter, on being informed by his servant that the King was restored'. He is really a great-uncle rather than a direct ancestor. But I start the family story with him because he makes such a good contrast to the sobriety of most of the others. And that contrast shows up well the amazing variety of ways in which we use our imagination.

Sir Thomas translated Rabelais into English and in doing this he is said to have expanded the long lists that Rabelais loves to many times their length. This is plausible in view of his other writings.

I have a little volume of his works in which he carefully traces 'the true pedigree and lineal Descent of the most honourable family of the Urquharts, in the house of Cromarty, from the creation of the World until the year of God 1652'. He names each successive head of the house, so this list allows later generations to establish comfortably their exact relationship with Adam, and thereby with God. Rather less expectedly, too, these earlier Urquharts turn out to have made some very good marriages. At various times, members of the family took as their wives (among others scarcely less notable) Narsesia the Queen of the Amazons, Arenopas the daughter of Hercules, Pharaoh's daughter Termuth (the one who looked after Moses), Panthea the daughter of Deucalion and Pyrrha, Hypermnestra, 'the choicest of Danaus's fifty daughters', Thymelica the daughter of Bacchus (What? Yes, that's right . . .), Nicolia the Queen of Sheba, Lycurgus' niece Pothina, Coriolanus' sister Aequanima, Diosa the daughter of Alcibiades and Tortolina, the daughter of King Arthur of Britain.

The author adds many absorbing scholarly notes in which he sharply rejects other people's alternative conjectures as 'fabulous'. Having thus traced the early history of his house, he promises that he will describe at some future time 'the illustrious families from thence descended, which are yet in esteem in the countries of Germany, Bohemia, Italy, France, Spain, England, Scotland, Ireland, and several other nations of a warmer climate, adjacent to that famous territory of Greece, the lovely mother of this most ancient and honourable Stem'. He will explain, too, how it is that the names of these noble houses have unfortunately become corrupted into forms that no longer reveal their descent from the Urquharts. He will also make it clear 'why the shire of Cromarty alone, of all the places of the isle of Britain, hath the names of its towns, villages, hamlets, dwellings, promontories, hillocks, temples, dens, groves, fountains, rivers, pools. Lakes, Stone-heaps, akers [fields] and so forth of pure and perfect Greek'.

After this pedigree, the book contains a treatise called *The Jewel*. This is nothing less than an offer to construct a Universal Language, a language 'wherein, whatever is uttered in other Languages hath signification in it, while it affordeth Expressions, both for Copiousness, Variety and Conciseness in all manner of Subjects, which no Language else is able to reach unto'. That proposal is, as we soon see, a cunning grant-application. Sir Thomas hopes that, by offering humankind this inestimable benefit, he can make the authorities let him out of prison to pursue his promising research programme and look after his estates. He wrote his book in the Tower, where the Commonwealth authorities had reasonably imprisoned him for several years for having fought on the King's side as an ardent royalist at the battle of Worcester.

They don't seem to have found his linguistic project persuasive and, in spite of strong family feeling, I am afraid this is understandable. The argumentative part of *The Jewel* turns entirely on the fact that it is inconvenient to have so many languages, all of which are imperfect. A new universal one is therefore clearly needed. Having settled that point, the book wanders off into Scottish history where it gets lost and never comes back to actually inventing the ideal new language. Sir Thomas did, however, get let out of the Tower on parole and for some years went abroad, where he was living when he was struck down by laughter on the fatal news of King Charles's restoration.

My aunt Jane, in her book on the family, describes Sir Thomas as 'imaginative', and few of us will want to quarrel with that. But what I find fascinating is the direction of his imagination – the use to which he wants to put it. His trouble is not exactly that he finds life too boring. He is not just trying to extend experience by adding extra colour to its greyness. What he wants to do is rather to impose extra tidiness – to introduce order into the vast chaos of the past. He wants to show a network of simple connections which will finally make sense of that huge unexplored region. He keeps indignantly rejecting attractive suggestions which would not fit in with this chosen order. And the maddening disorder created by the diversity of languages inspires him to organize them all round the one that he finds to be the best organized – namely Greek.

The trouble is, of course, that his idea of simplicity involves orbiting round a particular centre – his own family and his own favourite language, a pattern that is probably not the best one he could have chosen. But the ordering motive itself is surely identical with that which moves what we may unkindly call real scholars. Like them, Urquhart is a universalizer because he shares with them a kind of obsessive perseverance. He is not just normally egocentric like the rest of us. He does not just see neighbouring parts of the world as linked in a pattern round himself. He wants to extend that pattern of order to include the whole known world.

Far greater thinkers than he have shared that wish and have often been led into trouble by it. To name just one instance of someone who is only a little greater, Herbert Spencer, when he had formed his notion of evolution on a crude idea of survival of the fittest, found to his delight that this one idea could then be used to explain everything in the cosmos, from gas to genius. 'Bearing the generalisation in mind,' he said, 'it needed only to turn from this side to that side, and from one class of facts to another, to find everywhere exemplifications.'

By contrast, Darwin showed his stature by rejecting this obsessive over-confidence. He thought such generalizations empty. He probably wouldn't have been much impressed by Sir Thomas's theories either. But the same universalizing tendency keeps cropping up in our thought. And it does so with special power when the world around us seems specially chaotic – when, as in Sir Thomas's time, we are struck by political turbulence and civil war.

The seventeenth-century wars of religion were particularly horrifying because they were not just power struggles but were also conflicts between rival world views – disputes about how the world essentially is. If we ask why that century produced the tremendous crop of rationalistic philosophers who framed the Enlightenment and made way for modern science – Descartes, Hobbes, Spinoza, Leibniz – it surely makes sense to say that, at that time of profound disorder, the need for order was peculiarly strongly felt.

I am not trying to suggest that Sir Thomas belongs with figures like these. I am just noticing something about the motives for thought, something which is common to great and small thinkers, and is, in a way, easier to see in the small ones. Sir Thomas himself is not in much danger of being considered a great thinker, indeed, he is more likely to be suspected of being entirely mythical. Even a kind reader may well think that I have invented him entirely, or have at least drawn him by crudely exaggerating some of the people in Walter Scott's novel *The Antiquary*.

He and his book are, however, perfectly real and he may be found occasionally mentioned as a minor character by historians. Indeed, I should perhaps take this opportunity of saying quite generally that I am myself an almost pathologically truthful person. I attach great importance to the difference between fiction and fact and I hate the kind of literature that deliberately blurs it. I don't mean that I can't tell a lie in real life when one is absolutely necessary, but I always reckon that one should be quite clear about whether one is doing so or not, and there is very seldom any need to do it in books. Everything in this book is meant to be true and so far as I can I shall make it so.

Early Scruttons

The reason why the Urquharts come into my story at all is that, in the 1790s, one James Scrutton married Susannah Urquhart, heiress to the small estate of Kinbeachie, which was therefore, for a time, entailed in the Scrutton family. I had always supposed this to be a rather romantic connection, bringing into the bourgeois Scrutton world an element from the other kind of Walter Scott story – a flavour of Rob Roy and Fergus McIvor. On looking into my aunt's book, however, I see that the Urquharts' own family historian will have none of this. He wrote to my aunt:

> They (the Urquharts) were a 'Lowland' family to the extent that they were not Celtic and were never a clan. They were just the ruling family in an East Coast trading port . . . They were landowners and trading burghers, and would certainly have been shocked at anyone expecting them to wear the tartan appropriate to the wild savages who were the local nuisances . . . In no sense were they the clan chieftains of romance. I don't suppose any of them wore a tartan until the Victorian revival invented tartans for every family who had ever lived in Scotland at all.

I don't think Sir Thomas would have liked that. Nor, perhaps, would Susannah. In one of the two portraits that I have of her she appears wearing a small but becoming tartan scarf. And both portraits show her as a lass of character, who would have known what she was about in doing so.

The Scruttons themselves were much less exotic. The name is Saxon and comes from the village of Scruton on the banks of the river Swale, near Richmond in Yorkshire. Scrottons, Scuruetons, Scruttons and the like spread from Richmond to Hull, where some of them worked in various capacities for the much grander De la Poles, and may have moved with them to East Suffolk in the fifteenth century. From then on, many of them are recorded around Falkenham, near Ipswich, varying socially from being on poor relief to being named as 'Gentlemen', 'Church-Wardens' and 'Overseers of the Poor'.

From the mists of this uncertainty there emerges one Robert Scrutton who died at Ipswich in 1809, having run a successful tailoring firm there and having been a devout Congregationalist. (This deeply anti-clerical Nonconformist sect was strong in East Anglia, influencing its attachment to the Parliamentary side in the Civil War.) Two of Robert's sons came to London and the elder, also called Robert, built up a prosperous stationery business in Whitechapel. His brother James joined him in it, but, as my aunt plaintively puts it,

> His heart was not in that kind of occupation. Realising that there was money to be made in stockbroking, and finding that he had a flair for it, he spent quite a bit of time in the City coffee houses and became a sworn broker in 1801. He was one of the first members of the Stock Exchange and by 1802 he had joined a Mr Ellis, thus founding the firm of Ellis, Scrutton and Co, Stockbrokers.

This early representative of the Forsyte spirit was our ancestor. His portrait shows him as a lively character, and he seems to have shown taste and judgement by marrying Miss Urquhart. A number of Urquharts were living in London at that time, having probably come there to escape the depressing consequences of the Jacobite rebellion in 1745. In fact, they were part of that invasion of hungry Scotsmen who so much upset Dr Johnson. (Johnson himself in his youth had also been a penniless immigrant to London, but since he came from Lichfield, he thought that was quite different.)

Susannah's father Alexander was the illegitimate son of one Thomas Urquhart of Kinbeachie, a small estate in Cromarty. How Alexander come to London is not known – another Scott story seems to lurk here? Having arrived there, however, he lived in Wapping, and ran a bakery when he was not at sea. His eldest son Thomas, a successful merchant, was associated commercially with James Scrutton, and this commercial link between the families continued for several generations. This Thomas Urquhart too seems to have spent part of his life at sea, and was once nearly taken by the press-gang, which led him to campaign against that institution. Out of this partnership grew the large Scrutton shipping and stevedoring companies that are, I believe, still with us to this day.

Thus the prosperity of both families revolved round the owning, sailing, financing and insuring of ships in the port of London. This concern centred in Wapping, where the ships themselves were directly outside the windows and their captains called in to the offices to see their relatives. Wapping was – as its large houses still show – during the eighteenth century a respectable neighbourhood peopled by merchants. James and Susannah Scrutton started their married life nearby in Stepney in 1793. Soon after, however, they followed the suburb-seeking urge that was beginning to stir rising people like them and moved out to the then fashionable district of Kingsland.

This was surely a sign of prosperity. But in 1804, James Scrutton was suddenly thrown from his horse and killed while out riding, leaving Susannah with five young children to bring up. Here her family helped her. Her eldest son Alexander soon became established as a stockbroker, founding the long-lasting firm of Alexander Scrutton and Sons. Her younger son, our ancestor Thomas Scrutton (they are all Thomases from now on), was taken by his uncle Thomas Urquhart into the shipbroking firm and had a successful career there. He lived prosperously in a large Georgian house on the north side of the East India Dock Road – then also a country suburb.

So far everything goes well with the industrious shipbrokers. But when we come to this Thomas's son, Thomas Urquhart Scrutton – my great-grandfather, who lived from 1828 to 1896 – the plot suddenly thickens. My aunt, who has scrupulously given details and discoursed at length about much more remote figures, says scarcely anything about this man – her own grandfather – though she was eleven when he died. Giving him less than a page, she writes that he was

> an extremely lively person, impetuous to a degree and not a very careful businessman. A typical story was told of him that someone told him he could not run from his office up the Monument and back in eight minutes. He accepted the challenge (not a bet) and he did it.

This confirms what I have always heard about this character – not from my father, who was always discreet, but from other relatives – namely, that he made a considerable mess of the family finances. He seems to have broken with the immensely bourgeois ethos that has coloured most of this story so far. I don't think he can have done anything really scandalous because, if he had, he would probably have gone to Australia. Many members of his family did do that at this time, leaving descendants who can be found there to this day. (After all, this was the time when Mr Micawber, as well as Magwitch, went to Australia and made good there.)

Perhaps this Thomas Scrutton just poured his money into good causes, for my aunt adds that 'he was very much involved with his Congregational Church as were all his family, and he also interested himself in education, ranging from the "Ragged Schools" for the poor to the founding of Mill Hill Public School'. This school was a philanthropic Nonconformist enterprise, and he sent his sons to it. In any case, however, it seems clear that he got rid of money rather than making it. His portrait shows a fine pair of whiskers, a rather uncertain eye and a weakish chin.

The other thing that I remember hearing about him is that he was very cross when his eldest son, my grandfather Thomas Edward, insisted on going into the law rather than into the family firm – exactly as that son himself became angry, later on, when his own son, my father, insisted on going into the church rather than the law. I think the very discretion of my aunt's language confirms this story too. Writing of Thomas Edward, her own father, she says:

> At a very early age it was realised that he had a good brain and a phenomenal memory. It was therefore decided that he should concentrate on these gifts

and make his career on academic lines, by scholarships if possible. His brother, also with a good brain, was to succeed to the business.

No doubt that's how it turned out in the end, but the decision wasn't necessarily instant or unanimous, more particularly if the family exchequer was getting low. Good brains are all very well and with hindsight we know that they later produced a record crop of scholarships. But that could not be counted on in advance, and the Bar calls for some initial outlay. It was a much slower and more uncertain way for a son to make his living than a ready-made job in the family firm. And in fact, as I have mentioned, it was many years before this young man – Edward, or Ted as he was always called – could afford to get married. There is a touching story about his first meeting with his future wife, when they were both seventeen. It seems that he was lying on a sofa with a broken ankle, probably feeling bored, when some cousins came in bringing with them a pretty girl called Mary Burton who promptly said, 'Hello, long and lazy!' This went down very well and they quickly got engaged, but it was ten years before they could afford to marry.

Thus Ted the lawyer became successful in the end and so did his brother Fred, who ended up as a director of the two family firms – Scrutton, Sons and Co (shipping) and Scruttons Limited (stevedores). Like Hilaire Belloc's hero Charles Augustus Fortescue, Fred thus Became Extremely Rich and as far as I know he lived happily ever after. And I think the two brothers remained on quite friendly terms. But the conflicts that were started at that point have, I suspect, reverberated down to my own day. The passionate enthusiasm for the law that had made my grandfather insist so strongly on going into it in the first place surely sharpened his anxiety to see his son succeed him there, and the memory of that earlier conflict surely embittered his disappointment when this plan failed.

One more telling detail is recorded about my great-grandfather, Thomas Urquhart Scrutton. Apparently he was much attached to the little estate of Kinbeachie, which had long been entailed in the Urquhart family. My aunt reports that

> he frequently visited Kinbeachie and much improved the property; he intended building a handsome modern mansion on the estate, possibly on the site of the old castle, but he died before this could be accomplished . . . On his death, the estate came to Thomas Edward Scrutton [my grandfather the lawyer] who was a very practical person; he did not believe in absentee landlords and so arranged with Lyon King at Arms that the entail should be cut, and the estate was sold.

I often heard about this because he had to get the consent of his young sons to cutting off the entail. My uncles used to reminisce about it and would sometimes grouse, not too seriously, about having been tricked into losing their only chance of becoming country gentlemen.

Thus this story brings out the great gap between the world views of this father and son. So does the point about Thomas Urquhart's involvement with the Congregational church. Ted the lawyer wanted none of this. Though correct about religion in public, he was a hard-nosed Victorian rationalist. When he died, he left a note directing that he should be buried without any of the idle forms and ceremonies of the Christian religion. As, however, he died suddenly after a stroke on a Saturday afternoon while playing golf at the age of seventy-eight, the idle ceremonies had already been performed before anybody found the note, which he had not bothered to mention to anybody beforehand. This was something that, as a lawyer, he might reasonably have expected would happen.

The Lord Justice

When Ted Scrutton died, a crowd of obituarists went to town in recording him. The piece written in the *Manchester Guardian* is typical:

> Everything about Scrutton betokened strength and abounding vigour. A powerfully built man of towering stature, ruddy-faced, white-bearded and rather contemptuous of the tailor, he suggested a hardy old master-mariner rather than a man of law. He sailed his own course, and if it took him into a forensic storm he was, if anything, the better pleased. His considered judgments were often brilliant and always arresting, pungent and masterful, expressing a functional philosophy of law in strong, graceful English . . . Any failure of the law as an instrument of practical justice would provoke him to lively criticism . . . No poor litigant appearing to plead his own cause in person ever failed to find in Scrutton a genial, patient and helpful judge.

The forensic storms raged when he began, in 1910, to sit as judge in the special Commercial Division of the Queen's Bench, a court that had been set up in 1894 to modernize the treatment of commercial disputes. It employed expert judges with specialized knowledge, both of business itself and of commercial law, to adapt a common law that had changed little since the eighteenth century and had become desperately slow and inefficient. Merchants, exasperated by its delays, were deserting the law altogether in favour of informal arbitration so that two disconnected sets of rules were being used side by side. This not only worried the lawyers but led to widespread confusion. Drastic measures were needed.

Scrutton's radical style of thought suited him to the work of devising a new and more efficient system and he had great success as one of the leading counsel in the new court. When he became a judge, however, trouble set in. Lord Justice McKinnon reports it:

> Scrutton soon proved himself a very efficient judge, but not a popular one. He never had good manners (partly because he was in reality a very shy

> man) and he indulged in petulant rudeness to counsel, and to solicitors' clerks on summonses. Eventually all the chief city solicitors, his former clients, gave a point retainer to Alfred Chaytor, then a leading junior, to make a protest to the judge in court. Chaytor discharged this novel task with much tact, but with equal firmness. Scrutton listened without comment, but showed proof of his penitence in his subsequent conduct . . . With age, Scrutton's manners improved. The younger barristers, who only knew Scrutton as presiding in the Court of Appeal, would regard him as a dignified and imposing, even kindly person.

This unusual experience evidently chastened him. There were no further general complaints about his rudeness. But complaints did still come in from other judges who apparently sometimes 'felt the critical lash and were heard complaining of the way in which their judgments had been "scruttonized"'. He made enemies, which probably did something to prevent his being raised to the House of Lords, as he probably should have been by seniority and general standing. An American lawyer, Professor Llewellyn of Columbia University, comments

> Scrutton, a greater commercial judge than Mansfield, lived at a time when Parliament, and precedent, and the fate of private commercial law, had limited his scope. For fifty years he enriched legal literature by books which are classic, by occasional articles (sweetly wide in range) by twenty years of opinions which, in substance and in style, make the best reading on commercial law this century has seen . . . I have never sent a student to the opinions of Thomas Edward Scrutton who did not come back bubbling – and dreaming of a trip to England . . . Some day I hope to see in print an adequate study of Scrutton's crusty grimness, his hound-nose flair for sense and practice, his sure power with the clay of the law – whenever that clay proved soft enough to shape.

Sir Henry Slessor, who shared the bench with him in his later years, wrote:

> Scrutton was a magnificent figure, with the head and bearing of a traditional Norse Viking. He had great love of music and certainly would have made a most splendid Wotan at Covent Garden. He was at times quick-tempered and even severe, but entirely free from malice . . . He had a very robust mind and could not tolerate false learning. What he would have done in Parliament I cannot think; fortunately for him and for that assembly he was never a member.

He did, however, stand for Parliament as a Gladstonian Liberal in 1886 in Limehouse where, as he observed in his address to the voters, he had been born and had spent much of his life. No doubt there would indeed have been trouble if he had ever actually become a Member, but his political interests were real. He campaigned in support of Liberal candidates at other elections, concentrating on a particular set of causes. The first of these was Home Rule for Ireland. After this came reform of land tenure to distribute landownership more equally – a proposal aimed at the abolition of primogeniture and thus leading to his third favourite cause, reform of the House of Lords. The fourth cause was the improvement of housing for the poor, especially in London.

In his book about the law of land tenure, entitled *Land in Fetters*, Scrutton discussed the objections that reviewers had raised to his style of argument in an earlier book:

> The *Saturday Review* regretted that my treatise 'was marred by a pervading flippancy in tone', and expressed the hope that I might, when a little older, become 'less cocksure'. I naturally took this to heart, and was about to endeavour to mould my style on the sober and modest exemplar prescribed by the *Saturday Review* itself. But my intentions were bewildered by a critic in the *Law Quarterly Review* who informed me that 'the author's opinions are for the most part sound and sober, and are clearly and modestly stated', and on reflection, I felt that a style which was, in the opinion of two such authorities both 'sober' and 'flippant,' 'cocksure' and 'modest', was such a unique production as to be worth preserving.

He wrote, too, a classic book on the law of copyright, where he also called for serious reforms. Thus he ranged far beyond his original base in commerce, especially after 1916 when he was raised to the Court of Appeal. In one case he vindicated Marie Stopes, who had sued a Dr Sutherland for libel when he claimed that her writings on birth control were obscene. On appeal, Scrutton reversed the judgement of the lower court which had accepted Sutherland's claim, pointing out that obscenity does not depend on the subject matter treated but on the spirit in which authors treat it – something which many people have still not grasped today.

One more thing that shows him in tune with the spirit of the age is that, some time early in the 1890s, he bought himself a Stanley Steam Car. This, I find from the Internet, was then state-of-the-art:

> While the internal-combustion engine had been under development since 1860, it suffered mechanical complexities, not to mention being almost impossible to start . . . The Stanleys' first steam car was built for personal use but it gained immediate attention . . . It was light, quiet and perhaps the most powerful vehicle of its time; definitely the fastest . . . The thrashing, banging, clattering and smell of the internal combustion car was no match for the discernible hiss of a Stanley burner . . . Stanleys became the premier steam car to own.

Unfortunately the Stanleys did not develop their sublime invention but left the field open, as we know, to Henry Ford.

With this car went a chauffeur called Marr, who used to call for his orders every morning at breakfast time. The children were therefore repeatedly convulsed over their toast as the parlourmaid solemnly announced, 'Marr, m'lady'.

The industrious apprentice had certainly arrived.

As a judge Scrutton is now best remembered for the case of the Brides in the Bath murderer, George Joseph Smith, whom he tried in 1915. Smith was a bizarre man who had managed to murder three wives successively by drowning them in their baths as soon as he had arranged to inherit their money. He had also married, and promptly robbed, a number of other women. His counsel had to try and persuade the jury somehow that the three similar deaths were just due to a coincidence.

The judge's task was equally awkward. On the one hand, he had to make the jury set aside all irrelevant prejudice ('we are not trying him for bigamy' – 'The fact that we know he is a liar does not concern us except when we are wondering whether to believe him'). On the other, he showed that, though evidence of an accused person's bad character is usually not relevant to his guilt, evidence of similar behaviour on past occasions can rightly be used to interpret a person's actions in the case under trial. It is 'evidence of system' – a legal point that had not been clearly made before. Smith's elaborate behaviour in dealing with the last death could not be understood without noting how it was modelled on his equally elaborate actions in the other two cases. The question then was, what could possibly have been his intention in repeating all these actions three times?

The story of coincidence here was easily seen to be a non-starter and the jury quickly found Smith guilty. In passing sentence, the judge used words which were long remembered. He said:

> Judges sometimes use this occasion to warn the public against the repetition of such crimes; they sometimes use such occasions to exhort the prisoner to repentance. I propose to take neither of these courses. I do not believe there is another man in England who needs to be warned against the commission of such a crime, and I think that exhortation to repentance would be wasted on you.

Scrutton sustained his huge energy by a rigorous daily routine. His work days were exactly programmed and so were his relaxations – the same holiday at Sheringham every summer, games on the same golf course, seats at Covent Garden every year for the Wagner season and at the Savoy for all the Gilbert and Sullivan operas – not, I think, for anything Italian. And he was unconscious of the surroundings of his work. Here is Lord Justice McKinnon again:

> Scrutton got through an immense amount of work in the courts, or in the hideous room which he occupied in the hideous block called Temple

> Gardens, and in which it was characteristic of the man that a Spartan rigour reigned. He sat on a Windsor chair, without a cushion, at a battered writing-table, to the side of which was a table, loaded with papers, that had come out of one of his father's ships, with a rough piece of wood filling the hole that had enclosed the mast. When darkness set in the only source of light was a Victorian chandelier with fish-tail gas-burners. The other two rooms were filled with 'devils' and pupils. At 4.15 all the party met in one of the rooms for tea. The liquid was repulsive, and the only form of food was Bath Oliver biscuits. Scrutton, silently absorbed in thinking about his work, would stride about the room until, almost daily, the top of his head crashed into the knob of the chandelier . . . If he had any spare time, he spent it at home.

Here we come back to what my father told me. He, as the eldest and brightest son, had always been intended to follow his father at the bar and had been duly sent to read law at Cambridge. But his father never talked to him on this subject. Tom supposed that such talk would begin after he took his degree, when he went into his father's chambers as a pupil. But it did not. He found that he did not get talked to at all, nor, of course, did he get listened to. As I have said, for some time he had had powerful religious experiences. More and more he felt drawn to the church. And eventually, when he was about twenty-six, he picked up the courage to tell his father so.

I don't know how he did it, but there was little or no argument. He knew that his father was deeply upset, but he still didn't talk. He simply grunted to the effect that 'all right – if that's what you want I suppose that you must do it'. No further communication was possible.

Things might indeed have been a lot worse. He might have been thrown out altogether. But there was still no real openness with his family and matters got still worse after a strange misunderstanding that concerned the death of Tom's youngest brother Hugh. All Tom's three brothers got the Military Cross during the war, two of them as despatch-riders and the third in the Tanks. Hugh, however, was killed at Salonica in 1916. Not long after his death Tom's son (my brother) was born, and Tom asked his mother whether she would like the baby to be called Hugh. She, it seems, said that she would not, since she thought that 'there should never be another Hugh Scrutton'. But somehow he misunderstood her and supposed that she had said 'yes'.

The baby was therefore called Thomas Hugh. There was no open protest, but my parents were utterly mystified by an arctic chill which followed. Some time passed before it was discovered that there had been a misunderstanding. When this finally came out, they hastily nicknamed my brother 'Dan' and he had that name for about ten years till he himself got tired of having the wrong initials and insisted on becoming Hugh.

The whole thing was an absurd example of the policy of not mentioning things, which caused so many kinds of misery in that generation. As the song has it

O no, we never mention him/her
His/her name is never heard;
My tongue is now forbid to know
That once-familiar word. . .

An astonishing amount of this kind of thing used to go on. On this occasion, my mother was probably right in suggesting that the original mistake was simply due to disparity of heights. My father was about a foot taller than his mother and they had been out walking together when they had this conversation, so he could easily have misheard her. But of course the extraordinary thing is the failure to sort the matter out right away when it became clear that things were going wrong. In that way at least customs are probably better today.

The general point that interests me about the story of these grandparents is how hard it proves to be to bring together intellectual achievement and ordinary life – even when you are well aware, as Ted Scrutton clearly was, that some such combining is needed. He saw the gap between obsolete law and the changing state of trade and he boldly set about bridging it. But he found it much harder to bring his trained intelligence to bear on the state of things in his own family – or even, it seems, with his own pupils. Here he surely missed his chances to pass on and refresh his own thinking. He did not, however, develop into a real active tyrant. He simply froze the relation with his most gifted son at the point where there might have been an explosion, followed either by a parting or by some kind of increased understanding. It was a typical outcome for British people of his generation.

My mother, Lesley Hay (Scrutton), 1916

With my brother Hugh in the garden at 3 St Paul's Road, Cambridge, 1923

My Grandfather, Ted Scrutton, the Lord Justice, 1934

Olive Willis, the headmistress at Downe House, swimming at Lerici

As the Elder Brother in *Comus*, 1935

Just before my marriage in 1949

3

At Downe House School, 1932–7

The place

I moved to Downe House School, near Newbury, when I was twelve. When my parents suggested this change I was pleased, thinking it would be something of an adventure. And it was. Although I was sometimes homesick, it did give me a quite new sense of space.

This sense came partly from a much less restricted social atmosphere than that at St Leonard's, but it was also directly physical, caused by the school's situation. As Anne Ridler describes in her lively biography of its founder Olive Willis, the school stands on the edge of a hill overlooking a vast stretch of the Berkshire Downs. Though the hill is not really very big,

> you have the impression of a commanding height, for the ground drops steeply away from the school buildings, and the view extends over the lower wooded ridges of the Kennet valley, to where the sun sets behind the Newbury hills. Distracted from Pythagoras or Magna Carta, those who sat at work at certain windows would gaze down over the steep woods (now, alas, much denuded) to a pond where horses drank, in a field of toy-sized cows, and watch, mesmerized, the smoke of a train as it snaked along the valley. Oak-woods covered much of the hillside, and red squirrels lived there for years after the school came, wild daffodils and lilies of the valley are still to be found, and bilberries.

This was all true in my day and it struck me at once with delight. I loved that view and I loved the walk through the woods to the outhouse where I slept at first, as well as the further walks through the surrounding woods that we got when – as luckily often happened – it was too wet to play lacrosse or cricket.

The buildings, to which the school had moved from its original home in Darwin's Downe House in Kent, were quite attractive too. They had been built during the First World War by the architect Maclaren Ross for a mysterious contemplative order called the School of Silence. Little is known of these ladies except that their degree of spiritual advancement was marked by wearing robes of six successive colours ending in pure white – a colour that indicated perfection and was worn only by the founder, a certain Miss Curtis. In spite of perfection, however, the order did not prosper as she hoped and in 1920 she found herself compelled to sell the estate to Downe House. She then retired with a few faithful (if less than perfect) followers to a haven at Burton Bradstock in Dorset.

Perhaps moved by this mystical background to thoughts of Spain, the architect had produced friendly, quite domestic-looking buildings covered in white rough-cast and roofed with Mediterranean-looking red tiles. He used plain round arches, both in the cloisters (of which Miss Curtis had demanded many) and in all other arcaded places. Thus there was no trace of that gloomy and pretentious Gothic which has haunted the schooldays of so many people in Britain.

Buildings that were added later to this original range were designed by a most singular lady called Miss Nickel, devoted to Miss Willis, who had charge of all practical work about the place. As far as we knew, Miss Nickel was a White Russian or Polish princess, but she was not an entirely typical one. Anne Ridler says that in her later days she always wore

> a brownish serge overall, belted and reaching nearly to her ankles (generally stained with machine-oil and with a packet of cigarettes stuck in the breast pocket) and rubber boots. Seen in the distance going about her tasks she resembled a Russian moujik on some great estate. Her high cheek-bones and dark complexion showed her Slav origin; her voice was deep and musical; and as she spoke with a strong foreign accent it was no wonder that when war came she was suspected by the villagers of being a spy. Her blank refusal to say anything to the local tribunal was a considerable embarrassment to Olive.

In my time she looked more like a sinister priest in a Goya etching, wearing a dark slouch hat which extended hugely fore and aft and an ankle-length khaki coat and skirt. (We believed – and Anne Ridler says we were right – that the hats were made for her in batches by a West End tailor.) Her habit of constantly muttering to herself enhanced the priestly or magical effect she made as, with a cigarette in the corner of her mouth, she prowled endlessly about the place on her lawful occasions.

We certainly viewed her with awe. But she did add to the interest of life. In fact she was one of a number of features at Downe which were so unexpected – at times so weird – as to delight my taste for a bit of variety, without being alarming enough to undermine basic confidence. Her buildings were less exciting than her persona but perfectly adequate. Though plainer and cruder than those of Maclaren Ross, they stayed up and mostly kept the rain out. They were still built in the same attractive white roughcast and red tile, so the effect was quite harmonious.

As time went on, these buildings sprawled out all over the hillside – classrooms, gym and library down below, dining hall and extra dormitories, which were built during my time, at the side. This gradual expansion – by the time I left, the school had about two hundred pupils – meant that we spent a lot of our time running from place to place, sometimes out in the rain. In fact, as in so many schools, we were often cold and wet and usually had chilblains in winter. I particularly remember the blissful contrast that arose when, in the bitter weather of the spring term, one managed to get a temperature and was sent off to the san for a spell of flu or German measles. The bedrooms in the san had big brick fireplaces containing fires of logs and peat which stayed in at night, flickering peacefully in a wonderful manner. There were also lots of books and puzzles, and as I was never seriously ill I always welcomed the break.

We were all supposed to write something for the school magazine, and in doing this I soon wrote two poems which both express this sense of liberation:

April

One day like this, an ancestor of mine
(Dust on the hills now) went out from his hut
Sniffed the new air and heard the calling birds
Went in again, put on his Sunday woad
And strode off through the greening woods alone . . .
Pure foolishness – but then a man must stretch
His legs once in a while, and who could fear
Unarmed, to meet an unarmed adversary
In the woods of Gaul, in spring?

Then the other, a year or so later:

Rhapsody on Isaiah 58.11 'The daughter of Zion shall be like a lodge in a garden of cucumbers'

I dwelt in a lodge in a garden of cucumbers, quietly watching the cucumbers grow,
And for many a century rain falling silently beat on the roof, and the wind did not blow.
I gathered and ate of their leaves in the twilight – they sprouted again ere the morning was grey –
And at Christmas in Leap Year the oldest slug sometimes would bring me a worm for my tea on a tray.
But the cucumbers grew, and their reasons were few, and strange was the light of their stalks in the gloom,
Till – well I remember – late, late in November one looked down my chimney and started to boom!

Resistance was useless – I quoted Confucius and, gnawing a bread-knife, lamented my fate –
I had known, I had known, yet had let them alone, I had knitted them socks but had knitted too late –
For the lodge floated wide on the crest of a tide where they swam and blew bubbles through holes in the floor,
And with jubilant screaming their eyebrows were streaming as they shouted in Welsh 'Nevermore! Nevermore!'
But we passed by the Cape, and I made my escape, crying 'Vive la République!' and 'Auf Wiedersehn!'
Yet the things of this earth have no manner of worth – for I never shall see my cucumbers again.

The reference from Isaiah is wrong, having got corrupted in the course of the years. Since the index of my current Bible ignores cucumbers, I couldn't correct it till somebody lately told me that it should be Isaiah 1.8. The quote itself is real enough. I had been delighted by the phrase when I heard it, but I had forgotten it, and I was certainly not meaning to write a poem about it until I suddenly found myself doing so. This is a very convenient way of writing and I only wish that I had been able to make it a habit. By contrast, anything I write now usually costs me a lot of pains. I mostly do it on the gloomy assumption that the things that are easiest to write will turn out to be the hardest to read. You have to go round to where various readers are standing to see what it looks like from there, and this can sometimes be very hard work.

I am pleased to remember that, about the first poem, I defended my style to the editor of the magazine, even though she was a very senior girl. She objected to the shifting stress on 'unarmed' in the last-but-one line of 'April', and she said that 'adversary' had too many syllables. It ought to be 'enemy' instead. With a firmness that I have often lacked in later life, I insisted that both effects were intended. I still think I was right.

Why had I not thought of writing poetry before this? I really don't know. Plenty of people who are writers in later life have got an epic poem and half a dozen tragedies under their belts by the time they reach their teens, but I never thought of doing this sort of thing. The only kind of verse that I have ever written much of is squibs – Christmas pantomimes, staff plays, sudden spoof shows usually written in collaboration and put on at top speed in the various institutions I have worked in. A great deal of this kind of thing went on at Downe, both when I was on the staff and when I was a pupil. I was found to be able to write what was needed at amazing speed and also to suggest handy dodges for stage effects. Who knows? Maybe if I had kept on at this I'd be rich and famous today, with all the accompanying frenzies and neuroses. As it is, however, my texts and devices have long ago gone up in smoke, and a good thing too. Still, I love this occupation, both the writing itself and the hasty improvising of properties – masks, curtains, costume changes, noises. As an actual actor I may not be outstanding – my level at school was Death in *Everyman*, Old Capulet in *Romeo and Juliet* and the Elder Brother in *Comus*, which was about right. But as a stage manager and deviser of effects at the last moment – for instance in making a pack of bluebirds fly on to the stage and then change their minds and fly backwards off again – I have to say that I have had moments of real greatness.

Drama also played a large part in my life during my last years at school when my friends and I developed an occupation called Sunday Night. This largely grew out of an overdose of Corneille, Racine and Cyrano de Bergerac in our French lessons. On one occasion, after Sunday supper, four or five of us were gloomily wandering about the place, brooding on the Monday to come, and we just happened to be crossing the stage in the gym. Suddenly somebody – I think it was Jacobine – swung round, waved an arresting arm and cried, 'My lord, we are betrayed! The castle is besieged!' 'Gadzooks, can such things be?' shouted the respondent, probably Pandora. 'Oh rage, oh despair! Call in the Guards! Where is my dastard uncle?' or the like, and things went on from there. We found that we could generate a melodrama from scratch without the slightest effort. We did it enthusiastically every week, and after a time it developed into a most satisfactory serial soap opera. Pandora was usually the hero, Anne the heroine and Fatty was often the villain. Jacobine and I shot round to other roles as they became needed, while several other people joined in from time to time. The whole thing greatly improved our approach to Monday mornings, which somehow began to look much less important and disturbing.

This kind of thing was easier at Downe than it would be at many boarding schools because we had a certain amount of leisure. Olive Willis, the headmistress who founded it, had reacted strongly against the policy of her own school, Roedean, which was based on the principle that the devil finds some mischief still for idle hands to do. The authorities believed in filling every moment of the children's day by a mass of rules that were supposed to make any unexpected activities – especially any unscripted conversation – impossible. This idea seems, indeed, to have been rather widespread among girls' schools then and for a long time afterwards. Cheltenham Ladies' College was famous for filling every moment, and an early pupil at Wycombe Abbey said that 'our lives were so full and lived with such speed, all our programme so well-organized, that we had no idea of occupying ourselves in the holidays, and still less when we went home for good'.

Miss Willis did not design Downe as a full-scale 'progressive' school like Dartington or Summerhill. But she did try to minimize rules and to make life interesting rather than highly organized allowing us, for instance, to walk freely in the surrounding woods and to occupy ourselves at weekends and in the evenings. In the summer, we were allowed to bring campbeds and to sleep out if we wanted to, which I loved. (Most schools would, I think, have made an awful fuss about drying the dew off the blankets, but it all seemed to get done somehow.) Occasionally, too, in the summer Miss Willis would suddenly announce at breakfast that, since the day was so fine, we could have a holiday – we should all take our sandwiches and she didn't want to see us till evening chapel. On one such day my friends and I walked right across the landscape to the far horizon, about which we had always wondered, and saw the still further horizon that stretched beyond it. Traffic was slight enough to made such things much easier than they would be today.

The drawback about leisure is, of course, that it leaves you more space for getting bored and lonely. Thus, on a pouring wet Saturday afternoon in my second term, I was standing with two depressed friends in the cloisters outside the cloakroom, wondering what on earth we could possibly find to do. Miss Willis, however, put her head out of her window and said, 'Come up here'. Somewhat alarmed, we did so. She sat us down in her study and proceeded to read Browning to us for the rest of the afternoon – 'My Last Duchess', 'A Toccata of Galuppi's', 'De Gustibus' and 'Before'

> What's the leopard-dog-thing silent at his side –
> A leer and a lie in every eye of its obsequious hide?

And, I think, lots of others. We were entranced. Can anyone imagine a headmistress finding time to do this sort of thing today? Miss Willis was, of course, her own boss. She saw to it that she, as well as her pupils, had some leisure, and this was one of the ways in which she liked to spend it. She often suggested other ways to us, and of course after a time we found them for ourselves. I remember another wet Saturday afternoon, much later, that a group of us spent most fulfillingly and uproariously in the studio, painting a huge picture of Hell. It showed Mademoiselle and other hate-figures being suitably punished, but it also had a vast, varied, cavernous background that was much admired.

Miss Willis had some friends of note who used to visit. One whom we liked very much was the novelist Charles Williams. I can still hear his deep, rather grinding, cockney voice reciting Donne and taking us through *King Lear*, bringing out strange and exciting angles. Dr Scott Williamson talked intriguingly about the Peckham Health Centre. Myra Hess came from time to time and sometimes gave concerts; so did the violinist Jelli D'Aranyi.

Some of these occasions, it should be said, were less successful. There were some amazingly boring lectures with lantern slides, given by people who, for one reason or another, Miss Willis had felt sorry for ('And this is another corner of Fez . . .'). There was a lady in her seventies called Mrs Diana Watts who lectured on the body beautiful in a short Greek tunic, ending up by standing on one leg on a ball and shooting an arrow in the air in an alarming manner. This, however, wasn't exactly boring.

Early in my days at Downe I had the interesting experience of seeing pure sense-data, or, as they are now called, qualia. It happened like this. I was bending over a bath, stirring the water before getting into it, when I felt a light tap on the back of my head and the world before me suddenly turned into an expanse of white triangles. These gradually began to move and some of them went pale blue at the edges as the scene started to reassemble itself. What had happened was that the ceiling had come down, owing to revelry in the bathroom above. This ceiling was only a thin, harmless layer of plaster and it shattered on impact all over the room, filling the bath with neat white pieces which then gradually turned blue as they absorbed the water.

Later, when I started studying philosophy and began to hear about sense-data (which were then philosophically respectable), I remembered this scene. Later still J. L. Austin put these unfortunate sense-data quite out of fashion, indeed he devoted much of his career to demolishing them. They were tabooed for a long time, but recently, when consciousness itself came back into fashion, they have made a comeback under their new name as qualia. Dan Dennett doesn't believe in them. He is trying to repeat Austin's feats of exorcism, but I don't think he'll succeed. Of course it is true that items like this shouldn't be built up into solid substances, actual independent 'things', as sense-data were for a time. They are appearances. But appearances are part of the world; they do actually appear. I've seen them, and I'll back them to survive.

Another thing that happened to me at Downe was looking often at the stars. On winter nights one had only to go outside and there they were – a tremendous light-show, twinkling and various, unimaginably far away yet reliably always there. I never got told much about them and I only knew the names of the most obvious constellations – the Bears, Orion, Cassiopeia, the Pleiades. But the sense of distance that they gave – the realization that one was only a tiny part of a vast and beautiful universe – was immensely welcome and reassuring. Up till the past few years people have always had this resource, and the fact that light pollution now makes the experience impossible for many is surely rather disastrous.

Learning this and that

Miss Willis herself taught us Scripture. Her lessons might be about anything from Dante or Buddhism to Yeats or Albert Schweitzer – in fact almost anything except the missionary journeys of St Paul. They were sometimes scatty, but on the whole they went for things of real importance. This was all part of a very good strain of teaching on the humanistic side of our education. English, History, Languages were all invigorating. Other things, unfortunately, were not, no doubt because she herself wasn't much interested in them.

Geography was – as it is in many places – a vacuum, of which I remember only the oxbow lake. Botany I quite liked, but it dealt only with classifying plants – there was no more general biology. Science – Physics and Chemistry – struck me at first as rather exciting when I began to hear about heat and light and the chemical elements. But I soon discovered that what really mattered in Science was simply to produce neat and elegant homework, all in the passive voice, with the apparatus tidily drawn through a stencil and absolutely no blots.

My bugbear at that time was ink, a sinister fluid which lurked in little china pots let into our desks, collecting spidery foreign bodies that stuck to the points of our pens and spread trouble over everything in the neighbourhood. Fountain pens were available in principle, but they were easily lost and anyway they were liable to flood at the wrong moment. Since I never discovered how to control this stuff, my name in the scientific arena was usually mud. Later, when my sons went through these same ordeals at school, I was appalled to discover that their teachers would not, even then, allow them to use the ballpoint pens that were already available. They were sure that the agony produced by using a dip-pen improved the character.

This kind of difficulty rather put me off science and I did not begin to see the point of it until, at college, I made friends with people who were biologists and medical students. My parents and other relatives were not at all hostile to science; they just didn't happen to know much about it – except, no doubt, my grandfather Hay, who never discussed it. About evolution, my father took Charles Kingsley's view – that this was at least as good a way as any for the Lord to have created the world, and probably better than some others. In any case he knew far too much about biblical history to have ever taken the Genesis story literally.

He had no doubt that Darwin had, on the whole, got things right. He read books on this topic by Canon Charles Raven who – as I now understand – gave the Anglican church very sensible views about it during the 1920s. I saw these books lying about, but it never occurred to me to read them. About physics, my parents read, with some excitement, the cosmic doctrines of Arthur Eddington and Sir James Jeans, which linked astrophysics with tentative spiritual speculations in rather the same way that Paul Davies' writings do today. I suppose I took some note of these, but I didn't follow it up. I don't think anybody at school made much of them.

As for Mathematics at Downe, I was quite willing to be interested, but the lady who taught us did not make it very clear and she usually much preferred to talk about something else. The class encouraged this habit, laying bets as to how soon she could be got off the subject onto some other topic, such as drains, and how long it would take her to get back. I am sorry now to think that we didn't even attend to what she said about the drains, which might really have been worth hearing about. I think the more mathematically minded of us probably picked up enough from the textbook to keep ahead of what was supposed to be happening, but I soon lost interest in a way that I had never done at St Leonard's, so I got fatally left behind and have never caught up. I still liked Geometry as far as the Extensions of Pythagoras, because there one could still see in the diagrams what was meant to be happening. But after that the trail went abstract and invisible and I lost it.

About Latin I was much luckier. There it was noticed at once that I was far ahead of my class and I was put in a small group with some others in the same situation, which went ahead at speed. Later, a new and vigorous Classics teacher offered to teach a few of us Greek, and that too was somehow slotted into our timetables. We loved this and worked madly at it, which meant that, with considerable efforts on all sides, it was just possible for me to go to college on Classics – even though the teacher who had started us on Greek left before my last year and was replaced by a total zombie.

I had decided to read Classics rather than English – which was the first choice that occurred to me – because my English teacher, bless her, pointed out that English literature is something that you read in any case, so it is better to study something that you otherwise wouldn't. Someone also told me that, if you did Classics at Oxford, you could do philosophy as well. I knew very little about this but, as I had just found Plato, I couldn't resist trying it.

This red-letter event happened on a wet, discouraging Saturday afternoon when I was sixteen. I happened to pick off the school library shelf two battered Everyman volumes of Plato's dialogues in translation and that somehow settled the matter. I think I started with the *Phaedo*, which tells the story of Socrates' last day – of the conversation about life and death and the soul that he is said to have had with his friends on the day when he was about to be executed. And by the time when I was forced to run off to evening chapel I was hooked.

I was startled at how the arresting imaginative vision, vividly shown in the dramatic setting of the dialogues and in the various myths and metaphors, grew directly out of the sober reasoning and in turn contributed to reshape it. And as I went on reading Plato I found that this constantly happened. He seemed to extend thought on difficult subjects in a quite new way into the realm of the imagination. Thought and feeling did not seem to be at odds here. They were collaborating in real harmony.

As I went on reading, many haunting pictures emerged, but the one that increasingly gripped me – as it has so many other people – was the central image that dominates the *Republic*. Socrates there describes a remarkable scene. He says:

> Imagine an underground chamber like a cave . . . In this chamber are men who have been prisoners there since they were children, their legs and neck

so fastened that they can only look straight ahead and cannot turn their heads. Some way off, behind and higher up, a fire is burning, and behind the prisoners and above them runs a road, in front of which a curtain-wall has been built, like a screen at puppet-shows between the operators and their audience, above which they show their puppets.

I see.

Imagine further that there are men carrying all sorts of gear along behind the curtain-wall, projecting above it and including figures of men and animals . . . Some of these men, as you would expect, are talking and others are not . . . Do you think our prisoners could see anything of themselves or their fellows except the shadows thrown by the fire on the wall opposite to them? . . . If they were able to talk to each other, would they not assume that the shadows they saw were the real things?

(Book 7, section 514. Translation by Desmond Lee, Penguin 1955)

His respondent, astonished, remarks that this is surely a strange scene and a strange set of prisoners. Socrates simply replies, 'They are like ourselves'. They take the shadows that appear before them to be realities, just as we accept without question the things that we have always been shown by our culture.

This extraordinary cinematic image is Plato's way of explaining why we have such difficulty in understanding the world around us. We are (he says) just like those prisoners in the way that we treat the disconnected shadow-shows that pass before us as if they were the whole of reality. In our efforts to make sense of them we merely look for connections between various particular images. But this is useless when we have no grasp of their real causes.

What we need to do (he says) is to turn our backs on these shadows of puppets – to break out of our fixed places, to move away towards the mouth of the cave and to walk right out towards the world outside. There, instead of flickering phantoms in firelight, we shall finally be able to see real things by the true light of the sun. That sun was actually the source of all that we saw before, and of the light which makes all sight possible, but it is itself something immeasurably more important than any of its effects.

What does this parable mean? The message that people today can see most clearly in it is that we should not be satisfied with just perceiving the physical world but should learn to understand its inner structure, mainly through mathematics. And Plato, who was a mathematician, did indeed mean this and had deep confidence in this approach. It is the part of his thought that we now grasp most easily and it has become central to modern science.

But for Plato himself this was only the preparation for a much more momentous change. He was calling for a general clearing of our conceptual maps, a huge philosophic effort to see the real structure, not just of physical things but of the whole world that includes them. And this world contained subjects as well as objects. It was a world in which spiritual realities were much more important, and indeed actually much more real, than physical ones.

The prisoners do not only fail to see outside physical objects; they also fail to see themselves and each other. It is no accident that Plato mentions this incapacity before he touches on the physical aspect. Our grasp of this wider world must (he says) centre on a deeper understanding of ourselves, revealing spiritual values. This understanding does indeed require intellectual disciplines such as mathematics and logic. But it goes far beyond them to a mystical understanding of goodness itself, which (like the sun) is the source of all reality, and these insights have to start with self-knowledge. It was in order to make this understanding possible that he proposed the rigorous, highly organized way of life that is described in the *Republic*, a lifestyle which, to many of us, seems unduly one-sided and over-cognitive.

The cave imagery, however, is flexible and fertile. It can suggest other developments besides the ones for which it was invented. Its negative aspect – the point about the blinding effect of social conditioning – can work on its own. It does not necessarily have to suggest that there is only one way out, only one set of errors that must be corrected or only one discipline that will correct them. Fertility on such matters is indeed one of the virtues of a really useful image. It can suggest directions that its originator never thought of.

Thus Plato's pupil Aristotle gradually moved away from the drastically simple, black-and-white opposition between spirit and matter which dominates Plato's early work and developed a much richer, more hospitable, more continuous notion of human nature and its place in the world. Indeed, Plato himself in his later dialogues, from the *Timaeus* on, actually already began to do this. But most of these dialogues are so much harder to read – so much more complex in their reasoning – that they have never caught on in the tradition as the striking imagery that he used in his earlier work did.

This imagery is indeed a remarkable feat, a point on which Plato is surely outstanding among philosophers. Though other thinkers have used striking imagery, nobody else has used imaginative visions quite as explicitly and carefully as he did. He keeps them scrupulously separate from the argument, yet he uses them effectively to show the living background out of which it arises and out of which still more thoughts can always grow. This method is something that I still find wonderful even though I have gradually moved away from many of the conclusions he reached by it. I think that the gaps he saw – gaps between mind and matter, soul and body, feeling and reason – are real, yet they are not unbridgeable. It is possible to look behind them and find a background that makes sense of both sides, as Aristotle constantly tried to do. It is possible to see mind and matter, reason and feeling, as kindred aspects of our life, not as separate forces for ever hostile to one another.

I have been fascinated to see how Iris Murdoch, who studied the dialogues with me at college and always remained my close friend, has stayed quite close to

Plato's actual doctrines here while I have gradually left them. I have eventually come, as Aristotle did, to envisage a much more continuous world containing a much wider spectrum of values, a world so complex that we need to look at it from an indefinite number of different angles, not one that is split neatly between spirit and matter. Because it is complex, I don't think that there could ever be a single Grand Theory unifying and explaining it – a Theory of Everything – nor that there is a single basic moral solution to all human problems. Like William James, I go for pluralism. As he put it:

> *Prima facie*, the world is a pluralism; as we find it, its unity seems to be that of any collection; and our higher thinking consists chiefly of an effort to redeem it from that crude form. Postulating more unity than the first experiences yield, we also discover more. But absolute unity, in spite of brilliant dashes in its direction, still remains undiscovered, still remains a Grenzbegriff [an ideal limit] . . . 'Reason,' as a gifted writer says, 'is but one item in the mystery . . . Not unfortunately, the universe is wild – game-flavoured as a hawk's wing . . .' This is pluralism, somewhat rhapsodically expressed. He who takes for his hypothesis the notion that it is the permanent form of the world is what I call a radical empiricist.
>
> (Preface to *The Will to Believe*, pp. viii–ix)

That is surely the right sort of place to start from. I am sure that Plato's sharp alienation of soul from body is misleading and – in particular – that there is something badly wrong with his talk about the 'quarrel of philosophy and poetry' in the *Republic*, which Iris takes very seriously in her books *Acastos* and *The Fire and the Sun*.

It is notorious that Plato there shut out most of poetry from his ideal state. This gesture is usually discussed mainly in political terms, as an issue about censorship. But it seems to me to be much more interesting from a psychological angle, as marking the unresolved conflict between two parts of our lives. Tradition says that Plato himself wrote tragedies when he was young and later burnt them. Whether he did or not, he was obviously a supreme literary artist. Yet he sharply needed to attack the Athenian education of his day, which consisted largely of uncritical admiration of poetry, leading on to the practice of rhetoric as a preparation for a political career. Plato wanted to cut these things back so as to make room in people's thought for deeper philosophical problems. But what he wrote on this topic in the *Republic* strikes me as hasty and ill-balanced. He dealt with the conflict a good deal better in the *Phaedrus* and in the *Symposium*, though he never really resolved it.

Of course, in general, Iris's own philosophical work does show the characteristic virtues of his method – the systematic attention to the harmony of thought, feeling and imagination, the resolute refusal to let one of these run away from the others. But the relatively drastic, black-and-white character of his morality also appealed to her for reasons that are surely related to the traits that sent her into the Communist Party at an early age and kept her there throughout the war. She was constitutionally open, in a way that I have never been, to demanding and accepting monistic solutions.

To go back, however, to my life. The rather mixed education that I had at Downe, which I have just been describing, naturally meant that I arrived at Oxford much less well prepared than people from more highly organized girls' schools, and incomparably less so than boys from public schools with the old classical tradition. This became troublesome later. But it was a real testimonial to Downe's flexibility that the thing could be done at all. The wider education that I got there certainly was, on balance, a huge advantage.

At Oxford, I found that, while the male students working with me knew far more Classics than I did, they were often rather bored with it and were not always sure why they had done it in the first place. When Classics was the staple educational diet, this state of things must have been very common. Indeed, later on, when I taught the Classical Sixth in a boys' public school during the war, I found to my amazement that none of my pupils had chosen to study the subject at all. They had simply been directed to do it by the headmaster because they were clever. The idea was that they would do the school credit by getting degrees in this gentlemanly subject, since it was a conveyor belt to a safe career in the civil service – especially if it was done at Oxford in the course called Honour Moderations and Greats, along with Ancient History and Philosophy.

This kind of thing would have annoyed Plato very much.

Our French teaching at Downe was educational in a different way. We had a cross and slightly dotty traditional Mademoiselle, clothed in shabby black dresses, who could be heard muttering curses and complaints all the time as she pottered about the school. She yelled insults at us, threw chalk and books, and sometimes banged down the swinging blackboard on our heads when we slipped up over archaic totems such as the preterite and the pluperfect subjunctive (*Que vous ne marchassiez pas . . .*). Though some of this was probably rather a waste of time, we did get used to speaking and hearing French. I suppose that there was even some advantage in hearing something about the weird traditional French system of literary criticism.

The main advantage of the method, however, was that it showed us that being shouted at – in any language – doesn't kill you and may, indeed, sometimes not matter in the slightest. Mademoiselle was simply taking out her own unhappiness on the surrounding scenery in a way that was, to her, traditional. This sort of talk can in principle just be regarded as a noise, much like hearing a lawnmower or a thunderstorm. I don't think one ever gets round to viewing it quite like that, but one does largely stop taking the words literally. Those of us who survived the experience, rather than telling our parents that we must instantly be moved to another French teacher, probably did learn something from this.

Attending to History: Collingwood

History and English, however, were really well taught. In many schools this happens about English, but it is rarer with History, and it is something I am deeply grateful for. Our History teachers constantly brought together the many different aspects of life that history tells of, and they also connected the past with what was happening in our own day. One of them, Jean Rowntree, used to give a fortnightly talk to the whole school about current events. In 1932, when I went to Downe, this at once included things like the rise of Nazism, which I already knew to be important, and the international scene contained other dramatic and alarming matters throughout my time at school. She made it all live, yet she always made some sense of it. Because my parents had done the same, politics was always real to me, though many of her hearers just thought it all a bore and secretly read adventure novels during these talks.

She also reached back often into the past to show how the strange things that seemed to be happening now could have become possible – what people had meant by acting in this way, what states of mind had shaped our world. This way of getting at the meaning of the present by looking at the past has remained central to me. It is just as useful for understanding thought as it is for understanding action. At any time, the language of controversy is never new. It always takes for granted older ways of thinking that it shares with those it is attacking. Besides this, if the attack succeeds, after a time the ideas that were attacked get forgotten, so that the attack gets a different sense, often a more one-sided sense than was originally intended. That is one reason why debates so often seem to be going on between extremes, leaving the more useful middle ground unexplored.

For this reason, whenever I get interested in some new person's thought I always want to know more about their life and the conditions of their age. And when I manage to do this, I always find that it does add something important to the thought. This is not a matter of substituting irrelevant gossip and psychoanalysis for the ideas. It is a way of making the ideas themselves more intelligible by getting nearer to their full meaning. You need to see in which direction the thought is moving – what problems it arose from, what ills and errors it was intended to cure, what earlier doctrines it was contradicting and what hopes for the future lay behind it – if you want to use it and see where it needs to go next. You need the background to make sense of the story. Without that context thoughts appear as static patterns that can't really be developed. For instance, Hobbes's dramatic generalizations about the need for an all-powerful state only make real sense when one reads them against the background of the dire wars of religion raging in the sixteenth and seventeenth century.

By contrast, a lot of formalist analytical philosophy during the twentieth century has been carried on in a deliberately anti-historical style, in a strenuous effort to abstract the thought entirely from its context. The classic example of this is G. E. Moore's *Principia Ethica*, which rules loudly that the only project of any interest in ethics is the linguistic one of finding (or not finding) the definition of Good. Moore and Russell originally introduced this approach as a reaction against their predecessors' Hegelian emphasis on history. But among their followers it quickly escalated into an aggressive orthodoxy. This never became universal, but to some extent it still persists.

Thus Professor Ted Honderich, in his lively autobiography *Philosopher: A Kind of Life*, explains firmly that only contemporary philosophy interests him. He says that he was, therefore, at first rather unwilling to accept the editorship of a series of books called *The Arguments of the Philosophers*. But eventually he thought of a way in which he could safely do this:

> It would be analytic and critical philosophy, *rescuing the great philosophers from the past*. Plato could be understood, on the way to judging him, without the aid of noticing that he was an ancient Greek. The book on Kant might abandon the conceptions of Kant, and carry on his enquiry with up-to-date ones . . . Would philosophy not be better if it was like science, which left at least most of its past behind in museums?
>
> (p. 164. Emphasis mine)

This is a much more surprising proposal than it may look. We naturally ask, is this way of treating history also suitable for anthropology? Today, the study of other cultures is not usually undertaken in this drastic style. Theorists are not often heard to say – for instance about a Japanese or Russian thinker – 'We can investigate this foreign sage without troubling to find out about his local background or the alien language in which he writes. Indeed, it is our duty to rescue him from the inadequate surroundings to which he has, so far, unfortunately been confined. Ignoring that irrelevant material, we can translate his work directly into the much more satisfactory terms that are in use here . . .' Is this parallel between time and space an unfair one?

These two sorts of foreignness do, of course, differ in some ways. Supporters of Honderich might retort that it is more important for us to understand other contemporary cultures than it is to understand the past, because we may actually travel to countries such as Japan where these cultures prevail. But few people today would think that this was the only reason for bothering about them. The main reason is that they serve to set our own culture in perspective. They put it in context. They show us, by contrast, other ways of thinking, possible alternatives to it so surprising that we would never have thought of them if we had not looked outside it. They indicate the vastness of the world of possibilities that surrounds us. And past epochs obviously do this too.

Besides that, however, the past has a special importance of its own because it helps to explain the present. Past thought always has much more influence than we recognize on current ideas – including the ideas of those who most sharply disown it. The ancient Greeks, who were distant from us in both time and space, laid down patterns which still shape our thinking in countless unnoticed ways. There could be no such thing as a philosophy that was purely contemporary.

As for the analogy with science, what science leaves behind in museums is its details and some of its less interesting mistakes, not the philosophical conceptions that are its wider framework. These do not get out of date. They go on needing attention indefinitely. Problems about the meaning of concepts such as time and space, mind and matter, life, function, causality and evolution keep changing and give trouble all the time. In discussing them, the notions suggested by earlier scientists constantly become relevant, because they raise philosophic problems which are ongoing and don't have a final solution.

Ted Honderich tells me that he no longer feels as strongly committed to the anti-historical stance as he did when he wrote these remarks. This shift in his thinking may be a straw in the wind of a wider change in attitude. Some philosophy departments, I'm told, now run courses in 'post-analytic philosophy'. And even within the analytic tradition itself probably not many philosophers have felt quite the strong anti-historical fervour that Honderich expressed in this quotation – a fervour that was indeed particularly characteristic of Honderich's college, University College London, where A. J. Ayer had been head of the department. Things were rather different at Oxford because Greek philosophy was central for Greats, which meant that some regard for history was built into the syllabus.

All the same, the resistance to approaching philosophical problems historically has been real and influential because it is part of a much wider change in current notions of what it means to be professional and 'scientific'. Asking background questions about why the particular problem before you arises means looking up towards a wider horizon, within which there will always be many questions which you will not be able to settle conclusively. And the idea that scholars should discuss only things that they can settle conclusively is, unfortunately, quite widely held today. Professionals (it is thought) should always take their general background for granted and deal only with details.

This has been a general tendency across many disciplines, but it naturally produces what is now called a Whig view of history, a policy of assuming that the past has been been a simple progress through a series of errors towards current beliefs which are final and perfectly satisfactory. This attitude easily arose, I think, as part of that general exaltation of 'the modern' which prevailed during the first half of the twentieth century. As far as philosophy goes, R. G. Collingwood answered it resoundingly in his *Autobiography* in 1939. But at that time the fashions of the day prevented most philosophers from noticing this, so it may be worthwhile to look at his remarks now.

Collingwood noted how, when he arrived at Oxford in the early 1900s, the philosophers there had just changed their attitude sharply from that of the previous generation. In that earlier generation, the main influences had been thinkers with an idealist slant, such as T. H. Green, who were much interested in political philosophy. Their ideas had affected public opinion and public life far beyond the university. Oxford courses had been designed with that in view:

> The 'Greats' school was not meant as a training for professional scholars and philosophers; it was meant as a training for public life in the Church, at the Bar, in the Civil Service, and in Parliament. The school of Green sent forth into public life a stream of ex-pupils who carried with them the conviction that philosophy, and in particular the philosophy they had learnt at Oxford, was an important thing, and that their vocation was to put it into practice.
>
> (p. 17)

By contrast, (he goes on) their successors in the next generation told their pupils that philosophy was a purely theoretical study which should not be expected to affect their lives at all. 'If it interests you to study this, do so; but don't think it will be if any use to you.' Accordingly, the pupils

> whether or not they expected a philosophy that should give them, as that of Green's school had given their fathers, ideals to live for and principles to live by, . . . did not get it; and were told that no philosopher (except, of course, a bogus philosopher) would even try to give it. The inference which any pupil could draw for himself was that, for guidance in the problems of life, since one must not seek it from thinkers or from thinking, from ideals or from principles, one must look to people who were not thinkers (but fools), to processes that were not thinking (but passion), to aims that were not ideals (but caprices) and to rules that were not principles (but rules of expediency). The effect on their pupils was (how could it not have been?) to convince them that philosophy was a silly and trifling game, and to give them a lifelong contempt for the subject.
>
> (pp. 48–50)

In short, it turned out that the analytic approach to philosophy was not – as its prophets supposed – one free from ideology. Instead, it was one that called for an ideology of irrationalism. This resulted in public disillusionment, but that fact did not disturb the analytic philosophers, since, as Collingwood explains, they were happy to be considered as pure theorists:

> Unlike the school of Green, [they] did think philosophy a reserve for professional philosophers, and were loud in their contempt of philosophical

> utterances by historians, natural scientists, theologians and other amateurs . . . They were proud to have excogitated a philosophy so pure from any sordid taint of utility that they could lay their hands on their hearts and say that it was no use at all; a philosophy so scientific that no-one whose life was not a life of pure research could appreciate it, and so abstruse that only a whole-time student, and a very clever man at that, could understand it.
>
> (pp. 17, 49–51)

Philosophically, the root of this attitude was, said Collingwood, the unrealistic doctrines that fragmented thought and knowledge into separate propositions, supposedly distinct atoms of thought, each of which was supposed to be verifiable on its own. (Though he calls this approach by the name of a now-forgotten doctrine called 'realism', this fragmentation did indeed remain as a central feature of the logical atomism preached by Russell and the young Wittgenstein.) Against this atomism, Collingwood insisted that propositions only make sense as the answers to particular questions. To understand them, therefore, we need to grasp not only what question each one is meant to answer but also why that question arises – what is the wider background that is making people ask it? And to do this we always need the methods of history.

Collingwood describes how he came to this view about the centrality of history from his experience of archaeological work. You cannot (he says) start to understand a Roman artefact unless you have some idea of the purpose that it might have been made to serve – the question that it answered. And he adds another, still sharper example from his own reactions to the Albert Memorial, an object which, for a time, he passed daily on his way to work, and which, being a man of his epoch, he found unintelligibly awful:

> The Albert Memorial began by degrees to obsess me . . . Everything about it was visibly misshapen, corrupt, crawling, verminous; for a time I could not bear to look at it . . . recovering from this weakness I forced myself to look, and to face, day by day, the question: a thing so obviously, so incontrovertibly, so indefensibly bad, why had Scott done it? . . . What relation was there, I began to ask, between what he had done and what he had tried to do? Had he tried to produce a beautiful thing, a thing, I meant, which we should have thought beautiful? If so, of course he had failed. But had he perhaps been trying to produce something different? If so, he might possibly have succeeded.
>
> (p. 29)

Though we might today select a different hate-object, we will surely agree with Collingwood's point that we cannot understand such an object on its own, in isolation, but only by following out the network of connections that show why it has arisen. Similarly, we cannot deal with our knowledge by atomising it – by splitting it up into separate propositions and judging each one separately:

> This doctrine, which was rendered plausible by choosing as examples of knowledge statements like 'this is a red rose', 'my hand is resting on the table' where familiarity with the mental operations involved has bred not so much contempt as oblivion, was quite incompatible with what I had learnt in my 'laboratory' of historical thought . . . You cannot find out what a man means by simply studying his spoken or written statements . . . You must also know what the question was (a question in his own mind and presumed to be in yours) to which the thing he has said or written was meant as an answer.
>
> (pp. 26, 31)

Thought, in fact, does not break down into ultimate units at all. Like life, it comes in fair-sized, fairly complex patterns, always linked together as parts of a wider background, which we have to sort out and deal with on their merits.

This does not mean that our work is impossibly complicated. It does not mean that we cannot know anything until we know everything. Human cultures contain all sorts of convenient ways of breaking up the world into manageable handfuls and dealing with one part at a time. And we can keep continually developing these ways so that they can correct one another. In this way, quite a lot of the time we do get things right. Attending to the background pattern of questions and answers does not tip us into a helpless relativism. But it is perfectly true that this approach does stop us hoping for a universal scientific formula underlying all thought. We cannot, as Descartes hoped, find a single path to infallible certainty. But then, luckily we do not need to.

A world apart

As these reflections show, the teaching at Downe was thus something of a mixture, but on balance it suited me and there was certainly a lot to be got out of it. As for the social life there, the population was a mixture too and rather an interesting one. There was a sizeable contingent of fairly rich people, many of whom were horsey. Scribbled on the desks of the lower forms one found remarks like Jorrocks's 'Count all time lost time wot's not spent in hunting'. Many silver-framed bedside photographs showed mothers or elder sisters arrayed as debs in court dress, ostrich feathers and all, ready to be presented at court, and the owners of these pictures usually expected to do this themselves after attending finishing school. All of this was quite new to me and I found it rather impressive. A few destined debs objected to this prospect and meant to give their parents hell in order to avoid it, but most took it fairly calmly. There was one girl who claimed that her father had twelve Rolls Royces.

On the other hand, there were a lot of people from quite different worlds. Miss Willis often lowered her fees substantially for families who she thought deserving or pupils whom she wanted to have. She habitually did this for clergymen's daughters, which accounted for me. Two daughters of the anthropologist Malinowski were there with me and I remember one of them startling us, when the rest of us were busy agonizing over Edward VIII's abdication crisis, by saying, 'Well, why can't he have her as a mistress? After all, kings always have had mistresses . . .' And as the 1930s went on, there was an increasing contingent of German and Austrian refugees.

On the whole I managed to make friends well enough during my time at Downe, though up to the age of sixteen or so the kind of difficulties that I mentioned over my brother's early comment on Teddy Hobson (p. 6) did keep arising. At that stage in life people who find you odd simply say so, and it takes time to learn how to get past this alienating effect so as to know them better. One doesn't realize at first that being abused for being messy won't necessarily prove a bar to friendship later. I don't think that there were any large tribal divisions between us, whether on grounds of income or origin. But unforeseen obstacles did still seem to keep arising from time to time, making social life somewhat bumpy and unpredictable.

The main point for which I got picked on was still my untidiness, and at one stage I found that I had been elected form captain simply as a stratagem to force me to be more organized. This turned out to be part of a Brighter Scrutton Campaign and it was an ingenious idea if only the deep planning behind it could have been kept secret . . . It made me rather cross, and I retaliated by ostentatiously spelling STATIONERY right – to mark a contrast with previous holders of the office – on the notice which it was now my duty to put up every week.

In the Sixth Form, however, this kind of difficulty seemed to evaporate. There I made some very good friends who have remained among those closest to me for the rest of my life.

The obvious drawback of being educated at Downe was one that afflicts all boarding schools – the social isolation. Life was artificially simplified by being cut off from many practical complications. It was class-bound and extraordinarily single-sex. Though we were told a great deal about social problems afflicting the less-privileged population, and urged to take part in social service to help them, we never actually met them. And as for the sexes, except for a very occasional music master and some workmen, no men were to be seen. In some ways, our situation was almost like that of convent girls in earlier times, who were entirely kept away from what was bound to be a central interest and challenge of their later life until they were suddenly thrown in at the deep end when they 'came out'. I don't know of any good descriptions of what this felt like by those who had to make the adjustment, but the kind of way in which it could go wrong is terrifyingly described in the fate of Cécile in *Les Liaisons dangereuses*. Of course our isolation was nothing like as extreme as this, but it was still rather bizarre.

Its strangeness can be seen from a daring attempt that was made to circumvent it when we were about fourteen. At that point my friend Anne, along with three other girls, actually contrived to bicycle out to some distant woods and to meet by stealth some boys who were cadets at the Pangbourne Naval Academy. The boys' instructions had been, 'Bring a rug and don't split!' This sounds dashing indeed, but, as it turned out, nobody had the least idea what to do with the occasion. Conversation flagged and the boys quickly turned to climbing trees so as to show the girls how well they could do it. They had brought some sweets, which might have been the foundation of a feast. But the girls had brought nothing because at Downe we turned in all our sweets, along with our money, at the beginning of each term. (This was another way in which we were cut off from ordinary life.) The sweets were distributed after meals, but the money remained in purdah to be used as occasion required. So they could have made no contribution to the orgy even if there had been any shops near the school – which there weren't. The party petered out and nothing came of it.

As for sex, it was something that we had heard about and we were not at all against it, but we did not see it as any of our immediate business. It was one of the many things that mysteriously occupied adults. Of course there must have been many teenagers around who really were busied with pair-formation, but that did not hit the headlines and the schools I went to gave no opportunity for it. Some people, both at Downe and at St Leonard's, certainly put up photos of handsome actors or film stars and raved about them – Clark Gable and Leslie French were favourites – but this seemed to have only the vaguest connection with real life. Pashes on senior girls and staff were always part of our life, but, beyond that, any romantic attachments that the girls at Downe might have had were much more likely to be directed at horses than at boys. The whole background of frenzy about teenage fashion and its heroes that pervades life for schoolchildren today, and now seems so natural to them, has been built up since that time, largely by television and advertising. The fashion and showbiz industries had not yet started to pour the huge sums that have since made these things a constant concern into the national psyche. We were not, of course, as badly off here as our convent predecessors had been because we were not actively set against sex. But we were no better off over knowing how to place it or how to move on when we came to deal with it.

The kind of detached attitude that we had was, no doubt, quite common in earlier generations and I think it is quite suitable in childhood, but it gets less and less usable in adolescence. My parents had given me a book about the actual mechanics of sex when I was around twelve, and my mother had explained periods to me well and sensibly before I had them, which doesn't happen to everybody. But little more was said on the topic and there was no sex education at Downe. Homosexuality was something we had heard about vaguely in theory, but there were only the slightest of rumours that it could apply to women. Altogether, our situation was at the opposite extreme from that of children today who have sex pushed at them from their cradles. It seems rather a pity that people always find it so hard to stop pendulums halfway.

In my last few terms at Downe, as a sideline to the history course, I wrote a play, at Jean Rowntree's suggestion, about Charles James Fox and the Regency crisis. This was the occasion when George III seemed likely to go permanently mad, so that the Prince of Wales began to regard himself already as Regent and Fox to act as if he were Prime Minister, but the King recovered at the last minute and they were all covered in confusion. It was a good subject and I very much enjoyed doing it. I always find it fascinating to write dialogue. The play was called *Gone Away*, and was acted successfully after I left, but unluckily I couldn't get to it, so I don't know how well it worked. Apart from the odd departmental pantomime and so forth, it has been my only excursus into drama.

4

At Oxford, 1938–42

Preparations

I took the entrance exam for Oxford in the usual state of panic during the autumn of 1937. I went up to Somerville for the interview, desperately nervous, and – along with the rest of the candidates – was much depressed there by a smart girl who kept telling us all how much she had impressed the interview panel by explaining to them just what made Keats choose the words 'blushful Hippocrene' in the 'Ode to a Nightingale' . . . I wished he hadn't chosen them and I couldn't follow her theory at all. I knew I was ill prepared for the exam and expected nothing but disaster.

To my astonishment they gave me a scholarship because they liked my General Paper. I owed this amazing piece of luck to Jean Rowntree, who had made all her college-entrance candidates prepare for that paper by getting used to answering vast general questions in forty minutes. We became much intrigued by doing this and two of these practice questions still remain with me. One was, 'Nature is too green and badly lighted. Discuss'; the other was 'Attempt, by definition and example, to explain the meaning of the word *work*'. Plainly these are philosophical puzzles and both of them still seem to me worth thinking about. I suppose that this kind of preparation gave us an unfair advantage over other candidates, but it is too late now to do anything about that. There are many such factors and my bad preparation in Classics was quite a counterweight.

I now had most of a year to spend before I went up to college in the next autumn. Somerville had insisted that I should have some coaching in Classics, which I got from a tutor in Chiswick, a Mrs Zvegintzov, who had already given me some lessons during the summer. I travelled there twice a week from Kingston-on-Thames, where we now lived, my father having become Vicar of Kingston a few years earlier.

Mrs Z, a very shrewd and knowledgeable lady, was astounded by my ignorance of Latin and Greek, and I don't think that she ever quite got over the idea that I was being incompetent on purpose. My zombie teacher in my last year at Downe, who was extraordinarily ignorant, had landed me with some bad habits that must have seemed unaccountable. When she finally heard that I had got a scholarship, Mrs Z said, 'Well well, I'd rather lose my reputation as a prophet than my reputation as a coach . . .' If we ask why Miss Willis had appointed this bad teacher, I think the answer is that she was sometimes rather careless on these points, and occasionally gave people jobs simply because she was sorry for them. Her appointments were a lottery, but on the whole the top prizes balanced out the bottom ones.

Kingston was in many ways a more lively place to live in than Greenford had been. Though it was still near enough to London for easy travel, and is indeed now more or less part of that endless city, it was once an ancient market town and has all sorts of past associations. Kingston borders several attractive parks – Bushey Park, Richmond Park and Hampton Court Park as well as pleasant paths by the river. In all these we walked with my mother's dachshund, a talented animal who was a great runner, in spite of his impractical shape, and who sometimes sang to the accompaniment of the gramophone.

The place, then, was interesting, and we gradually made friends there, but there was no immediate social circle. My parents' closest friends were still largely at a distance and so were my own. My school friends and I exchanged an amazing number of long letters at this time when we were not actually visiting one another. Glancing through a few that have survived, I can't now make much sense of the imbroglios that they deal with, but I know that they seemed very important then and letters were the way to communicate about them. People didn't make long-distance phone calls much in those days and naturally there was no e-mail. But the urgent need to speak all the time to one's contemporaries was quite as strong as it is today. We were sure that our friends were the only people who could possibly understand our problems, and that our parents in particular – though well-meaning – were far too ignorant to do so. Today, a whole generation glued to its mobile phones evidently shares this belief. We shall see what is the next device invented to accommodate it.

Changing times, changing families

Though this sort of misunderstanding is always common to some extent I think there were things that made it specially intense at that time. My parents' generation, who were young adults at the time of the First World War, seem to have tried particularly hard to avoid imposing their ideas unduly on their own children, yet they still found themselves divided from them by a considerable gulf. The shock of that war violently dramatized the gap in outlook between the old who were organizing the conflict and the young men fighting in it. That change shook parental confidence and it lastingly altered relations between parents and children.

This was the time when the idea that parents naturally know what is best for their children was radically shaken. Of course, it was not news at that time that parents can be awful. Fathers in literature have always been liable to stamp in thundering, like Egeus –

> Full of vexation come I, with complaint
> Against my child, my daughter Hermia . . .[2]

Greek and Roman comedies often revolve round the problems posed by difficult parents, and so did many early novels, such as Richardson's *Clarissa*. But their authors usually blamed these troubles on particular personal faults. What was new at the start of the twentieth century was the general denunciation of parents.

The first fanfare here was Samuel Butler's novel *The Way of All Flesh*, published in 1901. Painting with relish a gallery of horrible elders, Butler reflected sadly on the hopelessness of families, and speculated – anticipating some later anti-psychiatrists – that

> Surely nature might find some less irritating way of carrying on business if she would give her mind to it. Why should the generations overlap each other at all? Why cannot we be buried as eggs in neat little cells with ten or twenty thousand pounds each wrapped round us in Bank of England notes, and wake up, as the sphex wasp does, to find that its papa and mamma have not only left ample provision at its elbow, but have been eaten by sparrows some weeks before it began to live consciously on its own account?

Butler's real target was actually the ideology of his parents' generation – the social conventions of Victorian Christianity. Being covertly homosexual, he felt these restrictions with a special force which he could not express openly in his writings. But he did express a more general revulsion against the beliefs and customs of the whole age that was passing, a revulsion that many of his contemporaries were beginning to share. It was later expressed in Lytton Strachey's *Eminent Victorians* and it caused the word 'Victorian' to remain a straightforward term of abuse for half a century.

Thus, the attack on parents was actually a way of trying to adapt to a rapidly changing world – an effort to make certain particular changes look possible by simply cutting the emotional link to the elders who resisted them. No doubt all rapid change strains the relation between generations in this way, making younger people see their elders not just as unsympathetic but as actively wrong. But, in the past, there were often quieter times when people could, so to speak, catch up

[2] *Midsummer Night's Dream*, Act 1, Scene 1, l.23.

emotionally with recent developments. Since the invention of railways there has not really been this kind of pause. We have lived in a continuously accelerating stream of new technologies which alter life deeply. They constantly force us to think and feel in new ways.

That is surely why, around 1900, people made a virtue of necessity and began to celebrate change as such. This was the time when the word *modern* became suddenly a crucial term of praise. Prophets such as Nietzsche and Wells glorified the idea of the future, replacing the old justification 'this has always been done' by the new one 'this is what we shall do in the golden age that is coming' – a very strange way of thinking that is still used today in spite of the nastier senses that the word *modern* has acquired more lately. In personal life, this approach was naturally dramatized by the hostile stereotyping of parents in fiction. Quasi-historical novels such as *The Forsyte Saga* continued the campaign that Butler had begun, and those written by ex-soldiers describing their experiences in the First World War made it still more bitter.

Generational apartheid

When things gradually settled down after that war, this alienation took the form of a chronic gap between the generations – an acceptance that old and young people are separate tribes who naturally can't be expected to understand each other. That division was exploited by the fashion industry, which saw to it that they were kept apart by their different clothes – uniforms supporting the assumption that only the young need try to keep up with the rate of technological change. Those who can't do that should move away to Sunset City and stop trying to influence the world.

The most obvious awkwardness about this arrangement is, of course, the difficulty that each individual finds in making the change from young to old during one lifetime. It guarantees an irresoluble mid-life crisis for anyone who doesn't manage to die before they are forty. There is also a wasteful break in the normal process of tradition, a difficulty in passing experience on across the gap. That difficulty makes it necessary to reinvent various kinds of wheels even more often than has usually happened. And in families – which is our present concern – the normal difficulties of understanding those of a different generation are intensified by being seen as part of a wider background warfare. We simply take sides instead of trying to think out the actual issues involved.

That certainly happened in my own generation. Although our parents tried quite hard not to repeat their own parents' mistakes, we still vaguely took it for granted that they did not know much about real life. This was strange seeing that they had just been through the First World War, but the point seemed obvious.

All through my childhood, that war loomed steadily in the background like a big dark hill overshadowing the landscape. Our ideas of what it meant were not very clear. (As a small child, I had difficulty at first in distinguishing between the words 'germ' and 'German'.) But because this hill was a place where only adults went, we gradually came to feel that it was not as real as the places that we ourselves could visit. Our elders' concentration on it began to make them seem alien, removing them from the rapidly changing world that we thought we understood. In the same way, when my own children were growing up in the 1950s and 1960s, all parties were easily seduced by the illusion of quite separate worlds for the different generations, again crystallized by talk about the recent war. And more lately, the people who were teenagers in the 1960s have found themselves becoming a remote piece of history in the same way.

Each time this happens, people in middle life – just at the point where they are beginning to suspect that they may need to revise the slogans of their youth – are suddenly faced with noisy children who aren't interested in helping in this work because they don't want to start from the same base at all. They are speaking a different language.

Both parties then have a choice of treating this tribal clash as ultimate – refusing to penetrate the differences of uniform and language at all – or trying to crack the barriers and understand the other side's ideas. Most of us shift between these moods. We do try to extend our understanding. But we find this hard, not just because the other side's ideas may be alien but because, in order to do it, we have to become more conscious of our own ideas than we normally are. We need to sort out our own thoughts, which are tangled up with our feelings. We have to make our own assumptions explicit. In fact, we become involved in trying to be a bit wiser. And as the word *philosophy* actually means the love of wisdom, it is not surprising if, at this point, we sometimes find ourselves actually doing some philosophizing.

Times of violent change always call for new thinking, so they do often throw up philosophers. In Athens, philosophical business did not start in the Periclean age, when the city was brilliant and prosperous. It arose when the Athenians began to lose the terrible and destructive war against Sparta which they had provoked and had caused to spread. That thirty-year war was an epoch of increasing confusion, of shattered and discredited ideals, ending in a sink of moral as well as military defeat. Plato's dialogues, set at that time, constantly show Socrates trying to arbitrate radical conflicts that are not of his making – conflicts that are already raging among the people around him. And many of those dialogues, notably the *Republic*, show those conflicts arising between the generations, between champions of a tradition that is already shaken and younger people producing new ideas which are not yet clear. Thucydides describes the background in terms that are remarkably familiar to us today, noting the conceptual chaos that spread through Greece as civil war broke out everywhere between factions allied to one or other of the two main superpowers, Athens and Sparta – in fact, as Athens became mired in the difficulties that always beset a democracy trying to run an empire:

> The sufferings which revolution entailed upon the cities were many and terrible . . . Words had to change their ordinary meaning . . . moderation was held to be a cloak for unmanliness; ability to see all sides of a question, inaptness to act on any . . . To succeed in a plot was to have a shrewd head, to divine a plot, a still shrewder . . . To forestall an intending criminal, or to suggest the idea of a crime where it was wanting, was equally commended, until even blood became a weaker tie than party, from the superior readiness of those united by the latter to dare everything without reserve . . .
>
> (*History of the Peloponnesian War*, Book III, ch.10)

That corrupting Cold War was the soil that produced not just Plato's outright immoralists such as Thrasymachus in the *Republic* with his Hobbesian doctrine that might is right but also the other, more central characters in that dialogue, tormented young men who are desperately worried by Thrasymachus' simple solution but see that the problem he raises must be dealt with somehow. Following Socrates' lead, they are taken into profound depths of philosophical discussion about the hidden meaning of life.

Time in Vienna

To come back, however, to my own story. The other obvious thing that I might do during this year before college (apart from exchanging letters and studying the Classics) was to spend some time abroad. Teenagers did not then hop on a plane to India, or indeed to anywhere else, air travel being still uncommon, but it was usual to go somewhere in Europe. I looked forward to doing this, not having been abroad at all before except for two brief idyllic holidays, one in Brittany and the other in the Salzkammergut. My family considered various schemes and for this the political situation at once became important.

A long series of gloomy events had been darkening the skies throughout the 1930s – the rise of the Nazis, the remilitarization of the Rhineland, the Japanese invasion of Manchuria, the Abyssinian war, the Spanish war and all the rest of it, so that Abroad now looked in general fairly menacing. Accordingly, some prudent advisers suggested that the safest and simplest thing would be to take a course at a French university – perhaps Grenoble?

Jean Rowntree, however, opposed this, arguing that it was very important to learn German. She thought that, though Germany itself was now too horrible to visit, one could still reasonably go to Austria. She told us – I think now with a good deal of wish-fulfilment – that Schuschnigg's moderate clerical-fascist government there was solid enough to survive for some time longer. My parents were doubtful about this because of the threats the Nazis were making. But they knew that Jean was familiar with the country, so they deferred to her advice.

It was arranged, then, that I should stay in Vienna with the family of a schoolmaster called (engagingly) Professor Jerusalem, whose daughter Lilli had previously stayed with us. Hugh, too, had later visited them to learn German, and had quite enjoyed it. So I set out for Vienna, arriving there on a very bad date – 1 March 1938, just a fortnight before the state of Austria ceased to exist.

I found the Jerusalem family amiable and friendly though not specially exciting. In their cosy big flat in a suburban alley (pleasingly called the Paradiesgasse) they led a placid bourgeois life of a kind thoroughly typical, as I've since been told, of many quiet middle-class Viennese Jewish intellectuals. Not a great deal went on. Towards me however the family was helpful and considerate. Frau Jerusalem took a good deal of trouble to teach me German and to send me off with a guidebook to see the sights of Vienna, which I found very interesting but a bit remote. She ran her household well and at meals, which were good and solid, she always sat, as custom required, beside her husband, buttering his bread and cutting up his apple for him. (When they later stayed with us as refugees we discovered that this arrangement was necessary; he couldn't sit on his own because he had never been trained to do these things.)

I liked Frau Jerusalem very much and I got on quite well with her two daughters. I'm sure that, if things had gone differently, I would eventually have settled in there and discovered Vienna properly. But from the moment I arrived the political shadows were deepening over the scene. The radio was usually on in the flat, partly with classical music but more urgently for the news. The Nazis, who had been meaning to annex Austria for some time, kept stepping up their menacing rhetoric, claiming that the country was part of Germany and must quickly be saved from the Jews (about a third of the population of Vienna was in fact then Jewish). The Austrian clerical-fascist government wanted to preserve its independence but for a long time it saw no way of resisting. Then at last, just over a week after I arrived, its premier Schuschnigg announced a plebiscite in which all Austrians would vote on the question of whether they wished to preserve the independence of their country.

The excitement in Vienna was huge. Posters appeared everywhere urging citizens to vote 'yes' and there were constant processions and demonstrations. We continually listened to excited discussions on the wireless. And then quite suddenly, on the evening of the 13th, on the very eve of the proposed plebiscite, Premier Schuschnigg came on air to say that it was too late. The project was doomed. The German government had decided to save Austria from itself by pre-empting the plebiscite with an invasion – an invasion which, in their terms, was, of course, not an invasion at all because Austria was already part of Germany. Schuschnigg told us this and he ended his speech with the despairing words 'God help Austria'.

This was all quite horrible. The Jerusalems were frantic and so were most of their friends. We kept hearing of suicides. People made desperate efforts to leave the country, but there were all sorts of difficulties in doing this. And overnight the centre of the city was dramatically transformed. The Nazis, though they called their arrival an *Anschluss* – which is supposed to be something voluntary – had of course stage-managed it with their usual theatrical talent as an ostentatious display of power. In Vienna, huge red floating banners marked with swastikas appeared at once, as if by magic, on posts all round the Ringstrasse, and a ceaseless procession of tanks and armoured cars continuously circled it, full of young men yelling and singing the Horst Wessel song: – 'Today we have Germany, / Tomorrow the whole world' – and so on, while large crowds continually shouted 'Sieg Heil!' Jewish shops – of which there were naturally many – were marked crudely in white paint and were quickly targeted by vandals who looted and smashed everything they could reach. Broken glass was everywhere. Amongst all this, there appeared a number of beaming blonde girls with German accents, evidently sent as ambassadors of goodwill, accosting people with Hitler salutes and (I think) handing out flowers to greet their new fellow citizens. Shops which were still open quickly displayed standard rhymed notices (obviously prepared in advance, like the rest of the stage properties) saying 'If you come in here as a true German, let your greeting be "Heil Hitler"'.

Most people complied. There was no fighting and indeed no resistance. Many Viennese actually welcomed the Germans and the others – including Vienna's Jewish population – knew enough to keep quiet. Visitors like me were not therefore in any danger and had no real role. I had not been there long enough to be able to help in any way, and I felt myself to be in an odious, unreal position as a spectator. The violence that did go on was efficiently directed to targets such as the Jewish shops. Besides shopkeepers, many other Jews and other suspected people were arrested and a few days later my host, Professor Jerusalem, was arrested too. His wife asked me to go to the local office of the Quakers in order to see if they could do anything for him.

I did not think that this could possibly work, but I went and waited there for a long time in a queue of frantic people. Eventually I was told – as I expected – that they could not help him because he was an Austrian citizen. I could not help crying throughout this interview, a reaction I was much ashamed since it could only serve to distract the poor overworked Quakers. My host was, however, released after a few weeks and he, with his family, managed to emigrate to Israel and to settle there successfully, after staying with us in Kingston, with their daughter Leni, for several months on their way.

There seemed to be nothing I could do by staying in Vienna, so I finally went home, having been there just one month out of the three that had been planned. This visit, then, was a bad experience. It did, of course, serve to give me some direct impression of the evils that I had already heard of, the actual glass on the pavement, the actual police standing by while the vandals smashed shops and the vile effect of the endless raucous chanting and yelling. I don't think, however, that it surprised me in any way or showed me anything that clashed with what I had already heard and read. This kind of destructive process is depressingly predictable and straightforward. Since 1933, my parents had gained many refugee friends, some of whom remained their friends for life, so we knew how these things were done.

During the two weeks before the invasion I did grasp the impending danger in a general way, but my German was still too poor to give me much understanding of events. The Jerusalems were naturally rather preoccupied and I hesitated to question them on anything beyond what was already obvious. When they got to Kingston, Leni – who was about fourteen – told me how she and her sister had been arrested and made to scrub off some of the painted slogans, calling for Austrian independence, from pavements nearby while hostile crowds looked on and jeered. But apart from that they had got away without too much difficulty.

While I was in Vienna I did get time to look briefly at the city. I loved the baroque buildings, whose style was quite new to me. Hugh had told me about them and I found them as good as he said. Like him, too, I loved many of the pictures in the museums, especially the Dürers and the Brueghels. I think this was the first time that I grasped the difference there can be between an original picture and even the best reproductions of it. I did learn a certain amount of German, enough to pick up the words of Schubert songs and to read a German book with a dictionary. I find it a beautiful language, one which sounds much better than it looks, but I am ashamed to say that I have never taken it much further. I did go with the family on a couple of expeditions in the Vienna woods, which was lovely. I also went once to the opera, but this was a non-event. The Jerusalems arranged it on the sober principles that prevailed in their household by sending me off on my own to see *The Bartered Bride* from the standing-room pen at the opera house, since, as they delightedly explained to me, standing-room cost only one schilling. I could make no sense at all of this ritual and it put me off opera for a long while.

The truth was that, even if there had been no political troubles, their quiet lifestyle would probably not have given me the wider social life which was what I really needed to shake me out of the narrow circle of school. Hugh, when he had stayed with them, had had other friends in Vienna so he had managed to see quite a lot of people. Not having that advantage, I would probably not have done so. In any case, as things were, I came back from Vienna not much changed, still an outsider in the public adult world where people came in many classes and two sexes.

During the summer after I returned to England, the political situation grew steadily worse, darkening steadily until in September of 1938 the Nazis made their threat against Czechoslovakia and Neville Chamberlain flew to Munich, returning with his claim to have established 'peace in our time'. Like most people on the left I thought this was nonsense, and during my first term at Somerville I became slightly involved in a by-election at Oxford on the matter, when the Master of Balliol, A. D. Lindsay, stood as an independent candidate against Quintin Hogg (later Lord Hailsham) on the issue of Hogg's support for the Munich agreement.

Lindsay lost this election, which should not have surprised anyone. A. J. Ayer – who also supported him – explains in his autobiography *Part of My Life* that

> Oxford City was then a safe conservative seat, but it was hoped that Lindsay's prestige, and the dislike which many people, including even some Conservatives, had come to feel for the government's policy of appeasement, would turn the scale. It would have been an illusion, even if the Conservatives had come up with a less eloquent and gifted candidate.

That, however, wasn't at all obvious to us as undergraduates. I, with many others, eagerly ran errands and addressed envelopes in support of Lindsay. We felt much uplifted by these efforts, but we did not impress the electors of Oxford. I remember feeling some doubts about our approach myself one day when I heard a small, excitable, strangely dressed Polish student whom we called Popski loudly describing to an audience in the front hall the crushing arguments by which she had just expounded the Marxist theory of the state in canvassing the voters of Jericho, which was then still a working-class suburb. But these confusing tactical aspects of politics don't easily strike one in the course of one's first exciting election.

First impressions

It was in the October of that fateful year, then, that I duly went up to Somerville. One of the first people that I met there was Iris Murdoch – also just arrived and about to take the traditional course of Mods and Greats along with me. I liked her at once and she quickly became one of my closest friends; she remained so throughout our lives.

I shall say a good deal about Iris in this memoir – more than I normally would in proportion to the other people in my life – because she has been so much in the news lately in a way that makes everything about her of interest. Recent talk about her has, however, been distortingly concentrated on her painful last days. A word about her earlier life and thought seems needed to balance that emphasis. I can understand how this has happened – why people who wanted to remove the veil of silence that isolated patients with Alzheimer's disease should have used a high-profile case like Iris's to break that taboo. They may have been right to do this. But, unfortunately, the workings of the publicity machine see to it that people are usually remembered for only one thing. And to be remembered only – or even primarily – for the disease that destroyed one is surely a horrid misfortune, an especially unsuitable fate for someone the rest of whose life was as full and active as hers was.

In my own life she was indeed important, but not more so than many other people about whom I shall say much less because they are not public figures. In our first days at Oxford she did stand out among us because she was exceptionally relaxed and easy to know. This was largely, I think, because she was far less self-conscious, less frightened of making a wrong impression, than most of us, so one could get to know her more easily. Iris was always much less interested than people generally are in wondering what others would think of her, and this was a central reason why these others in fact liked her so much. She was never beautiful but always attractive, in those days looking rather like an art student, with a blond fringe – blonder than it became later – and slightly dirndl-ish clothes, but this effect was fresh and not at all excessive. She had, I think, indeed been taking some course in art before coming up, after her schooling at Badminton. She had a sunny room in East, Somerville's modern front quadrangle, which made a nice change from my own dark one at the other end in the oldest building, West. Middle-sized, lively, with a slightly buxom Irish figure and a bouncy, swinging walk, she was altogether a cheerful and encouraging element in a confusing scene.

Probably the move from school to college is always pretty confusing. One has to get used to a new life. But the problem was deepened at that time by ongoing changes in the position of women students. The protective structures that had shut them off from the rest of the university were beginning to crack, but new ones had not yet developed. The unfortunate chaperones who for a long time had had to guard them on all social occasions were at last excused this duty in 1925, and, by 1938, girls were actually allowed to have men undergraduates to tea on Saturdays.

But why only Saturdays? As it happened, that was the first question that came before the Junior Common Room committee in my first term, when (having no doubt opened my mouth on some subject or other) I became a member of it. I can still hear the anxious voice of the JCR President (one Barbara Brier) as she urged us to consider this decision long and carefully. Please (she said) don't let us be led by our sudden excitement into doing something that we might later regret . . .

However, carried away by the Zeitgeist, we did go ahead and duly derestricted Sundays. But anyone who looks at the history of women students in Oxford and sees the bizarre defensiveness with which the university constantly shut them out of all its more attractive activities will see the reason for such caution. The Dr Pusey who, in 1884, described the establishment of the women's halls as 'one of the greatest misfortunes that has happened even in our own time in Oxford' had loyal and determined heirs. Sixty years later they still kept high barriers fixed between the sexes. Vera Farnell, the very sensible Dean who welcomed my year on its arrival, spoke from experience when she said that we must always remember that 'the women are still on probation in the university'. This, she said. meant that if we did anything awful it would not just injure ourselves. It could be seized upon to justify wider bad effects on the general position of women.

Earlier generations of female students had reacted to these restrictions by turning inwards and building communities of their own. They formed societies for all sorts of activities such as sports and they often acted plays – which, of course, had to have single-sex casts. But after the First World War the general loosening of convention gradually made these segregated goings-on seem ridiculous so that, by the time I arrived, the internal college activities were dying. Thus, Somerville had had a tradition that the first year should always produce a play to entertain the rest of the college. But this custom died out because eventually the freshers simply refused to do it. This apparently happened in my time, but I don't even remember the proposal being made.

Rituals like this had been part of the introverted lifestyle that was forced on the women in the early days. When you read their history, it is touching to see how much ingenuity they put into this way of life and how much they managed to get out of it. But essentially it was a prolongation of boarding school, and not many people want to stay at school for ever – indeed, many don't much like going there in the first place. In *Dusty Answer* (1927), Rosamond Lehmann shows a couple of depressed girls trying to cheer themselves up after a dismal arrival at Girton:

> 'I say, let's make our rooms absolutely divine, shall we?'
>
> 'Mother told me to get whatever furniture and things I wanted', said Judith. 'But what's the good with that carpet?'
>
> 'I've turned mine upside down', said Jennifer. 'Come and look . . . I say, Judith Earle, do you think you're going to enjoy college?'
>
> 'Not much. It's so ugly and vulgar.'
>
> 'It is. And the students are such very jolly girls.'
>
> 'Yes. And I'm frightened of them. I don't know a soul. I've never in my life been with a lot of people and I don't feel I shall ever get used even to the smell of them . . .'
>
> 'Isn't it awful,' said Jennifer, 'to have enlightened parents? They never ask you whether you care to be enlightened too, but offer you up from the age of ten to be a sacrifice to examiners. And then expect you to be grateful.'

The range of student styles that this conversation lights up came out rather nicely in my time in the way that we arranged ourselves for meals in hall. Crossways, custom determined this for us by seniority. The third year sat at the three long tables by the windows, the second year in the middle and the freshers next to the serving hatch. But longways a much more subtle system prevailed. A thoughtful anthropologist would have noticed that, in each year, the top table – the one nearest to the dons – was largely occupied by slightly anxious girls, dressed mostly in navy and beige, who could often be seen to troop in *en bloc* from the library when a meal began and to troop out there again when it had ended. The bottom table, by contrast, harboured a mix centring on long-haired doe-eyed lovelies, variously but always intriguingly dressed and often late for meals. (In my year one of these, a Russian princess, actually eloped and went off with somebody, which should have been exciting, but unfortunately she had so seldom been there in the first place that nobody even noticed.) And in the middle things were pretty much intermediate.

Most of us settled for this arrangement without noticing it, but Iris somehow did not. Though she often joined me and most of my friends at the middle table, she also often visited the bottom one and sometimes the top one as well. This was part of her general tendency, which many people have remarked on, to have many sorts of friends separately without wanting to bring them together. (Perhaps this is part of being a novelist?)

But the choice presented by these different ways of living made things difficult. Even the most blasé of us must have taken a good deal of trouble to get to this place, and when you do that you are bound to have at the back of your mind some vague notion of the lifestyle you are going to find there. Since reality never fits this formula you look round for what seems to come nearest to it, and it sometimes happens that there is no clear candidate. You only see a set of possibilities, none of which you much care for.

This must still be troublesome for new students today, but their problems are different. The special difficulty in my generation was that the school life we were used to was far more separate from adult life than it is now – far more enclosed in its separate bubble – and college life was still largely expected to be a continuation of life at school. This was true for day schools as well as for boarding schools, and indeed it was true for boys as well as girls, so that the men undergraduates often found us as remote as we found them. Oxford and Cambridge colleges were still closely linked to particular public schools. Yet many of us were already becoming uneasy about this prolonging of childhood. Segregation by age, as well as segregation by sex, was beginning to seem artificial.

This puzzlement about roles surged up during my first year when a number of us received a mysterious questionnaire asking about our intentions in life and centrally raising the question, Do you aim at marriage or a career? Those who got the document were indignant at getting it, What business is it of theirs?, they asked, speculating that the authorities were somehow trying to winkle out their secrets. But they were also intrigued, and I think those of us, like me, who didn't get it felt rather left out. We all discussed it. The trouble was, of course, that we didn't want to face this question, but we knew it was there. There still existed a strong background idea that this was indeed a stark choice that would have to be made – you couldn't have both, and going to college put you already some way on the career path. But we certainly didn't want to vow ourselves to a life of celibacy.

The bubble of speculation finally burst when it was discovered that the enquiry did not actually come from any sort of authorities, however devious. It was a quite private initiative by a girl called Peter Ady, who later became known as a social theorist but was then simply an undergraduate at another college. *Well*, we said, feeling rather foolish, and dropped the topic.

Marxist dreams

One activity, however, which really was open to both sexes was politics, and this was an absorbing interest for many of us. Most students who noticed politics at all were more or less left wing and the Labour Club, which I promptly joined, had over a thousand members. The main question then was, how far left do you want to go?

Here again Iris is a significant figure. She started to investigate Communism as soon as she reached Oxford, and quickly joined the local branch of the Party. This was, of course, not just a part-time occupation like joining another political party but a commitment to unconditional devotion, more like joining a religious order. She remained a dedicated member until just after the war when she went to work for the United Nations Relief and Reconstruction Agency which cared for refugees in various parts of Europe. There she saw with her own eyes how appallingly the invading Russians had treated local political activists, including their own supporters, whom they regarded simply as alien competitors to be eliminated.

This dose of reality was enough to disenchant Iris. She left the movement at once. In this she contrasts favourably with a lot of Communist intellectuals such as Brecht and J. B. S. Haldane, many of whom went on supporting Stalinism until the Russian invasion of Hungary in 1956 or even longer. They postponed the shock of disillusion by believing that the stories of Russian atrocities were exaggerated, and they found it possible to do this because there had been indeed been lies on both sides. By contrast, those, like Iris, who honestly faced that shock underwent a sharp bereavement. It is not surprising that some of them reacted by joining the Roman Church.

Why was this fascination so strong? It is not possible now to convey the powerful part that Communism played at that time in all our intellectual lives. The point was that, among the manifold horrors of the age, Communism did make it seem possible that there was one force that was working steadily – however poorly and imperfectly – for good. This is an immensely powerful kind of hope, a hope whose power becomes stronger the more the surrounding horrors darken.

It is clear now that some people were determinedly credulous about it. Well-informed social scientists such as Sidney and Beatrice Webb, people who were thought to be particularly hard-headed and anti-sentimental, managed to visit Russia repeatedly and to see nothing there that clashed with their beliefs. They came back with statistics supporting favourable judgements. Numbers of others, less deeply committed, still centred their hopes for humanity on this cause, even when they knew that it was not being well served by its current champions.

In many ways this moral situation is quite like the one that we saw in reverse during the Cold War. During that time, many people who dreaded the Evil Empire in the East idealized the West absurdly because they saw it as the only bastion of freedom. It is also quite like the position that followed the first French Revolution, when what some saw as barbarism seemed to others, such as Wordsworth, the true rise of hope for humanity. 'Bliss was it in that dawn to be alive.' In these situations people form tribes, supporting and attacking the new development, about which they actually know very little. This tribal division hardens the conviction on each side that the development is simply good or simply evil.

Over the Russian Revolution, Western thought became further confused because it tried to fit these new events into an existing set of ambitious political theories – theories which had not been around in 1789, but which were framed afterwards in its shadow. Even in the early twentieth century many progressive people still had, I think, a residual sense of unfinished business from 1789. They were still gripped by the tremendous hopes formed then. They longed somehow to repeat the event without its former disasters, and this nostalgia was a central element in Marxism. Marx himself had wanted a successful replay of the failed 1848 revolts in which he had taken part. Those revolts had themselves been expected to complete the work of that first revolution, so that 1848 has been called the turning point at which modern history failed to turn. Marx thought this replay would occur in Germany and was sure that it could not do so in Russia. Yet, since expecting a great revolution was central to Marxism, Lenin's claim that the Russian revolt was indeed this promised Messiah looked quite plausible.

This kind of hope affected people's moral response to excesses in Russia in the 1920s and 1930s deeply, even in those of us who never considered becoming Communists. If one fitted the Bolsheviks at all into this tremendous historical story, one could see their political errors as merely unfortunate lapses occurring in the course of a wonderful and necessary experiment. These excuses did indeed begin to wear thin after a time – for instance after the liquidation of the kulaks, the systematic destruction of peasant farmers, in the late 1920s. But just at that point the rise of the Nazis began to make the situation in Germany so alarming that it became increasingly urgent to have some confidence in Russia as a counterpoise. Stories about Bolshevik excesses appeared constantly in the right-wing press, while left-wing papers featured equal atrocities committed by fascist governments. One had to choose whom to believe, and it was easy to make a habit of simply trusting one set or the other. It was much harder to accept that there might be a lot of truth in both.

This was the background that generated the remarkable state of student politics in the 1930s. As Peter Conradi explains in his life of Iris:

> The Labour Party in 1935 had permitted fusion of Communist and Socialist societies . . . The Labour Club at Oxford, dominated by Communists, had [in 1940] over a thousand members; nearly all its committee were in the CP. But then, *all of the committees of the League of Nations Union, the Liberal Club, the Student Christian Movement, two of the five Conservative Club committee, and two even of the then British Union of Fascists were also in the CP*. It helps give the atmosphere of the time to point out that Robert Conquest, later to pioneer the objective history of Stalinism, while an open Communist, was a member of the university's Carlton Club, with the approval of both bodies, and that the CP included John Biggs-Davidson, later chairman of the right-wing Monday Club. Probably there were dons also in the CP . . . Of the over two hundred student-members at Oxford, thirty were 'open', among them Robert Conquest, Denis Healey and Iris.
>
> (pp. 130–1, emphasis mine)

Even Kingsley Amis, in his first year at Oxford in 1941, was a member of the Communist Party's student branch and was co-appointed to direct its policy on culture. The pattern of confusion, naive idealism, entryism and general corkscrew deviousness involved here is hard to penetrate today. But then the threatening state of international politics did set a real dilemma.

In this predicament the *New Statesman*, edited by Kingsley Martin, made a real effort to present both sides. So did the Left Book Club, whose varied and exciting red volumes reached my parents and a whole host of other concerned people. These publications expressed the current ambivalence clearly, making it plain that left-wing people were themselves much divided. As the 1930s went on, many of them already experienced the bitterness of disillusionment and were reacting violently against their former heroes. The point at which I, along with my parents and many other people, finally became disenchanted about this was the series of treason trials that were held in Russia in the mid-1930s. Here there were simply too many similar stories coming out to be disregarded, and their details seemed to ring true. It gradually emerged that we were indeed seeing what Arthur Koestler later described so well in *Darkness at Noon* – a set of paranoid rulers engaged in sacrificing their most loyal supporters in a senseless attempt to protect themselves from non-existent plots. Unmistakably, what ought to have been the seedbed of Utopia was now displaying the classic behaviour so often reported in decadent empires.

From that time, I could never support the Communist Party and I found it increasingly hard to see how other people, such as Iris, could do so – especially, of course, after the German–Soviet pact was signed in August 1939. Yet the magnetism of Communism was still powerful with most of us, simply because of the impressiveness of the people who did accept it. It still stood for idealism. The guilty feeling that, in spite of the difficulties, we all ought somehow to be Communists played the same sort of role in our lives that thoughts of being a missionary, or joining a religious order, had played in those of earlier generations. This feeling had been intensified – at least for men – by the thought that they ought somehow to fight in the Spanish Civil War.

This sort of guilt is not very clear-sighted, and it is often mixed with motives which distort any action that is taken on it. But it is a start towards taking some sort of action, perhaps a necessary step in doing so. Our idealism needed some channel, some direction to flow in and, for many of us, neither convents nor the mission field could now provide that channel. But those Communists whom we met and heard of in the West did often seem to be moved by a genuine flame of idealism, even if the ones in Moscow had now betrayed it.

This was the moral strength of Marxism, and its loss when the doctrine was discredited has been a real disaster. People do need some direction for their hopes, some ideal that seems to be working, some vision of possible upward movement, and in a fast-changing world it is not easy to base these visions on realistic expectation.

Fantasies about the future therefore grow like mushrooms in our undisciplined imaginations. At present, for many people these tend to take two forms. There are hopes concerned with technical miracles such as artificial intelligence, space travel and genetic engineering. There are also economic hopes based on a faith in market forces. (These last have of course been conceived in a direct reaction against Marxism and they share many of its obvious drawbacks.)

Both these kinds of proposal deal in means, not in ends. They make no suggestion about what we should be trying to do, only about how cleverly we are going to do it. They aim to increase our power, not to make us use it differently. However, destruction being easier than construction, an increase in power can always do more harm than good unless real efforts are made to prevent its doing so. One obvious example of this distorting effect is the invention of explosives, from gunpowder on to nuclear bombs. Another is the series of advances that people have laboriously made – from goats to chain-saws – in converting forests to pasture, thus finally producing deserts. The Sahara and much of the Central Asian Desert seem to have been made by humans long ago in this way, and as knowledge of the earth's history widens, people are finding many similar examples. We need somehow to get it into our heads that most of our troubles do not come from lack of power but from our own abuse of it.

Have we, then, moved to a more rational and realistic view of how the world works now Marxism is gone? It has certainly been a clear gain to get rid of the idea of confidence in a violent revolution. The twentieth century's savage wars have probably been responsible for this de-romanticizing of violence. Today's currently popular ideologies therefore centre on evolution rather than revolution.

This ought to be an improvement. But, unluckily, it is still none too clear that the change has made us any more realistic. With surprising speed, a whole forest of myths has grown up about techno-based futures, viewed as coming instalments of evolution. In these the migration of our species to outer space, or its improvement by genetic engineering, or its conversion into cyborgs, or the mere accumulation of information, take the place of the Marxist revolution to produce a final Utopia. This Lamarckian vision is often loosely grafted onto Darwin's theory of evolution – with which it is quite incompatible – by devices such as Teilhard de Chardin's conception of progress towards Omega Man.

Stories like these are no better than the Marxist myth, in fact in most ways they are worse. They are even less realistic and – what is more serious – they completely lack any moral core. There is no aspiration in them comparable to the deep sense of indignation at political inequality and oppression that lay at the root of Marxism. Essentially they are just power fantasies.

By contrast, any serious idealism today has to centre on saving the environment – on attempting somehow to halt and reverse our ferocious destruction of the natural world. This does not mean that social justice no longer matters. Suffering passengers on the sinking ship still need to be cared for. But all schemes, such as Marxism and monetarism, which try to provide for human welfare without attending to the damage we are doing to the system we live by are hopelessly unrealistic.

I do not want to go on about these various competing ideologies, which I have discussed elsewhere. Marxism, however, is central to my story because it was a real issue in our lives at that time. Along with the problem of pacifism, Would it be justifiable to fight in the war that seemed to be approaching?, it was a constant topic of thought. Iris's concern about it was not unusual. Though there must, of course, have been plenty of students who managed to ignore these matters, I think most of us were aware of them and certainly most of those whom I got to know well took them seriously. This included a number of scientists who became my close friends and thus provided a trickle of light to lessen my ignorance of the physical world.

One of these was Charlotte Williams-Ellis, daughter of the architect Clough Williams-Ellis, a zoology student. She had incidentally a hot line to the political debates because her uncle, John Strachey, was one of the editors of the Left Book Club. She too became a lifelong friend and is now a distinguished environmentalist and a professor of zoology in New Zealand. Another, Greta Myers, was then a medical student, one of a nice group whom I got to know through Charlotte and who began to put a bit of biology onto my mental map. It was also Greta, bless her, who did me the important service of telling me, soon after I arrived at

Somerville, to stop doing my hair like a girl guide and do something about my shoes. Greta later worked with Professor Trueta on the rehabilitation of children damaged by Thalidomide and did important research on the concept of handicap under her married name of Margaret Agerholm. She too remained my close friend until she died.

Studying the classics

All this time, of course, we were supposed to be doing some academic work, and we actually did do quite a lot of it. Iris and I plunged at once into a desperate race to catch up with our male contemporaries, attacking a syllabus in Classics that had been evolved during several centuries for public-school boys who had – rather bizarrely – spent their whole early life in learning Latin and Greek. This work in Classics occupied our first five terms, till we took Honour Moderations. It may be best to describe it as a whole now, ignoring the break caused by the start of the war at the end of our first year, and go back to the topic of war later.

With the best will in the world, Mildred Hartley, our tutor at Somerville, made the bad effects of our inadequate classical training even worse. Like so many academic women in the early days she was determined not just that that her students should do well but that they should do exactly as well as the men by exactly the same standards. ('Anything you can do I can do better . . .') In the days when Emily Davies insisted on this policy at the foundation of Girton, it may well have had a political point. But it always distorted things because the girls usually had so little preparation before college that they were not actually leaping the same hurdles as the men at all but others grotesquely higher. Mildred, though benevolent, was quite unrealistic about our patchy training. Right away, she kept explaining very advanced things to us without noticing that we didn't have the equipment to understand what she was talking about. And, in choosing our options, she told us firmly to take Latin and Greek composition in verse as well as in prose.

Composing verses in strict metre in a foreign language does not have to be a pointless activity. When Milton, or even Dr Johnson, made Latin verses, they were working within a still-living tradition of Latin poetry. In fact, Latin was then still the second language of educated Europe, to the point where Johnson could converse in Latin in Paris rather than in his less fluent French. Writers like him were so soaked in this literary tradition that they naturally thought in the language and could naturally add to the literature.

Even then, however, it was surely bizarre that writing these verses was a regular, compulsory school exercise. Most of the boys who had to do it can't possibly have had the background that would give sense to the proceeding. Done simply as an exercise, it doesn't have the value which prose composition in foreign languages has of making one rethink the meaning in different terms. It simply requires that one should somehow find words that will more or less scan so as to fit the metre. These boys were usually translating English poetry into Latin or Greek and they could do it only as a rather desperate kind of crossword puzzle. And this was what we found ourselves doing too. In more recent times, I can only think of one educational exercise that has been carried on in this sort of way – namely, the state of things in English Studies a little time back when students had to learn the bizarre language of post-structuralist literary theory in order to write their essays in it.

I am told that this sort of theory has now become less fashionable, but I suspect that the same kind of thing still goes on. Samuel Butler pointed out the objections to it in 1872, when he described the Erewhonian education system:

> They are taught what is called the hypothetical language for many of their best years . . . The store they set by the hypothetical language can hardly be believed; they will even give anyone a maintenance for life if he attains a considerable proficiency in the study of it; nay, they will spend years in learning to translate some of their own good poetry into the hypothetical language – to do so with fluency being reckoned a distinguishing mark of a scholar and a gentleman. Heaven forbid that I should be flippant, but it appeared to me to be a wanton waste of good human energy that men should spend years and years in the perfection of so barren an exercise . . .

Butler, incidentally, was educated at the same public school as Darwin, namely Shrewsbury, where his grandfather was headmaster, a school which Darwin thought wasted his time abominably. He wrote in his *Autobiography*:

> Nothing could have been worse for the development of my mind than Dr Butler's school, as it was strictly classical, nothing else being taught except a little geography and history. The school as a means of education to me was simply a blank . . . Especial attention was paid to verse-making, and this I could never do well. I had many friends and got together a grand collection of old verses, which by patching together, sometimes aided by other boys, I could work into any subject . . . The sole pleasure I ever received from such studies was from some of the Odes of Horace, which I admired greatly . . . When I left the school . . . I was considered by all my masters and by my Father as a very ordinary boy, rather below the common standard in intellect.

But the steam roller still rumbled on in my own day. In 1945, when I taught the boys of the Classical Sixth Form at Bedford School, verse composition in Latin and Greek was still a compulsory subject.

For our other options we chose texts that we liked and got a great deal out of reading them, but we were often bewildered by the way in which we had to study them. Two subjects that I had never even heard of before suddenly loomed up as central. One was philology, the study of the origin and relationships of particular Greek and Latin words. The other was textual criticism, the attempt to find out what the original wording of each text had been by discovering how repeated copying had corrupted it.

Both of these are actually fascinating and necessary studies, but the way in which some dons presented them did not make this obvious. I particularly remember one lecturer embarking on a long list of various different ways of spelling the name Pyrrha – variations that copyists had introduced in one of Horace's Odes. Before starting he grunted in sepulchral tones – 'Absolutely insoluble problem – of not the slightest importance – However – Here goes . . .'

No doubt, teachers were liable to develop this sort of attitude when they had a captive audience of boys forced to study the Classics. They didn't even need to pretend to be interested. But not long afterwards, when the long monopoly of Classical Studies was broken after the war, these scholars got their comeuppance. Classicists, like other people, began to have to explain why what they were doing mattered and to make the point clear to students. It was very good for them.

There were, however, some dons at Oxford in my day who were already doing this. One was E. R. Dodds, Gilbert Murray's successor as Professor of Greek. Like Murray, he had a deep understanding of the texts he lectured on and, though he may have been rather sterner than Murray about exact scholarship, he always went to the heart of the meaning in his lectures. We were lucky enough to go to his lectures on the Greek dramatists, and also on Plato.

Another was the Professor of Latin, Eduard Fraenkel. He was one of the many Austrian and German refugees then working at Oxford and was an immensely cultivated humanist. Listening to his lectures, I began to hear of something quite unknown to me – the long and fascinating history of how European scholarship developed, a story that makes sense of textual criticism and indeed of philology too. He told us how the shape of the books – scrolls or codices – affected the habits of copyists and scholars: how much more troublesome it is to check a reference on a scroll, what conventions people used for abbreviations, how gaps were not always left between words, how punctuation only gradually developed, how scholars had gradually become skilled in penetrating the resulting confusions, and what had been happening to the ideas that lay behind our literature.

As he talked, the whole process came alive. The generations of copyists and other workers who, till then, had seemed to be mere blockish obstructions to our efforts gradually emerged as colleagues, fellow toilers in the effort to understand and use the work of the great writers. The names that were attached in our texts to various conjectures and interpretations – Stephanus, Bentley, Porson, Housman – proved not to be just meaningless formulae but to belong to real people, people who, at actual dates, had looked at the muddles that were developing and had thought hard about how to resolve them. It was by their efforts (we now saw) that we were often able to enjoy clear and sharp sense in a poem instead of the blurred cliché that a weary monk had drifted into writing at the end of his day. The sense of being part of a great timeless effort – a sense that one gets to some extent anyway from the buildings of Oxford – became much clearer and more immediate. This continuity is something that has a value independent of current errors – something whose beauty persists however stupidly universities may at any given time be behaving.

I was specially impressed to hear how Porson succeeded, in the eighteenth century, in making his colleagues attend to the metre in Greek tragedy, something that had gradually become quite neglected when Greek was no longer spoken and the lines were no longer heard as speech. By working out the rules of these metres, he managed at a stroke to restore both the sense and the music to a host of lines that had become apparently hopelessly distorted. And in doing this he made it possible to see once more that the stuff had actually been spoken – that it was not just schoolwork but living drama

I don't think that Iris went to Fraenkel's Horace lectures. But she certainly did go to his class on Aeschylus' *Agamemnon*, which was a much more serious affair. This was a long, ongoing investigation that gradually worked its way through the whole play at a snail's pace over many years, dealing with every conceivable problem of text, interpretation, metre, style, character and background history that arose. Each week from five to seven o'clock around twenty people – about half undergraduates and half dons – sat round a long table with Fraenkel in a ground-floor room in Corpus Christi College – a visibly ancient room with Tudor windows, so that one had a strong impression of forming part of a timeless sequence of scholars. Tradition says that this class was followed by drinks at the Bear, but I think this must have been only for the elders. Undergraduates who wanted their dinner in college had to get it pretty soon after seven, so we certainly did not linger.

Those who came had somehow to be certified as seriously interested. Iris and I were told about the class quite early in our course by our tutor Mildred Hartley. She explained that this would be a great privilege; it was a most distinguished affair. A condition of entry was that we should promise to take our part in the work of interpretation and should never miss a session. If we were ill or dying, we must just tell Professor Fraenkel so in advance and in writing. So when – as will be explained later – I broke my leg and also hurt my right wrist during the spring of 1940, I duly scrawled my excuses for absence to Fraenkel, who graciously replied by sending me a little book. And it certainly never occurred to me to miss another session. I think we attended the class all through our first five terms.

For each session, the passage being discussed was prepared by two participants, one an undergraduate and the other a don, both of whom had to say exactly what they thought it meant and to defend their view about it. I remember conferring anxiously with Iris and a male undergraduate who was also involved in the passages that had been set to us, and finding with surprise how much better equipped than us he seemed to be about the language, and how much less idea he had of the point of what was being said. The procedure was that the undergraduate started in first, proceeded to get tangled up in fearful difficulties, was told by Fraenkel that he was hopelessly mistaken and was then supplemented by the don, who was also told firmly where he was wrong. After this Fraenkel himself took over and the discussion, becoming general, might go on for weeks, citing other relevant passages and ranging over most of European history. It was a terrifying procedure but also totally fascinating.

Agamemnon is a play that – as I knew already before I came to college – can stand up to all this investigation and more. It is about the problem of evil, the mysterious and dreadful entanglement of right with wrong that starts to pervade the story in the first great chorus. Fraenkel kept coming back to that chorus even though it is much earlier in the play than the part that we were actually supposed to be working on. When Peter Conradi recently asked me about this class for his biography of Iris, I thought that I would be able to name the exact passages we had studied by looking for places where my text was heavily scribbled. But in fact I find it scribbled almost throughout. I do know that the passage I particularly had to deal with was the wonderful speech in which Clytemnestra tells Agamemnon that he is being contemptibly mean when he hesitates to tread on the purple tapestry she has laid out for him to walk on into the palace (lines 958–74): 'There's plenty more purple dye in the world, and even in your own palace', she says. 'There is a sea, and who shall drain it dry? . . .'

Biographers also want me to tell them whether Frank Thompson, who was later Iris's lover, was also at this class. I think he probably was, but I don't remember him. The trouble is, of course, that everybody remembers their own affairs. I remember just one undergraduate who was there – Nick Crosbie, with whom I was then in love. (He joined the Fleet Air Arm not long after and was lost at sea.) I also remember a couple of very impressive older dons, one called Geary, the other, whose name now escapes me, the author of a little book of very funny poems in Greek and Latin which I've still got somewhere if only I could find it.

It will be clear that there was a great deal of passion around in this class – not only Fraenkel's own passion for literature, and his passion for dominance, but lots of other elements as well. When Iris asked Isobel Henderson whether we should take the course, Isobel said briskly, 'Yes, do go to Fraenkel's classes. He'll probably paw you about a bit, but never mind.' Iris didn't mind that. She got a rich mixture of private tuition and harmless cuddling and, as Peter Conradi explains, she developed a deep friendship with him. But she mused on the strange, intense atmosphere of these classes later in a poem that she wrote for Frank Thompson (which Conradi quotes in full):

> Did we expect the war? What did we fear?
> First love's incinerating, crippling flame,
> Or that it would appear
> In public that we could not name
> The aorist of some familiar verb?
> The spirit's failure we knew nothing of,
> Nothing really of sin and pain.

It was a strange mixture. I remember one occasion that showed the best and the worst of Fraenkel in sharp conjunction. After one class he started to invite Iris to his room, meaning (I think) to get her on her own. But she was giggling with me and Nick, and it ended with his taking the lot of us. He then showed us the passage in Goethe's *Faust* where Mephistopheles says 'Ich bin der Geist der stets verneint' – I am the spirit who always says No – and talked very interestingly about its connection with the nature of evil. This was good. But then, shortly after, we met him in Mildred Hartley's room and, on somebody's mentioning Nick, Fraenkel said, 'Ach, he is the Cherubino of my classes'. This meant that he cast himself as the Count, a bizarre thought totally disconnected from real life.

Mary Warnock, a few years younger than us, went to Fraenkel's classes some years later. She got the same mixture of tuition and cuddling to supplement these classes that Iris did, and she discusses it interestingly in her *Memoir*. She thinks that Fraenkel and the other refugee German scholars who were then present in Oxford had a very good effect on classical studies there, and beyond that (she adds):

> I believe they had an effect on philosophy as well . . . We learned from [these classes] the uselessness of wild interpretation without evidential support; we learned always to ask what a particular word could have meant at the time when it was used; we learned to treat classical authors, as far as we could, as coming from a culture vastly different from our own, a culture we had to study in all its aspects if we were to understand the texts . . . This deep desire to get things right, even quite small things, undoubtedly reappeared in post-war philosophy.

She is surely right about this. As for the erotic element, she remarks:

> When Iris and I started talking about him . . . nearly thirty years later, we discovered that we both felt exactly the same. In one way, the impropriety of his sexual behaviour seemed utterly trivial compared with the riches he offered us, and the vast horizons he opened up. In another way, the conjunction of the physical with the intellectual seemed the most natural thing in the world, a conjunction of mind and body which it would have been silly and ungrateful to attempt to disjoin.

Evidently she found it rather more disturbing than Iris did, but clearly neither of them was the worse for the experience, though she mentions another friend who was seriously disturbed by it. (I didn't get involved in this aspect myself so I can't give an opinion.) Peter Conradi comments, speaking of Iris, 'That there was anything dangerous or degrading in his behaviour, which would nowadays constitute a shocking example of sexual harassment, never occurred to her'. Standards in these matters are always changing. We shall see what sin moralists pick on next.

Thus, being taught in ways that varied between these two extremes, we worked our way through to our first big exam, Honour Moderations, which occurred after five terms (leaving seven more terms for Greats) in the spring of 1940.

What I chiefly remember about that spring term is the bitter cold. This did have its advantages. Heavy rain during the Christmas vacation had swelled the rivers, flooding the whole of Port Meadow (the big common north-west of the city, conveniently near to Somerville), and when term began the flood froze over, becoming a vast skating rink. Everybody bought skates and we used them euphorically for every minute when we could manage it. The trouble with this is that the better you get at it, the faster you go . . . So, a couple of weeks later, I went too fast and skated into a sunken log, fell over, broke my ankle and sprained my right wrist. After that I was naturally fixed indoors for quite a long time with little choice but to revise incessantly for Mods. I did this rather badly, since I can never work properly if I don't get breaks to move about and revive my concentration. Our rooms were miserably cold because (the war, to which I'll come back shortly, having now started) we were kept very short of fuel. And outside, slushy snow and Oxford fog during most of the term compounded the difficulty of stumping around with my leg in plaster.

When we finally took the exam in March 1940 the climate had not relaxed in the least, nor was the heating any better. We bicycled down clutching our hot-water bottles and took them into the exam room, but they were nothing like enough to last us through the three-hour papers. The one beauty of the situation was that, for some reason connected with exceptional wartime conditions, we did not take this exam in the usual rooms but in the seventeenth-century Divinity School attached to the Bodleian Library. This is a wonderful building, amazingly serene in its atmosphere and roofed with a particularly splendid fan-vaulted ceiling. My degree for this exam was a Second. I think I owe the fact that it was not a Third or even a Fourth to the inspirations that I got when, from time to time, I looked up at that ceiling.

In the spring vacation after that exam, I went with some Oxford friends on a wonderful sailing holiday on the Norfolk Broads – a holiday that stands out sharply in my memory because there wasn't a lot of this kind of thing during the war. It was organized by the Cozens-Hardy family – John, who was then a medical student and is still a friend today, his brother Graham and his sister Mary who was at Somerville – and we all set out from their house in Norwich. Charlotte Williams-Ellis came too, so did my school friend Pandora who was now also at Somerville. So did John Insley, my father's godson who had come up to Oxford when I did; we had been helping each other to get used to the place. Most of us couldn't sail but, trained by the Cozes, we became very spry at it by the end of the week, shouting fiercely 'Ready about . . . Lee oh!' with the best.

The broads gave us a peculiarly delightful impression – at that time, without many other boats – of being alone in an infinite space. Sailing across the open water, you only saw the vast sky above and its reflection below, with just a slight fringe of reeds and their upside-down reflection to mark the barrier between the two. And in the winding channels between the open broads, where the banks were often wooded, you never knew what you would see round the next corner. We might just as well have been somewhere on the Amazon.

The small scale of the whole thing didn't seem to matter at all. I recall one frantically exciting and satisfactory morning spent tacking up the little winding river Ant against a fierce north-east gale. We covered a huge distance, but we were quite happy to arrive somewhere not very far from where we had started. Now when you are actually sailing at sea – as I have occasionally done since – the sea around you all looks the same. You don't get half the sense of achievement from going quite a long distance that you have when you have managed at last to round an obstinate point on a narrow river without actually running into anything.

We slept five girls in one boat and five men in the other – a simple arrangement that probably seemed more obvious then than it would today – but of course we mixed up completely and harmoniously in the daytime. I am not sure by what stages I had gradually got used to having men around during my time at Somerville, but plainly I had done so by that holiday. Actually, though no one predicted it at the time, two of these mariners – Peter and Moira – did later get married, and as far as I know they lived happily ever after.

I took a lot of trouble writing up the log for this voyage and I can be seen doing so in the photo on the cover of this volume. I would have liked to look at this log afterwards, but someone went off with it and I have never seen it since.

This holiday had one other feature which may sound rather strange today. On the morning when we were about to set off from Norwich, the radio gave out the news that the Germans had started to invade Denmark and were probably about to invade Norway.

What were we to do? At first we thought that we must simply cancel the trip and go straight home. But then we began to consider; what good would that do? We could do nothing useful by it. The Coz parents said no, go ahead and have your week. And gradually we began to think that they were right. Then somebody – I think John Coz – said, 'Well, if we're going to do that, let's do it properly. Let's not take a radio or buy any papers during the week. Let's have time off from the war and get back to it when this week is over.' This is what we did, and I have never seen any reason to regret it.

A changing world

To return, then, to the war. We had, of course, seen it approaching all through my first year at college. In the spring of 1939 the Germans invaded Czechoslovakia, which Neville Chamberlain revealingly described as a far-off country whose name, in his view, most English people probably could not spell. Then the Germans threatened Poland, whose name people could spell. On 23 August they concluded their non-aggression pact with the USSR so as to make sure that the Russians would act as allies and fellow-bandits rather than opposing them. That point being settled, on 3 September both they and the Russians invaded Poland, after which Britain and France declared war on Germany.

For us bystanders this invasion was by now no surprise. There was even a certain relief in finding that our country had at last come out as an opponent of Nazism rather than being cast as its ally. This was the start of something welcome for people like me and my friends that persisted throughout the war – the sense of being at last in agreement with the rest of the country rather than struggling against it. I think that, despite all sorts of cross-currents, the anti-Nazi feeling that reigned in the war was genuine and did reflect some understanding of the actual evils involved. But, strong though that feeling was, it had not looked inevitable in advance that it would lead to action.

During the previous year indeed this had sometimes seemed very doubtful. Prominent British supporters of Nazism – some of them in very high places – had campaigned to exploit the Munich accord by cementing the friendship with Germany that they believed Hitler was offering. Organizations such as The Link and The Anglo-German Fellowship had painted rosy pictures of European harmony secured on this basis. With remarkable naivety, the leaders of this movement, flattered by Hitler's personal assurances of respect, had deluded themselves into supposing that he would be merely a harmless and manageable ally for them against the USSR, which they saw as the only real menace.

This fantasy may look incredible now, but at that time some quite influential people took it seriously. And when one remembers the Fifth Column networks that welcomed the Germans in France and other countries after they invaded, it seems clear that such things were not impossible. That, anyway, is how it came about that, during the summer of 1939, I worked for a month or two as a volunteer researcher for some subdepartment of the Labour Party (name now forgotten) trying to investigate what these potential Fifth Columnists were intending to do – whether, for instance, they were already plotting treason. Jean

Rowntree had, I think, played some part in arranging this, but other fairly senior people involved evidently thought the investigation necessary.

Cycling up from Kingston every day I worked on this strange project from an office somewhere in Westminster which was run by the MP John Freeman. My position there did not really make much sense. The work I was supposed to be doing could only have been done properly by an experienced journalist with suitable contacts – or at least, failing that, by someone who was enough of a natural-born detective to make such contacts on their own. Unfortunately I was neither of these things.

John Freeman was friendly enough and he gave me a number of starting points. But these were in libraries, and it was in libraries that I mostly continued to circulate, mainly finding stuff that was already in the public domain – schemes and pronouncements that were already on record. Much of this I found straightforwardly, though time-consumingly, in the British Museum Reading Room, often tracing it in old copies of *The Times* which were then stacked in enormous frames round the central issue desk

I have to say, in defence of my sanity, that even by these hopelessly primitive methods I did find a pile of thoroughly damning and sinister material. Pro-Nazi schemes had not been concealed; they were frequently on record. I don't doubt that some of my suspects were indeed up to no good. My efforts, however, would not have been likely to hinder them much if events in the world had happened to move their way. But of course they didn't. These people had backed the wrong horse. War on Germany was duly declared, and during the following year Winston Churchill, taking over from Chamberlain, made sure that the dangers of Nazism were taken seriously.

I stopped work on this research at the end of August 1939, leaving behind in that office a stack of files on potential Fifth Columnists. These no doubt met the usual end of all earthly files at some suitable date – perhaps at the point where they stopped being needed because, during the war, many of the characters I had enquired about were duly interned in the Isle of Man.

This work, though quite interesting, was much less use to me personally than it should have been because it was so solitary. Like my visit to Vienna, it ought to have presented a chance to get out into a wider world and meet more kinds of people, and it was undoubtedly partly my own fault that it didn't do so. If I'd been a different sort of person – if, for instance, I'd been that natural-born detective – I would surely have insisted on meeting some journalists. I would have gone to pubs rather than to the British Museum. I would probably have insisted on somehow meeting some of my suspects themselves. As it was, I simply didn't think of doing any of these things, which just shows how narrow my focus was. I did what people told me, assuming that they knew best. This amounted to treating the project like a large-scale history essay and producing those files at the end of it.

When that end came, I breathed a deep sigh of relief at not having to cycle twenty-two miles through London traffic daily any longer. It was about this time that I discovered that, irritatingly, I am not physically inexhaustible. If I do too much, my digestion packs in and I have to rest rather sooner and longer than other people do. A couple of walking tours had already begun to make this clear to me and I now began to see that I had to believe it. This slight weakness has remained with me throughout my life, going under various names as medical fashions have changed – it has now voguishly acquired a set of initials, IBS for Irritable Bowel Syndrome. It has become less troublesome since I discovered, in middle age, that panicking in crises doesn't help and is usually a waste of time. But I still always have to keep watching it.

Life in wartime

War, then, had begun. And when people now ask what it was like, it is hard to convey just how it was that we managed to get used to it so quickly.

Certainly it was horrifying. It was the supreme disaster about which everybody had been saying for the past twenty years that it must never happen again. But such big disasters, as they approach and become real, always break down into a number of separate elements – into anxieties about particular people and questions about what to do next. Except for some born black-marketeers, I suppose most people wondered what they ought to be doing, and at once there were so many answers to this that many of us quickly became involved in routine, which domesticates almost anything.

When talking about that now, the natural thing is to make light of the difficulties of wartime because many of them aren't important in themselves and don't cause lasting distress in later life. That is the line that I would certainly have taken in writing this memoir if it weren't that I want to correct a certain pernicious mistake which has crept into our language recently about what it means to be 'at war'. Today it is a widely accepted cliché that we are now engaged in a 'war on terrorism'. This is apparently not supposed to be just a metaphorical war, as in 'war on poverty' or 'war on crime', but in some sense a literal war, one that justifies the use of real weapons and the curtailment of civic liberties.

In this situation I want to point out, from experience, what it is like to be literally 'at war'. First, when you are at war you personally are almost certainly not doing what you would normally be doing or what you would have chosen to do. You have been sent somewhere else because you have either been called up or directed to work of national importance. Most of your friends and family, too, have also been moved around in this way – some of them are in danger, some may already have been injured or killed. It is often hard to find out what has happened to them.

Food, clothes and petrol are strictly rationed. Everything that is not rationed is getting scarcer and scarcer. Many ordinary goods vanish entirely; to find others takes a lot of effort and queuing. A tiny example occurs to me: at some point late in the war I wanted to buy a nail brush. The girl in the chemist's shop started to say, in a completely offhand mechanical way, as she obviously did for everything else, 'Oh no, those are gone, there aren't any of them now –' Then suddenly an exciting thought struck here; her eyes lit up and she whispered, 'Actually we have got One, but it's incredibly expensive. It's an experimental one, made of a quite new stuff called Nylon. It costs *nine shillings*.' Carried away by the splendour of the occasion I bought it, and it was a very good one, it lasted me till quite recently. But such luck was most unusual.

To continue the list of troubles. Public transport isn't working normally; when you can get it it is slow, overcrowded, unheated and liable to keep stopping or going to the wrong station for unexplained reasons. Everyday life is cluttered with extra difficulties caused by matters such as air-raid precautions, even if you don't have actual air raids. The news, though clearly censored, tells you of enough troubles bearing directly on the survival of your country and perhaps of your civilization to let you know that your own future, as well as other people's, is profoundly uncertain.

And so on. I could go on, but perhaps that is enough to show that we are not living now in that rather extreme state. The people who do live like that now are the Iraqis, whose war is supposed to be over. We ourselves, by contrast, are living much as usual, though we anticipate possible terrorist outrages. But conceiving these as 'a war' is surely a bad way of understanding them. Terrorists are not a fixed batch of enemies. Terrorism is a set of methods used by a shifting band of disturbed and desperate people who are being recruited all the time from among those who are provoked by various kinds of political oppression. Military weapons used against these populations simply recruit more terrorists. Angry populations are like the Hydra which sprouts ten more heads for every one that you cut off. The unsuitability of war imagery for these situations was made plain enough in the years when the colonial empires were being disbanded. It is surely perverse to go back to it today.

The Second World War, by contrast, was a real war, not a metaphorical one, and, as I have explained, by the time it started most of us thought, however reluctantly, that it was necessary. Young men like my brother Hugh had then to decide whether to enlist or to become conscientious objectors. Hugh, who had just finished taking a history degree at King's College, Cambridge, had already been arguing with his friends there about this for years. They now had a final series of intense arguments, after which some went one way and some another. Hugh was among those who thought it was now necessary to fight, so he joined the army, enlisting in the Green Howards. After training with them for a year or so he was sent to India and spent the rest of the war there, mainly at Dehra Dun which was then a large military station in the foothills of the Himalayas. He didn't have a bad time there but I don't think he found it very interesting. We got a lot of those miniaturized air letters from him but they didn't tell one much and I haven't kept them, though I do have a photo of him on a camel.

Women students like myself also had the option of leaving university to join the forces and quite a lot did do this. But it was not national policy to close down higher education altogether. We were told at some point quite early in the war that women might well make themselves more useful by finishing their courses than by enlisting at once. The country would still need highly educated people for work in places like the civil service, and most men students would now be taking only short courses at university before enlisting. This advice seemed sound to me. I was also keen to finish my course, and I was fairly sure that my digestion would make a lot of trouble if I tried to join the women's services. So I stayed, along with Iris and most of my Somerville friends, though my friends Pandora and Jacobine went into the forces after their first year at college.

All round us however uniforms appeared, and they too quickly became a matter of routine rather than of drama. Our friends in the services often turned out not to be doing anything particularly exciting. In civilian life, air-raid precautions – especially blackout curtains – fire-watching, rationing and all sorts of changes in business arrangements kept everybody busy. My father had a tin hat so that he could go out and help people in air raids – somebody stencilled VICKER on it but this was later corrected. He grew terribly expert at fuel-saving, priding himself on making one lump of anthracite last all day in the dining-room stove. My mother quickly became very good at black-outs and at devising good food to meet new difficulties. The council began to keep pigs, so bins to collect food for them appeared on the lamp-posts in our street. We put our potato-peelings and cabbage stalks (but *not* orange-peel) in the bin near our front gate. People in the street became much more friendly, instead of ignoring each other most of the time in the London style as they had done before.

Kingston did not have air raids at first, during the so-called Phoney War before the Germans began their real bombardment. But later in the winter of 1939–40, when the Blitz did start, we began to have alerts every night, and to hear bombs often elsewhere, along with a good deal of anti-aircraft fire. My parents then arranged the wide shelves in our cellar so that we could all sleep down there, and for a time we did do this, going down as soon as the siren sounded or even before. This arrangement, however, irritated my mother's auntie Nan, who at that time was living with us. She liked to pee in the night and at some point she asked whether this cellarization was really worthwhile. My parents agreed that it was not, and after that we mostly slept upstairs. When I had my twenty-first birthday party, however, in September 1940, raids did seem to be a little alarming. The first big air raids on central London had begun in August and they intensified early in September. But we managed to have our party. We arranged to put up a dozen guests or so to avoid their having to go home through the shrapnel. Some of them slept in the cellar. It was a particularly jolly occasion and had no bad consequences of any kind.

It may sound strange to some readers now that we should mostly have stopped bothering to sleep in shelters. I can only refer them to the reports of many other people who did the same thing. I think that, for many of us, the nuisance of sleeping in an awkward place was simply too troublesome an addition to all the extra confusions of daily life in wartime conditions. This may actually chime with the thought that some people are now expressing – that concentration on risk, even real risk, easily distorts practical thinking. It can be quite hard to keep one's sense of danger proportionate to realities because, if you attend to it, it is inclined to take over. In the war, too, one could estimate to some extent the sort of risk that threatened one's own district. Kingston was not central London and we were not living next door to a power station.

The flying bombs, which began to arrive in 1944, certainly were alarming and at first there seemed to be something almost supernaturally weird about the fact that they were unmanned. This didn't seem to make sense . . . But again, after a time we got more or less used to this peculiarity. Calling them buzz-bombs or doodle-bugs defused the spooky element and it grew quite interesting to realize that their engines always cut out well before they came down – so, if you could still hear the engine noise you were probably all right. One of them did land on Surrey County Hall, which was in Kingston not far from us, but it did us no harm.

I don't remember just when it was that a bomb actually did fall in our back garden. It was a small one – 110 pounds as I recall – and it didn't hurt anybody, though we were all sleeping upstairs at the time. It smashed the greenhouse, broke the back windows including mine, knocked down the garden wall and left quite an impressive hole in the flower bed. I later filled in this hole, and we grew tall artichokes there to replace the wall. The greenhouse never recovered so all the grapes after that were sour, but the windows were mended quite soon. My parents were emphatic that such things were done much more quickly and fairly in this war than they had been in the earlier one – notably, as is well known, in the matter of rationing. Those responsible at the Ministry of Food made a very good job on the whole both of fair distribution and of nutrition, arranging for things hitherto unknown like the wholemeal national loaf and the orange juice for children. People grumbled about the grey loaf, but they ate it and it must have done them good. Mostly we got enough to eat, though of course it did tend to be rather dull. There was a lot of excitement to be got out of unexpected things scrounged and sudden windfalls. I remember one time when some friend who was stationed in the Hebrides suddenly sent us a huge box of Stornaway kippers. They were wonderful, but how on earth could they all be eaten at suitable speed? You can't go on eating kippers for ever, and there was no fridge to keep them in . . . We bicycled round delivering them to everybody we could think of.

During that September, and in other vacations, I did some fire-watching while I was at home in the shelter under the marketplace, but this never involved any actual fires. It simply meant sleeping in a bunk in a rather noisy cellar from time to time. I also took a minimal nursing training – a rather futile course of first-aid lectures and fifty hours working in the local hospital. This was better because it involved meeting the patients – mostly, of course, bringing them their meals, fetching bed-pans, cleaning these up afterwards and 'doing backs' – rubbing people's bottoms and heels with spirit to save them from getting bedsores from long stays in bed. (I'm told that this essential work doesn't always get done today, with bad results.)

More surprising jobs sometimes varied the scene. Once the ward sister sent me over to a distant part of the hospital with orders to ask for 'alligator forceps and a sphigmoidoscope'. She didn't write these words down, but she made me repeat them so carefully that I not only managed to bring the things back but have remembered them ever since. Perhaps she needed this method of supply because the telephone lines had been bombed. But I got the impression that the procedure was normal.

Mostly the nurses were too busy to give us any real training; we simply got used to hospital routine. But this would have been quite helpful if we had been involved in such things later, and it's actually worthwhile anyway to understand it, even when you are only a patient. I got on well on the whole with the nurses and liked their attitude, but I did think that there was sometimes something a bit obsessive about it. One of them once said to me 'But why *don't* you want to be a nurse? What else is there that is as well worth doing?' which was hard to answer but, I thought, not conclusive.

When I went back to Oxford in October, I walked into one of those colourful muddles which afflict administrators who have to deal with sudden events such as wars. It concerned the time when college gates shut at night. Up till now, the men had had to be in at midnight and the women at 11.15 – presumably so that the men could see the girls home before running for their own deadline. Now, however, those in charge of the men's colleges had ruled that, since it was wartime, the men must be in by eleven. So the women's colleges responded by telling the girls to be in by 10.15.

Somerville students weren't having this. They began to shout, and as I came into the front hall one morning, I found a noisy indignation meeting going on. But just as I came in, this meeting was sternly addressed by an indignant anti-indignation protester, a third-year student who was President of the University Conservative Association. Why, she asked, did we suppose that we could understand the reasoning of our elders who had the burden of authority? If they made this regulation (she said), there could be no doubt that they had good reason for it. They were much better informed than we were about the complexities of security in wartime. They were skilled in such matters, and we were not. It would be deeply irresponsible to rock the boat, disturbing their delicate work with our ill-thought-out suggestions . . . But at this point she had to stop because the Principal's Secretary quietly came in with a notice to say that the offending announcement had actually been due to a mistake. All colleges alike would now close their gates at eleven.

Since Somerville was next door to the Radcliffe Infirmary, some of its buildings were taken over for wartime use as hospital wards. About thirty of us therefore moved out into Lady Margaret Hall for the year, and I was one of these. In the First World War, when the same thing had happened, the Somerville girls had been lodged in Oriel and, at the end of this occupation, a bizarre comedy was played out when the Oriel undergraduates startled the Principal by knocking a hole in the wall and coming through to visit the girls in the middle of the night. I don't know whether LMH was now chosen in order to avoid this happening again, nor indeed how that college hospitably found the space to accommodate us. But it did. We were put into one of its oldest parts, the Victorian Gothic mansion at the end of the range, by the entrance to the University Parks.

In winter, this had the drawback that our rooms were even colder than most others, being heated only by ancient grates containing very little coal, as I found when I was shivering over Homer before Honour Mods. In summer, however, there was quite a lot to be said for being there because the gardens reached to the river, making it possible to bathe before breakfast. In all my summers in Oxford, my friends and I spent a heap of time on that river, punting, canoeing, swimming and picnicking at all sorts of hours. The Cherwell is now supposed to be too dirty to bathe in, and no doubt it was dirty then – I certainly remember one time when a dead sheep made a dignified progress down it and was last seen below Magdalen. But it didn't seem to do us any harm. I should mention too that in those days the Cherwell certainly never had fallen willow trees wallowing helplessly across it, making a fearful obstacle course for punts, as it does today – I saw them when I was taken on it last summer. I don't know what authority it is that is supposed to tidy up fallen willow trees, but it doesn't seem to have got better at its work with time.

Some of our rooms – though not mine – were on the ground floor and had locked metal grilles on their windows, but, because of the danger of fire, those living in these rooms were given keys. So these girls, though in my time they were sedate and law-abiding citizens, had to deal with quite a brisk traffic of people wanting to get in after hours. This arrangement is just one more instance of the muddles that follow – I suppose inevitably – on efforts to regulate the essentially unregulatable elements in student life. I never used this route myself. On the two occasions when I was late, I swam in, just to be different – once across the river, once over the little backwater by the Parks – and found handy doors conveniently open.

College food, never of the most exciting, naturally became duller with the war and a lot of ingenuity was used in supplementing it. If you got up very early and bicycled to Summertown it was possible to get celestial cakes by queueing outside the cake factory there, which still went on producing them, but not very many of them. These queues sometimes led to quite hard feelings.

During term as well as in the vacations we all did some war work, of which I chiefly remember freezing afternoons spent in digging stiff clayey soil to plant potatoes on Headington Hill, after a strenuous bicycle ride to get there. It was my first acquaintance with wireworms, and I have never wanted to get to know them any better. There were lots of them and we were told to squash them, but if you are using a fork rather than a spade this is far from easy. I also worked at one point in an office – probably for the Red Cross – that sorted out requests from prisoners of war who wanted books sent to them. This was rather worrying because we had to reduce their requests, which were often quite complicated, to certain recognized categories for a standard form. I'm sure there was a reason for this arrangement, but it sometimes left me with a worried feeling that they were going to get something quite different from what they had asked for.

Marxism in decline

In the spring of 1940, the nature of the war changed. Things suddenly began to happen. Just after we took Mods, the Germans invaded Denmark, then Norway, Holland and Belgium and swept on towards France. At the end of May, the British Expeditionary Force had to be evacuated from Dunkirk, and Churchill replaced Chamberlain as Prime Minister. Italy declared war on Britain and France. France fell, and on 14 June the German troops entered Paris.

All this changed many things and along with everything else it transformed undergraduate politics. Until now, the people who ran the Labour Club had stuck to the Marxist position that the war was essentially something negligible, just an attack by the imperialist West on the Soviet Union – a capitalist trick designed to delay the onset of the Revolution that would save the world. This never looked very convincing, but the German invasions in the spring of 1940, coming on top of Russia's invasion of Finland in November 1939, made its hollowness finally unbearable. The story that Russia was engaged in a noble enterprise to save the oppressed Finns from a dictatorial government was absurd. So a number of Labour Club members, led by Roy Jenkins and Tony Crosland, called a protest meeting to demand a change of the club's policy.

This produced a split, half the members joining the newly formed Democratic Socialist Club at once and many of the rest following soon after. Tony Crosland chaired the new club, Roy Jenkins was treasurer, and I – having made a fiery speech at the initial meeting – found myself suddenly elected on to the committee. I didn't stay there long, however, because I quickly found that the nitty-gritty of undergraduate politics wasn't my thing at all. Not only did it involve far more work that I was prepared to find time for but it also seemed at once to draw me into a world of faction and intrigue which I found disturbing. However, while I stayed I enjoyed the drama of the committee meetings, which always ended in song – often with that slender youth Roy Jenkins performing *Frankie and Johnnie* to great applause.

Iris, however, naturally moved the other way. She joined the Executive Committee of the Labour Club in April and at once became a leader of those still defending the sinking ship of orthodoxy. During the next year she became Secretary, then Chairman of this surviving remnant, and as its co-treasurer she carried on a Byzantine correspondence with Roy Jenkins about the division of the club's remaining debts and assets ('Dear Miss Murdoch' . . . 'Dear Comrade Jenkins' . . .).

But trouble hit her long before this. In that terrifying spring, indignation at the old Labour Club's pro-Russian – and by implication pro-German – attitude to the invasions was widespread and intense. On May Day, when they tried to hold a march through the city, its leaders were shouted down and pelted with all kinds of (non-lethal) missiles. I met Iris coming back to Somerville from this demo in rather a mess and she told me – without surprise – that she was just going to wash the tomatoes out of her hair. So I wrote up the occasion as follows:

Oh where is Iris Murdoch, tell me where? tell me where?
She has gone to help the workers demonstrate!
Plutaristocrat tomatoes in her hair, in her hair
Cannot wean her from the proletariate.
Though the gilded youth are baying in the High, in the High,
And the Bullingdon are calling for her head,
Crowned with gory drops and golden, in her heart she is beholden
Shown at last in her true colours as a Red!

I did not, of course, actually believe that it was only people like the Bullingdon (an aristocratic club) who were throwing things on that occasion, nor that Iris's demo had anything to do with the workers. But it seemed more friendly to use Labour Club mythology for the purposes of the rhyme. This dialect provided a kind of Newspeak to smooth over all kinds of awkward facts. Thus later on, in June 1941 when the Germans invaded Russia, the remaining faithful had suddenly to change sides again, converting the war in an instant from an irrelevant imperialistic feud into a crucial battle for civilization. Iris told me on that occasion that they were exhausted after being in almost ceaseless session night and day for a week, 'straightening out the party line'. (This is the kind of thing that Orwell had in mind when he described the sudden change of government policy in the middle of a political speech in *Nineteen Eighty-Four*.) After they finished this straightening, the comrades spent the rest of the war putting up posters that read 'Start The Second Front Now!' which meant, invade German-held Europe so as to take the pressure off the Russians. This, of course, got done in the end but probably not at their urging.

During these appalling events we continued to live our student lives, though with an increasing sense of unreality and confusion. At the time of the fall of France, I remember a philosophy don saying to me, 'I don't expect that there will be another term, do you? This is probably the end.' And this did seem likely. But, like everybody else, we lived on from day to day and kept finding that the Germans had not invaded us yet.

Starting Greats

Workwise, Iris and I now began to do Greats – Greek and Roman History and Philosophy. I enjoyed the History a lot. A History essay each week made a welcome change from the vastness and confusion of Philosophy. It did seem that History questions sometimes had an answer.

I am inclined to think, both from my feeling then and from my later teaching experience, that Philosophy at undergraduate level is always better done along with some other subject which provides some solid material to philosophize about. Doing it on its own – as half our students did at Newcastle – is inclined to lead people to get their minds stuck in various strange twists, twists which have their uses, but which need to be used when they are needed, not to become habitual all the time. Joint courses tend to give a better education.

Our History tutor, Isabel Henderson, being a widow and in delicate health, did not live in Somerville but with her parents in Lincoln College, where her father was Rector. She therefore stood a little outside college affairs and was notably free from a certain anxious perfectionism – a sense of being indeed on probation in the university – that radiated from most of the Somerville dons, including Mildred Hartley. She took life in a much more relaxed sort of way. She taught us Roman History herself and sent us to an amiable don called Tony Andrews in Pembroke for the Greek part.

Of course Greece and Rome aren't the whole of Ancient History. But they really are very interesting because they have influenced our own civilization so much. Moreover they are at the kind of distance which makes it possible to study them – unless you insist on doing their very earliest parts – on the grand principle laid down by E. Clerihew Bentley, that Geography is about Maps, but History is about Chaps. You can see particular people and try to understand them.

Fascinating personalities stand out from the stories, and some of those who wrote about them are themselves fascinating personalities too.

There is Tacitus, who made the proper remark of all time about empire when he reported a speech supposedly made by a British chieftain rousing his troops to resist the Romans and their 'pax Romana'. 'These men make a desolation', he said 'and they call it Peace'. And there is Thucydides, who tried so desperately hard to understand how it was that the Athenian dream had gone wrong – how the young and thriving democracy that was called upon to unite Greece against the Persians, had, after getting rid of the Persians, gradually turned the alliance into an empire, oppressed its allies and divided Greece by drifting into a deadly war against Sparta – how it had finally lost that war and lost also the moral authority that had been its real strength.

History is not actually all about chaps nor is it made up entirely of striking stories like these. In studying it you have to get down to a lot of much less delightful detailed evidence, and you end up balancing probabilities in what often looks more like a wrecked building site than the stage for a Greek tragedy. I did work on this background engineering and I came to enjoy it too, but I always found it hard – more especially in dealing with Rome, where the proportion of literature to indigestible facts is lower than it is with the Greeks. When I came to my final exam, I found this the hardest part, and it was certainly what made my examiners dither and put me through a very long viva before finally giving me a First. They did let me through, but I spent the night after the viva in an endless exhausting dream, repeatedly counting the legions that had to be sent to the various provinces and trying to remember how I had lost the ones that would be needed.

One reason for this long viva was undoubtedly that these Greats examiners had lately been having a lot of trouble in grading previous students whose work was good in one part of the course and resoundingly awful in another. People like me who had not had a traditional classical education were naturally prone to set them this dilemma. I believe, indeed, that there had been a specially bad case of this in the previous year over Elizabeth Anscombe, who had hardly looked at any part of the syllabus except the bits of philosophy that interested her, but had done so well there that they could hardly deny her a First. I can actually bear witness to this because, as it happens, during the course of her final exam she wandered in to see me one evening and explained that she would be taking the Political Theory paper next day, so she had just been glancing for the first time at the set books for it. 'And,' she said thoughtfully in her beautiful quiet voice, 'some of the stuff is actually quite interesting. But there's one thing here that I don't understand. As far as I can see, this man', and she drew out Hobbes's *Leviathan*, 'is just saying that you mustn't revolt unless you can. Can that be what he means?' I told her that indeed it is, and that plenty of other people have made the same complaint about him. But naturally in your finals papers you are supposed to do this at rather more length.

Since that time, Oxford has made more flexible arrangements for combining subjects in Greats so as to let people take only the ones that they are actually prepared to work at. It was not at all silly in the first place to link Philosophy with Greek because Plato and Aristotle and the Stoics really are first-rate philosophers and they have influenced later thought profoundly. But of course there are plenty of other good approaches. Philosophy can (I believe) now be combined with other subjects such as Psychology and Physics. In our day the only other way of doing it was in Modern Greats – Philosophy, Politics and Economics – a course introduced by G. D. H. Cole between the wars to meet demand, and to cater for the increasing numbers of people without Greek. But not everyone wants to do Economics or Politics either.

I think Oxford still does not provide an unmixed undergraduate course in Philosophy, as some other universities do, and here I believe Oxford is right, for the reasons just mentioned. Joint courses are best. The trouble with joint courses is only that the people teaching them seldom manage to do much about bringing the two subjects together. They come from separate tribes using separate dialects, and it is quite hard to dovetail their approaches properly. So usually the students have to do it for themselves.

They can do this without too much trouble provided that they talk together freely, and it does strike me that we did a great deal of this casually in Somerville. 'Did you understand that bit?' 'No, I didn't; it sounds mad. Look, there's Jean, let's ask her about it . . .' In spite of all the warnings about being on probation, on the whole the atmosphere in Somerville was sensible and positive. People had time to help each other. I remember a lot of casual talk in the evenings in people's rooms that brought things into perspective. Today, when most of the colleges are mixed, I hear that the girls spend a good deal of their time looking after their boyfriends and washing their socks. I'm sure this is educational too, but I think there was something to be said for not having to do it. Thus, in spite of a certain amount of nonsense in the single-sex days, I was sorry when Somerville went mixed.

When we started on philosophy I went to a lively discussion class run by Heinz Cassirer, the son of the polymath Ernst Cassirer. It was something of a bumpy ride in which we toured a lot of major problems – I think he rather enjoyed rushing us up to one question and then whisking us away to another. But this did mean we got a notion of how everything hung together, so we wanted to go on. This was just as well because my essay tutor at that point was a terribly cautious man who insisted on always keeping problems in their separate boxes.

It was quite early in this term that I first encountered Elizabeth Anscombe. She was a year senior to me and was reading Greats at St Hugh's, but she was having lunch in Somerville one day with Jean Coutts (also in her year, who later married the philosopher J. L. Austin) and somehow over lunch we began to talk about

Plato. I said that I thought Plato was actually right about the Forms – there did have to be Goodness Itself and the Man Himself behind the particular examples of men and goodness. Yes, said Elizabeth, but then we have to ask, what does this mean? What sort of behindness is it? What are we saying if we say that they are there . . .? So we all went off to Jean's room and dug on at this matter for most of the afternoon.

Elizabeth was not being in the least destructive in asking these questions. Her approach was as far as possible from the standard triumphant 'But what could that possibly *mean*?' which was the parrot cry of brisk young men who had picked up enough logical positivism to be sure already that it couldn't mean anything. She could see that it did mean something – Plato wasn't just being foolish – but it was still very hard to say just what.

This was Elizabeth at her best. I was lucky enough to catch her in this mood repeatedly as things went on. I got enormous help from her in a lot of directions; she helped me with the deepest problems that I tried to grapple with. It is notorious that she wasn't always accessible and helpful like this – that she was sometimes fractious, intolerant and unreasonable. But one got used to these moods and learnt to take her as she came on each occasion. It is my impression, however, that her devils were a good deal less active in those early days than they became later after she moved to Cambridge and came under Wittgenstein's influence. Wittgenstein was a truly great philosopher, but he was a tortured man who gave those around him a hard time and I think he trained them to do the same to outsiders. Tolerance was not in his own repertoire, and he liked to remove it from other people's.

I remember a comical instance of this other mood of Elizabeth's that occurred later on, after the war when we were all graduate students. She and Iris and I were having coffee together in Lyons' teashop in the Cornmarket and we were discussing the meaning of rudeness. I think this topic must have come up out of background discussions that Philippa Foot finally expressed in her splendid article called 'Moral Arguments' (which appeared in *Mind*, Vol. 67, 1958), where she used the example of 'rudeness' to show that a word's descriptive and evaluative meanings are not separate and independent. 'Rude' has to carry both. This discussion went on quite peacefully until Iris happened to say, 'Of course, the evaluative meaning of rudeness might not be all bad. For instance, Elizabeth, I should imagine that some people might sometimes describe you as "rude"?'

She didn't mean this remark to be in the least offensive. Elizabeth's unbridled rudeness was so proverbial that it simply didn't occur to Iris for a moment that she herself might not be perfectly well aware of it and indeed take pride in it. Iris couldn't have been more wrong. Elizabeth froze and was wholly silent for a long time, removing herself to an arctic distance. She then stood up and made a short speech, showing that she regarded any such suggestion as an intolerable and extraordinary insult, after which she marched out in dignified silence. Dumbstruck, we looked at one another and asked each other how we could possibly have known that she would take it like that? What on earth was Iris to do in order to make her peace? In fact this took her quite a long time and a lot of diplomacy, at which she was luckily very good. But since then I have found that this isn't an isolated phenomenon. People who go about treading on other people's toes all the time often are peculiarly unaware of what it feels like to be trodden on, so they are naturally much surprised when it happens to themselves. But of course on balance what one got from Elizabeth was something unique and hugely worthwhile.

In the autumn of 1940 Iris and I were moved from our boring and cautious essay tutor to be taught philosophy for the rest of our time by that remarkable character Donald MacKinnon. This was an enormous stroke of luck, without which I might well have drifted away from academic philosophy altogether. MacKinnon is a kind of Oxford legend because of his eccentricity, but he was an amazingly good teacher. This was entirely a matter of his direct response in tutorials, not of his lectures or his writing. It was when he shared a question with a student that he drew on his enormous powers of intellectual digging.

The eccentricity was certainly a nuisance at first. It was of a kind that (like so many other things) has now acquired a medical name. It centred, I suppose, on what is now called Tourette's Syndrome. Like Dr Johnson, MacKinnon often made strange unpredictable movements and, in particular, strange grimaces, which often seemed to express profound anguish. A lot of the stories about him are true enough. He did wave pokers and other things about in an alarming way and apparently did try to lever the fireplace off the wall with them. He did lie on the floor or beat the wall violently. In these spasms, he often seemed to be in distress and to be asking for help, which one could not give. He was prone to long silences, sometimes not seeming to hear at all what was said to him.

Besides doing these odd things he often failed to do the obvious things that anyone expects in conversation. Indeed, until you got used to him it was quite impossible to predict how he would react to anything that you said or did. All this was peculiarly alarming to new pupils, even when they had been warned about it, and at first I was quite terrified. But in time one learnt the language. It became clear that no actual disasters were going to follow.

The upside of all this was that he had wide and deep philosophical interests. He attended to all the big questions and took his pupils sympathetically through very varied approaches to them, showing the point of diverse surprising positions and suggesting how they might be related. In particular, he grasped the full breadth and importance of Kant's enterprise and made the time to get us used to its various aspects. I remember one tutorial when he had given me two hours – not one – in discussing a particular Kantian topic and he ended by saying 'I don't think we've really got to the bottom of this. Come back on Thursday', which I did. It was only when I taught philosophy myself and realized how desperately short of time one is that I understood his generosity. It was the more remarkable because he had at that time a heavy teaching load because so many dons were absent at the war. He himself was unfit for military service because of asthma, though he was quite young.

The philosophical scene

To show the exceptional luck that we had in having such a tutor, a word is needed about the background of Oxford philosophy at that time.

Apart from the standard teaching of classic texts such as Plato's *Republic*, this consisted of various slightly moth-eaten traditions, all of which equally had come under attack from the Cambridge analytical philosophers, Moore and Russell, and more recently from logical positivism. The fighting text here was A. J. Ayer's book *Language, Truth and Logic*, published in 1936. Its first chapter, called 'The Elimination of Metaphysics', begins with a trumpet blast:

> The traditional disputes of philosophers are, for the most part, as unwarranted as they are unfruitful . . . *If there are any questions which science leaves it to philosophy to answer*, a straightforward process of elimination must lead to their discovery. (Emphasis mine.)

So Ayer listed these possible kinds of question and decreed that they were all meaningless – indeed actual nonsense. He thus proved philosophy to be unnecessary, not just by citing its failures but *a priori* from the very nature of language, by ruling that no sentences had any meaning except those that were verifiable, which – rather surprisingly – were all held to be only the propositions of science. The Verification Principle dictated that the meaning of a sentence consists only in its verification, and this verification was only possible through sense perception, always – again rather surprisingly – within the context of science. Any meaning that might seem to belong to other kinds of talk, especially to metaphysics or ethics, was merely an emotive effect.

It never became clear how the vast range of intelligible human speech could ever have been squeezed into the bounds of science in this way. (Ayer was not much interested in science itself and did not discuss its difficulties.) Nor indeed was it explained how books such as *Language, Truth and Logic* could themselves be considered to mean anything. Did they perhaps count as parts of science? Or were they simply emotive noises? In an ordinary sense such books are obviously metaphysical – that is, they deal with very general questions about how the world is and how to choose among the ways in which we can and should think about it. But it never emerges how they can find a place for their own enquiries.

This same difficulty comes up, of course, about the famous earlier fanfare on which Ayer's was obviously modelled – the manifesto that concludes David Hume's *An Enquiry Concerning Human Understanding*:

> When we run over libraries, persuaded of these principles, what havoc must we make? If we take in our hand any volume; of divinity or school metaphysics, for instance: let us ask, *Does it contain any abstract reasoning concerning quantity and number?* No. *Does it contain any experimental reasoning concerning matters of fact and existence?* No. Commit it then to the flames; for it can contain nothing but sophistry and illusion. (Emphasis Hume's.)

So what happens if, instead, we decide to take in our hand *An Enquiry Concerning Human Understanding*, or one of Hume's other philosophical works . . .? Surprisingly few of Hume's readers ever ask him this question and he certainly never answered it. Empiricists are not often seen committing their own writings to the flames, nor explaining that they are actually part of science.

Destructive doctrines like these that look completely sweeping are almost always meant as contributions to an existing feud. Their real aim is narrow and familiar. Each is a stick designed to beat a particular dog with, and people know already what that dog is. Hume, suffering greatly from the Calvinistic Scottish church, marked his real target – which was already clear to his Enlightenment readers – by his talk of 'divinity or school metaphysics'. Logical positivism too had its own clear political aim. The philosophers of the Vienna Circle used it as a handy piece of artillery against religious doctrines which they identified with the clerical-fascist regime that ruled Austria in the 1920s and 1930s. They were calling for opposition to such doctrines as a part of the socialist struggle against fascism.

Ayer's use of it, however, was looser and wider. He did often take pot shots at religious doctrines, which are always soft targets for such treatment ('That a transcendent god exists is a metaphysical assertion, and therefore not literally significant' – *Language, Truth and Logic*, p. 29). But his brand of weedkiller was packaged so as to be spread much more widely. His formula could be used at will against almost any form of thought that went beyond the direct reporting of sense-data. (This would, of course, also have included a great deal of science, but that was not usually noticed.)

In this way, a whole generation of undergraduates was excited to find that all they needed to do if they wanted to refute some inconvenient doctrine was to say loudly and firmly 'I simply don't understand that' or 'But what could that possibly mean?' and the opposition would have to wither away. *Not* understanding things became the unanswerable one-up default position for arguers and remained so for several decades.

Indeed, that notion is still influential today. *Language, Truth and Logic* was one of the most widely read of twentieth-century philosophical books published in English, reaching a large public that normally never hears about these topics. And its central destructive doctrines were reinforced in 1946 by the last section of another widely read and apparently solider book, Bertrand Russell's *History of Western Philosophy*. In his conclusion, Russell resoundingly endorsed the positivistic approach of recent analytic philosophy, crediting it, rather remarkably, with having *invented* the virtue of philosophical impartiality:

> In the welter of conflicting fanaticisms, one of the few unifying forces is scientific *truthfulness*, by which I mean the habit of basing our beliefs upon observations and inferences as impersonal, and as much divested of local and temperamental bias, as is possible for human beings. To have insisted upon *the introduction of this virtue into philosophy*, and to have invented a powerful method by which it can be rendered fruitful, are the chief merits of the philosophical school of which I am a member. *The habit of careful veracity* acquired in the practice of this philosophical method can be extended to the whole sphere of human activity.
>
> (p. 78. Emphasis mine)

So, did earlier philosophers not actually know that they ought to try to be impartial and to tell the truth? And do analytic ones always succeed in doing so?

What is empiricism?

Russell's claim is significant because it flows from a mistake that empiricists often make. They suppose that all they are doing when they emphasize the importance of experience is impartially reporting experience itself. They see themselves as neutral instruments, channels for the obvious, using no special assumptions that need to be criticized and justified. Not noticing their own metaphysics – the background network of concepts that shapes their thought – they suppose metaphysics itself to be simply a vice of their opponents. This conviction is particularly marked in Berkeley, who keeps innocently observing, while he makes his most startling suggestions, that he is merely stating obvious and unanswerable common sense. Similarly, Russell claims that now, with analytical methods, a large part of former philosophy can simply be dismissed because 'many questions, formerly obscured by the fog of metaphysics, can be answered with precision, and by objective methods which introduce nothing of the philosopher's temperament except the desire to understand'.

How (we might ask) are philosophers supposed to decide which questions they want to work on – which concepts to use in dealing with them – or what counts as a satisfactory understanding, without their own temperaments playing any part in the choice? Different things look obvious at different times to different people. Selection is needed at all these stages. Will a computer program be found to make all these proceedings quite impersonal?

Actually in all serious philosophy (including Russell's own) the individual philosopher's temperament sticks out a mile. Even in mathematics it is recognized that each thinker's personal style affects his or her reasoning, and on matters that bear more directly on life its effect is still more obviously important. Attempts to suppress one's individuality usually fail, and if they succeed they can be positively dangerous. We need to see what kind of person a particular sage is so as to allow for his or her bias in judging his or her ideas. It is a real virtue in many great philosophers, from Plato to Hobbes and Nietzsche, that they make their general attitude to life so clear that their readers are most unlikely to overlook their individual value systems. It is not a virtue in today's typical philosophical articles that they are often designed to conceal that factor altogether.

Personality is not an irrelevance to thought, an obstacle to philosophical enquiry. It is an essential element in the solutions offered. All thinking is a human activity, radically linked to feeling and action. All thoughts are thoughts that somebody thinks. The impartiality that we have to aim at is not impersonality but simply the avoidance of irrelevant bias.

In attacking an existing doctrine we never aim merely to leave a blank in its place. We always have views on what ought to be there instead and our method of attack normally makes those views clear, even if we have not thought them out fully ourselves. Wreaking havoc in libraries may be good fun but it cannot be useful unless we are somehow making them better for the future. Thus, the idea that the logical positivists promoted, and that other empiricists have often suggested, of philosophy as pure weedkiller – simply destructive, just a way of getting rid of other people's tiresome thought systems – is not workable

Empiricists have often found this destructive conception plausible because they took it for granted that they had only one natural target – usually the ideology of Christianity. Russell displays this absent-minded assumption in the passage just quoted by his astonishing remark that 'ever since Plato most philosophers have considered it part of their business to produce "proofs" of immortality and the existence of God', and by failing to notice that, in his own day, other metaphysics such as Marxism were as suitable candidates for weedkilling. (Karl Popper promptly filled this gap by writing *The Open Society and Its Enemies*, but that book is scarcely likely to count as an example of philosophical impartiality.)

What, then, ought empiricists to be doing?

The wider answer is that they are not there just to get rid of particular dogmas but to control the general habit of dogmatizing. It is their business to bring out the actual complexity of life – to resist the crude, oversimplified doctrines that continually narrow our options as we try to impose order on the foaming chaos around us. In philosophy, rationalists are the people who keep trying to refine and complete that half-framed order, hoping to build it into a clear, universal system. Empiricists are the ones who keep saying, 'No, that won't do. Things are a bit more complicated than that.'

This dialectic is unending. Both things are needed; both can be done together. (Both are also found within science itself, which is far from being just a tidy store of established facts.) But in making their protests, empiricists naturally tend to introduce rival thought-systems of their own. The resounding example is Hobbes, who put forward a wonderful construction of naive materialism, psychological egoism and political absolutism to replace the Christian metaphysic that he denounced as meaningless. Then in the eighteenth century, just to even things up, Fate produced a couple of very sharp empiricist bishops who shot the other way. Bishop Butler showed the crudity of Hobbes's psychology by pointing out the real complexities of desire and choice. And Berkeley astutely turned the empiricist critique back against the dawning materialist ideology that was growing up around Newtonian physics – an ideology which Locke had thought followed necessarily from empiricism.

Hume followed Berkeley here, combining the attack on scientism with his own attack on religion, and ending up with a very strange atomistic account that reduced the world to an ultimate disconnected mass of individual perceptions. This story is impressive and often useful because, like other extreme positions, it maps out a wide sweep of intellectual country. It makes clear the terminus towards which some apparently much more ordinary ideas are tending. But it is certainly metaphysical. Equally certainly, it is not the only clear alternative to the complicated common-sense world picture that Hume so stoutly rejects. From one angle Hume is the greatest of empiricists, the greatest constructor of empiricist thought palaces. But the business of empiricism is not just to build these palaces.

Each empiricist, in fact, puts forward a world picture of his or her own – often a good corrective to the one he or she is opposing, but still not necessarily a right and final view. John Mill saw how this tendency could distort the empiricist enterprise and he took great pains to resist it. But the philosopher most aware of this difficulty – the most careful and balanced of them all – is surely William James. I am cheered to find that James's work is now coming back into fashion after its deliberate eclipsing by behaviourist psychologists. James is a grown-up empiricist. He has really learned something from his predecessors' mistakes. He looks around him at the intellectual landscape to see where his suggestions should fit in and to deal with their unexpected implications. Among empiricists he stands at the opposite pole from the dogmatic purism of the ageing Russell and the logical positivists. As he says:

> The thing as actually present in a given world is there with *all* its relations; for it to be known as it *there* exists, they must be known too and it and they form a single fact for any consciousness large enough to embrace that world as a unity. But what constitutes this singleness of fact, this unity? Empiricism says, Nothing but the relation-yielding matrix in which the several items of the world find themselves embedded – time, namely, and space, and the mind of the knower. And it says that were some of the items quite different from what they are and others the same, still, for aught we can see, an

> equally unitary world might be, provided each item were an object for consciousness and occupied a determinate point in space and time.
>
> (*The Will to Believe*, p. 278. James's emphasis)

He is arguing here against the Hegelian view of the world as a necessary whole. But the same objection – the insistence on the importance of context – holds against the radical atomism of earlier empiricists such as Hume and Russell who have tried to imitate physics by splitting the world into a single set of ultimate components. To my mind there is no doubt which of these examples we should follow.

One philosopher whose lectures I went to throughout my Greats course did practise this more positive, hospitable kind of empiricism and that was the Professor of Logic, H. H. Price. He was a delightful lecturer (his book on perception begins with the beguiling sentence, 'When I see a tomato there is much that I can doubt') and he was deeply interested in the complexities of experience. Notably, he paid attention to the problems raised by queer phenomena such as telepathy, which many analytic philosophers now tend to bar from consideration on the grounds that they ought not to happen because nobody is allowed to break the laws of physics. This does not seem to me to be a very empiricist response.

By contrast, logical-positivist destructiveness promotes casual irrationalism, suggesting that, outside science, all serious thought is useless. This is, incidentally, contrary to the ideas from which logical positivism itself originally developed, which were those of the young Wittgenstein. Wittgenstein did indeed say in his *Tractatus Logico-Philosophicus* that 'everything that can be said at all can be said clearly', and that science provides the model for such clarity. But, far from believing that everything outside science is nonsense, Wittgenstein himself thought (even then) that what could not be said was far more important than the relatively trifling things that were sayable. What lay beyond speech was, he said, the mystical, by which he did *not* mean nonsense but the profound, the true stuff of our lives.

In fact, he had intended the *Tractatus* to show the inadequacy of language. The slick interpretations that people such as Ayer put on his teaching put him in a chronic state of volcanic fury. But of course the *Tractatus* is so obscurely written that there was nothing very surprising in its being misinterpreted. In fact, Wittgenstein might be said to have proved his own depressing proposition. The *Tractatus*, after all, was only words, and words alone, not fully backed by explanation in a suitable form of life, do indeed often prove inadequate for human communication.

Thus – to return to my story – if Iris and I (and Philippa Foot) had not been sent to Donald MacKinnon for tutorials, we would probably have gone to someone who was occupied with the rather barren disputes that arose at once about this attack. The analytic philosophers who later developed these positivistic ideas in a more usable way – Gilbert Ryle, Stuart Hampshire, Ayer himself – were then away at the war, probably solving ciphers at Bletchley or doing mysterious intelligence work in the Near East. (J. L. Austin was at Oxford and we went to his lectures, but he hadn't then published his books.) So we missed their messages. But this meant that we did not have to spend our whole time in following out their debates, as the undergraduates had to who followed us after the war, when these people had formed the new analytic orthodoxy.

As it was, we certainly studied Ayer's book, and also John Wisdom's much more subtle version of Wittgensteinian views. But we did not spend a long time on them. We looked at many other things, among which I'm always glad to have been made to read Bradley's *Appearance and Reality*. This is written in a Hegelian jargon that I would certainly never have penetrated if left to my own devices, but it deploys a fascinating idealist view about the way in which everything hangs together. Reality, says Bradley, is simply the whole thing; error is always due to incompleteness, partiality, the premature jamming together of parts. Thus, because there are degrees of completeness, there are also *degrees* of reality and degrees of truth, and this is why we should always approach disputes hospitably, with a view to synthesis.

Gender queries

As we went to lectures and classes and philosophical meetings something rather interesting began to emerge about gender. When we were reading Greats not many students were taking the course at all and there were as many women as men among them. Male undergraduates then mostly came to Oxford only for a year's course, leaving the rest to be finished after the war. Since Greats was a course for the later years, the only men taking it with us were conscientious objectors, disabled people and a few ordinands – Benedictines and Dominicans I think. The effect was to make it a great deal easier for a woman to be heard in discussion than it is in normal times. (I have seen enough of a number of universities, both here and in the States, in later life to have checked up fully on this comparison.) Sheer loudness of voice has a lot to do with the difficulty, but there is also a temperamental difference about confidence – about the amount of work that one thinks is needed to make one's opinion worth hearing.

I think myself that this experience has something to do with the fact that Elizabeth and I and Iris and Philippa Foot and Mary Warnock have all made our names in philosophy. Not everybody will think this was a good thing, and I am certainly not suggesting that it is worthwhile waging wars so as to make such results possible. But I do think that in normal times a lot of good female thinking is wasted because it simply doesn't get heard. Perhaps women ought to shout louder, but of course there is still the question whether men are going to listen.

Later on, all five of us used our voices – which for better or worse we had found in this way – to resist in different ways the bizarre irrationalist climate that had been encouraged by logical positivism. In varying ways, we all attacked what may be crudely called the boo-hurray view of ethics – more politely, the idea that facts are split off from values by a logical gap that makes it impossible to think rationally at all about moral topics. Though Richard Hare had by then modified this extreme position, treating moral judgements as recommendations rather than just emotive noises and allowing that they might form a structure, the reasons that people give for these judgements were still seen as outside criticism. 'Values' were treated as a kind of arbitrary opinions, and it was widely held – not only by analytic philosophers – that, since all people are entitled to their own opinions, argument about them made no sense.

I cannot here go into the objections that we brought against this notion. The idea of summarizing them exhausts me as much as it would probably exhaust my readers. But the point is still important because subjectivism of this kind has certainly not gone away, though some extreme ways of expressing it are no longer fashionable. I am inclined just to quote here what I wrote and cited about it fifteen years ago in *Wisdom, Information and Wonder* (p. 156):

> Facts are data – material which, for purposes of a particular enquiry, does not need to be reconsidered . . . And the data of any serious moral problem always incorporate quite complex pre-existing value-judgments and conceptual schemes. *The word fact, in its normal usage, is indeed not properly opposed to value, but to something more like conjecture or opinion*, as Geoffrey Warnock reasonably points out – 'That it is a bad thing to be tortured or starved, humiliated or hurt, is not an opinion; it is a fact. That it is better for people to be loved and attended to, rather than hated or neglected, is again a plain fact, not a matter of opinion'. (Emphasis added.)

Humans, in fact, are not disembodied minds but earthly creatures whose original constitution and circumstances determine a great deal about what can conceivably be good or bad for them before they ever start thinking about it. We cannot, as J.-P. Sartre suggested, just 'invent values' from scratch. To pretend that we can do this is to exaggerate our freedom grotesquely.

All the same, at that time this subjectivist scepticism strongly attracted people because they thought it was necessary for freedom. Judging other individuals was seen as interfering with their liberty. As one of my students later exclaimed indignantly, 'But surely it's always wrong to make moral judgements!' It didn't occur to her that this remark is itself a moral judgement. Freedom is just one value among the many between which we have to choose, and even given the importance of freedom we often need to choose – that is, to judge – between different freedoms. Being 'judgemental' or 'moralistic' in the sense of interfering is indeed a bad thing. But we do not have any way to avoid judging, except through the grave. And if we are going to make value judgements, it seems plausible to think that we might as well do it sensibly and co-operatively rather than just by making emotive noises.

Some of the best responses to this kind of philosophical subjectivism were contained in a series of short but lethal articles which Philippa Foot published in various journals during the 1950s, deploying most useful ideas which she has lately developed further in an admirable little book called *Natural Goodness* (Oxford University Press, 2001). At Somerville Philippa was a year junior to me. I took to her at once when she arrived and I saw a certain amount of her then, but we became close friends only later, when she was married and we were both living in Park Town. When she was an undergraduate Philippa seemed to me a little formidable – her standards, I felt, would be very high, could I hope to meet them? She tells me now that she had exactly the same impression about me. We were both being shy and frightened of each other. This just shows how easy it is to waste the opportunities that crop up in one's life.

What Iris said

So in the summer of 1942 we prepared for our final exams and also tried to make arrangements for what we would do after them. During that term those of us who had opted for the civil service received notices of the jobs to which we had been assigned. (Were we interviewed for them? Or did the authorities just take us on our tutors' recommendations? I really don't remember.) So the letters arrived. Nancy and Christine are going to the Board of Trade. Charlotte will go to Cambridge to do research on how to artificially inseminate pigs. Myself, I am going to the Ministry of Production. (Ministry of what? Yes, there was one; we will have a look at it shortly.) But what about Iris? She is still waiting. Does the civil service not want her? 'Of course they won't have me', she said. 'I never thought that they would, with a political record like mine.' Next day the letter arrives; they are delighted to employ her. They have a place for her at the Treasury, where she will stay for most of the war. We can forget about the future for the moment and get on with taking our exams.

This we did, with anguish mostly similar to that of Mods but less pain from the climate, since we took them in June. I had my agonizing three-hour viva and the job was done. At this point all that we wanted was to sleep. But our tutor Isabel Henderson, bless her, wanted to celebrate our Firsts properly. As a special treat she arranged a dinner party for us with two highly distinguished contemporary sages – the historian A. L. Rowse and the Cambridge musicologist J. B. Trend. We duly dressed up and through a long evening we listened attentively to their distinguished contemporary opinions.

Bright moonlight flooded down St Giles's as the two of us eventually stumbled home to Somerville. 'So finally,' I asked, 'what about it? Did we learn something new this evening?' 'Oh yes, I think so,' declared Iris gazing up at the enormous moon. 'I do think so . . . *Trend is a good man and Rowse is a bad man*.' At which exact, but grotesquely unfashionable, judgement we both fell about laughing so helplessly that the rare passers-by looked round in alarm and all the cats ran away.

Iris, however, never minded being unfashionable. It may be worthwhile to point out here that this is what makes *The Sovereignty of Good* such a good book – what makes it, still, one of the very few modern books of philosophy that people outside universities find helpful. It shares that distinction with C. S. Lewis's little book *The Abolition of Man*, which shoots with equally deadly aim at the same target. Both titles are misleading; they are both actually books about the nature of freedom. Both books effectively debunk the colourful, fantastic screen of up-to-date ideas inside which we live – a screen which, despite a lot of surface activity, has not actually changed much since those books were written. As Iris puts it, 'a smart set of concepts may be a most efficient instrument of corruption' (*Sovereignty of Good*, p. 33). As she explains, 'We are anxiety-ridden animals. Our minds are continually active, fabricating an anxious, self-preoccupied, often falsifying *veil* which partly conceals the world' (p. 84). What chiefly pierces that veil is a sharp, direct perception of things that are no part of our own being. For instance;

> I am looking out of my window in an anxious and resentful state of mind, oblivious of my surroundings, brooding perhaps on some damage done to my prestige. Then suddenly I observe a hovering kestrel. In a moment everything is altered. There is nothing now but kestrel. And when I return to thinking of the other matter it seems less important.
>
> (p. 84)

The veil, however, is persistent and terribly hard to detect. In every age it subtly provides new, unnoticed ways of evading reality. Detecting those new forms is a prime function of philosophy, but philosophers often find it no easier than other people. ('It is always a significant question to ask about any philosopher; what is he afraid of?', p. 72.)

During the twentieth century, intellectual fashions provided escape by claiming to isolate individuals progressively, first from God, then from their own societies ('there is no such thing as society'), and finally from the rest of nature, thus crediting them with an extraordinary, supernatural kind of independence. At each stage, the reformers were resisting genuinely oppressive claims. But at each stage the real, practical reasons for this resistance were gradually forgotten as one theorist after another (Nietzsche, Freud, Skinner, Heidegger, Sartre, Hayek,

Dawkins) dived in to contribute to the exaggerated rhetoric which, when these elements were combined, added up to an extreme and reductive individualism.

That extremism made it increasingly hard to think out any intelligent reconciliation which would bring together only the best parts of the various campaigns. So (as Iris points out) what we got instead was a strange half-thought-out jumble composed of the most dramatic parts of each doctrine because these were both the most exciting and the easiest to remember:

> The very powerful image with which we are here presented . . . is behaviourist in its connection of the meaning and being of action with the publicly observable, it is existentialist in its elimination of the substantial self and its emphasis on the solitary omnipotent will, and it is utilitarian in its assumption that morality is and can only be concerned with public acts.
>
> (p. 9)

In short, it is carefully designed to distract attention from what analytic philosophers least want to think about, which is the inner life. As she said, it is indeed always a significant question to ask about a philosopher, 'what is he afraid of?', and the chronic fear that these doctrines all show is a fear of the world within. The names of these theories may not now be familiar to all of us but, as she says, we are all familiar with the ideal figure who personifies them because he dominates the stories that we read and watch:

> He is the hero of every modern novel . . . This man is with us still, free, independent, lonely, powerful, brave, the hero of so many novels and books of moral philosophy. The *raison d'être* of this attractive but misleading creature is not far to seek. He is the offspring of the age of science, confidently rational and yet increasingly aware of his alienation from the material universe which his discoveries reveal.
>
> (p. 80)

Since Iris wrote, environmental dangers have made us much more uneasy about this last form of alienation. Yet the power fantasy she describes is as potent as ever. What upholds it is still 'the domination of science or rather . . . *the domination of inexact ideas of science which haunt philosophers and other thinkers*' (p. 27). For it is not science itself that makes this wild, fluttering escape seem necessary. The demand comes from ideologies (such as that of behaviourism) which have usurped the name of science and have grotesquely exaggerated its power.

Put very crudely, what frightens us is our superstitious belief that there exists a single, vast, infallible system called science which completely explains human existence and proves that the familiar kinds of freedom that we experience every day are illusory. To escape this threat, theorists have invented a special kind of metaphysical freedom, sending us up, like autonomous hot-air balloons, to a stratosphere beyond the reach of nature and science. Is that where we want to live? Iris comments:

> I find the image of man which I have sketched above both alien and implausible. That is; more precisely; I have simple empirical objections (I do not think people are essentially or necessarily 'like that'), I have philosophical objections (I do not find the arguments convincing), and I have moral objections (I do not think people *ought* to picture themselves in this way). It is a delicate and tricky matter to keep these kinds of objections separate in one's mind.
>
> (p. 9)

This difficulty faces anyone who tries to penetrate a contemporary myth. Intellectual and emotional aspects of the current veil are so intricately meshed that it is hard to make any special point without seeming to say something morally objectionable. Throughout the past century the concept of freedom has been treated with an unconditional reverence which has made it seem illicit even to ask, on any particular occasion, *which* freedom? Freedom from what? Freedom from scruple? Freedom from friendship and the bonds of affection? Freedom from principle? Freedom from all tradition? Freedom from feeling? These are the easy privileges of psychopaths, depressives and oafs. They are not what the prophets who exalt freedom are really aiming at. What then (Iris asks) are they proposing?

> Existentialism, in both its Continental and its Anglo-Saxon versions, is an attempt to solve the problem without really facing it by attributing to the individual an empty, lonely freedom, if he wishes, to 'fly in the face of the facts'. What it pictures is indeed the fearful solitude of the individual marooned upon a tiny island in the midst of a sea of scientific facts, and morality escaping from science only by a wild leap of the will. But *our situation is not like this.*
>
> (p. 27)

Under the term 'existentialism' she includes, of course, a wide tradition stretching from Dostoevsky, Kierkegaard and Nietzsche to Heidegger and Sartre, a tradition that is less mentioned today that it used to be simply because its cruder elements are by now accepted and taken for granted. They are also echoed in a different accent by American libertarians.

She concedes that, in facing hard dilemmas, we may indeed feel our situation to be hopelessly unintelligible and irrational. But this (she suggests) is because we concentrate arbitrarily on the moment of apparent decision, ignoring the mass of imaginative work that was done earlier, work which depends above all on *deliberate and selective attention*. She instances a woman who has been half-consciously despising her daughter-in-law D and who, wondering whether she is being unfair, 'reflects deliberately about D until gradually *her vision of D alters*' (p. 17). This woman now sees facts that she did not see before, not by deceiving herself but by using 'just and loving attention'. The imagination (that is) can itself be used to pierce and unweave the veil with which it has helped to blind us. It is not just a deluding factor or a luxury item to amuse humanists. It is itself a vital organ, a workshop where we forge our view of the world and thereby our actions.

That kind of reflective, imaginative attention – not arbitrary, sudden decision – is, of course, what chiefly marks out people who are acting relatively freely and responsibly from those who are not. Certainly we have only limited control over our attention. But not even the most bigoted and fatalistic of determinists ever actually doubts that we are able to make a vast difference by exercising the measure of control that we do have over it, and that the power to do this is a part of our natural heritage. The business of the various sciences is (as serious scientists know) to help in the understanding of such natural processes, not to deny that they take place. That kind of denial is ideology, not science.

For much of the past century, modern libertarians of various stripes have been fighting a ghost war here, not against science itself but against false scientistic prophets. A glance at *The Sovereignty of Good* might perhaps release them for better and more cheerful occupations.

5

Wartime Jobs, 1942–5

In the civil service

So we left Oxford. We did not, of course, have the option of doing graduate work at once. We were expected to do something publicly useful. Thus, while the war lasted I found myself in a number of jobs, none of them very exciting but each with an interest of its own. I have always been glad to have had that varied experience instead of going straight through the regular graduate mill.

To explain why, I must look ahead a little. People often ask me why I did not start to write the books and articles for which I am now known until I was over fifty. The answer is simply that I needed time to think. Before then, I did not know what I thought clearly enough to want to go public with it.

The graduate mill is an excellent device for training scholars in the various techniques needed for academic thoroughness, which is indeed an important process. But, during that training, students easily become entrenched in whatever assumptions are currently accepted in their discipline. Doctoral theses are expected to be well defended, so supervisors naturally discourage candidates from saying things that will be hard to defend against current criticisms. This probably would not matter if only the Ph.D. were followed by a reverse process which re-educated its subjects in saying something different and surprising. But it isn't.

When I did come back to do graduate work in 1947, the situation was unusual because the post-war graduate generation was abnormal. Its members had been outside academia for some years and brought with them quite varying ideas. Thus in philosophy, the graduate students of that time ranged from fairly extreme exponents of positivist denial, such as Jack Smart and Anthony Flew, through more moderate people such as Peter Strawson, Stephen Toulmin and Geoffrey and Mary Warnock to fully fledged Thomistic Wittgensteinians such as Elizabeth Anscombe and Peter Geach, along with some mavericks trying to say things that were altogether different. This made for dialogue and a lot of noise in graduate classes. H. H. Price's class and a class on Aristotle, conducted I think by Dr Walzer, were particularly exciting.

The rows that went on there formed part of a series of conflicts that were convulsing the intellectual world at that time. Besides the rift between various ways of doing philosophy there was also the gap between the 'two cultures', the gap between the various political ideas that we might follow once we got away from Marxism, and many other debates. It seemed to me that, in most of these controversies, people were trying to take sides tribally on issues where both positions offered were wrong. One had somehow to dig deeper in order to bring together the various half-truths that were involved – to find a synthesis that did not just paper over the cracks.

If I had been put in the position where most academics are today – if I had been forced to publish articles all the time whether I had anything to say or not – I should, no doubt, have settled for one of the grooves that were available within the current programme. But the only quick and safe way to do this is to be negative. Those who accept the terms offered must go on doing what they did in their doctorate theses, sharing their predecessors' background assumptions but complaining about details. This is the only way in which their departments can be sure of publishing articles fast enough to satisfy the assessors and stop the authorities from closing them down – as happened to the Newcastle Philosophy Department under Mrs Thatcher.

I have said that I don't think this system a very sensible one. Even where talents and intentions are good, it produces a flood of mediocre prose which nobody has time to read, since all those who might be interested are busy writing articles of their own. The whole set-up flows from the political notion that academic life is an industry that must justify itself by displaying a *product*, and this product is not – as might be expected – well-educated students but mountains of printed paper. These mountains are much easier to count.

To get back to my own career. Naturally, I am not saying that I anticipated these later troubles when I decided to spend so much of my youth doing other things. I did nothing so clear-headed. I made my decisions according to the circumstances at the time. During the war I had no choice anyway but to do the kinds of work that were open to me and were deemed (however oddly) to be 'of national importance'. And I was happy to go along with this. When the war was over, I did have a fascinating three years, from 1947 to 1949, doing graduate work at Oxford and after that I worked for four terms lecturing at the University of Reading. Then I got married, and much later I found that my ideas were becoming clear enough to be worth writing down. Thus, in the long run, the question that embarrassed us so much when Peter Ady put it in her questionnaire did get answered. I ate my cake and had it – marriage and some sort of a career.

All this certainly doesn't demonstrate any talent for planning. It was mostly luck. But it gave me – what, I suspect, most women who have children at all would like if they were given a choice – a chance to be with them fairly continuously when they were young, then part-time work as they got older, and then full-time work later on, using more mature powers on matters that I really thought important. If more women – and indeed more men – got a chance for a life shaped like this I think they might be able to contribute something quite important to their society, as well as fulfilling more of their own aims and wishes.

The main trouble about this recipe today is that part-time work hardly ever gets adequate treatment in the normal scheme of things. People are supposed either to work themselves to death all day or to do nothing significant at all. This is a desperate arrangement, both for women with children and for people growing old. Part-time work, if it were well arranged, would greatly mitigate the alarming vision that is now held before us of a tiny workforce killing itself in trying to support a huge helpless geriatric mass. Being now a part of that geriatric mass, I would like to say that it is time to do something about this.

To go back, however, to 1942 and the civil service. I arrived, then, at the Ministry of Production, which functioned at the bottom of Whitehall in the same buildings as the Cabinet Offices. It was a liaison ministry, fairly recently invented in order to arbitrate between the sharply conflicting demands that were made on resources by the three armed services and the Board of Trade, which provided for civilian needs. My part of it was the Raw Materials Section, which was supposed to introduce some order into the allotment of zinc, rubber, steel and so forth to these various users. It became clear at once how hard this was when I heard about the priority system that had been set up to arbitrate between their demands. Apparently, each department had been told to grade the urgency of its various requirements on a scale reaching from A to C. They all responded by declaring unanimously that all their needs were either A, AA or AAA.

When I arrived I was told at once to prepare a report on the history of something called the Combined Production and Resources Board – a body that had been established to play some crucial part in this arbitration. Piles of paper were put in front of me and I beavered away at them for about a month, after which I produced a report – one more of my history essays. I was told, both at the time and afterwards, that this report was a very good one. But then the downside of the situation emerged.

It gradually turned out that my boss – Betty Ackroyd, who later became eminent in the consumer movement – hadn't the least idea what to do with me once this piece of work was done. She had applied for an assistant because she wanted someone to write the report. Beyond that, she was a classic case of the lady who can't delegate. She herself operated like a whirlwind – rushing in early, constantly engaged on the telephone, dialling telephone numbers at twice the usual speed, often with a pencil, then rushing out to a meeting – and it was almost impossible to catch her attention for long enough to find out what I was meant to do, much less how to do it.

This, in fact, was another situation – like the one at Downe where I found myself landed with an incompetent Classics teacher – where I ought to have seen that things actually were wrong and taken firm steps to get them changed. The world is divided at any time into those who can see that it is possible to do this and those who can't. At that time I was one of the can'ts. I worried a lot, but it didn't strike me that change was in my power. The dilemma of how to share out raw materials was genuinely important and I'd have been very glad to find out more about it. But I never did. An extra piece of bafflement was the situation of our office. This was at the top of the building, so it ought to have looked out over St James's Park, but – by a strange aesthetic quirk – the architect had built an ornamental parapet in front of it, so that our windows looked out on the dirty white bricks at the back of this parapet, three feet away, getting little daylight from above and forcing us to have the lights on most of the time.

I was told much later that Betty ought really to have sent me for a regular training, after which I would probably have been allotted where I was needed, so that if she didn't need me I would have gone somewhere else. She didn't do this, either because she didn't want to lose the vague asset of having an assistant or – just as likely – because she never paused long enough in her whirl to give the matter a thought. Any time when I tried to talk to her she started irritably, obviously thinking me an interruption. I still find it hard now to insist on talking to people who behave like this, and I found it much harder then. Occasionally I did manage to get her to give me a piece of work, but there was never enough explanation to make it possible to do it properly. Sometimes, in despair, I just sat reading up the facts in the Raw Materials Handbook. This is why I still know a lot of odd details about things like wolfram, vanadium and essentials oils.

I lived meanwhile with my parents in Kingston, commuting by train to Waterloo and reading a lot of novels in the process, from *Clarissa* to Anthony Powell. (If you have to stand for half an hour in a crowded train in the rush hour the best thing is to have a novel to read that takes you to somewhere quite different.) In the lunch hour I quite often went to look at city churches, whose architecture I have always loved. Wren, Gibbs, Hawksmoor and the rest seem to me to have got it right. For some reason I also find a special meaning in the music of that time – I love Purcell. So I went and looked, sometimes indeed at St Paul's and sometimes, as Eliot said,

> where the walls
> Of Magnus Martyr hold
> Inexplicable splendour of Ionian white and gold.

It is good to have had some time to look at these buildings before they were dwarfed, as they now are, by an arrogant crowd of huge banks.

In other lunch times I sang for a time in Dr Jacques's Bach Choir. I also went more than once to have a sandwich with Iris in the flat that she had somehow managed to find, against all probability, in the heart of Westminster. She had got this flat – which she later made thoroughly habitable and shared with Philippa – cheap because it had been bombed, and at first it looked much like a stage set for a school performance of something by Dostoevsky. It was an attic with cracks in the roof revealing the sky and cracks in the floor revealing no ceiling below, so that nothing blocked the alarming rumble of the underground trains passing beneath us. What furniture she had then was mainly orange-boxes. She was however well settled there and seemed contented at the Treasury.

Not very surprisingly, after six months of this kind of life my digestion began to give trouble which could no longer be ignored, so my doctor sent me to the Middlesex Hospital for tests to find out what was wrong with it. My innards have been investigated in this way several times in my life and to date, after the barium meals and the rest of the palaver, the verdict has always been roughly the same, though of course the language varies with medical fashion. The advice is: nothing seriously wrong, but you will have to live differently.

I caught at this chance to leave my frustrating situation in the Ministry. I had kept in touch with my headmistress at Downe and she had been saying how much they would like me to come and teach Classics there if I ever wanted a change. Teaching, equally with the civil service, was a reserved occupation and I would be allowed to move to it. So I told her that I did want that change, and explained to Betty Ackroyd that I was going to resign on health grounds. She was astonished and evidently rather annoyed, but she could make no objection.

Interlude at Downe

I was cross with myself at having to withdraw in this way from what ought to have been interesting work, but I settled down for the time to teaching. I remained at Downe for four terms, at first with a light schedule so that I could recover my strength, which I quite quickly did, and then full-time. I enjoyed teaching those pupils who didn't mind learning Latin, and I gradually began to find ways of dealing with the ones – usually younger – who did mind, but who unfortunately had to do it for syllabus reasons, because it was a required subject for university entrance. (I once put an optional essay question in an exam paper, 'Would you rather have lived in ancient Rome or now? Give your reasons.' One girl's essay ran, 'I would rather live now, for all reasons.')

It is a good thing that this unfortunate subject no longer gets demanded as a qualification for advanced courses, presenting a needless block to other kinds of education. (It is a pity, however, that the teaching of other languages seems to be tending now to get dropped as well. This is a real loss.) I had one very interesting assignment of teaching a sixth-form girl enough Latin from scratch to take her through school certificate, which she needed for some career, in one term. It was striking to see how fast some things – for instance gerunds – which you are used to seeing treated as fearfully difficult, can be learnt when the learner's motivation is straightforward. She and I whistled through this course successfully.

Socially, Downe was less lively at this time than it had been earlier. A good many of the brighter teachers were away doing war work – Jean Rowntree was now with the BBC – and those who replaced them tended to be either very young or a good deal older, some of them long retired. Miss Willis, who had been ill, was less active than she had once been. She still, however, came up with bright ideas, and one of them was that I should teach the sixth forms a subject called Plato – essentially just a bit of philosophy – and this I did. I made some good friends among the younger teachers and one of them – Jewel Smith the pianist, who was a visiting teacher and brought a welcome whiff of outside air into our convent – is still one of my closest friends today. I went on seeing a lot of her during my next avatar at Bedford, since her mother lived there.

Because of the lack of petrol, the isolation of Downe was even deeper than it had once been, and this was more annoying for adult staff, including me, than it had been for boarding-school pupils who took it for granted. On our half-day off each week, we could bicycle three miles down into Newbury – get our hair done, do a bit of shopping if we could find anything to buy, go to a café for a tea which, though better than the school one, was rarely anything dramatic – and bicycle laboriously up again in time for supper. Without cars, it would have been fairly hard to get away for weekends, though I sometimes managed it. After a time, this life did begin to pall.

One way and another I would probably not have stayed there very long anyway, but during my fourth term something cropped up which I thought might make a welcome change. By some channel that I can't now remember, I heard that a job was vacant to teach sixth-form Classics in a boys' public school. I thought I would give this one a try.

At Bedford School

This had originally been an ancient grammar school but, like many others, it had managed after long and strenuous efforts to turn itself into a Public School – that is, of course, not actually a public school but a rather grand one, intended for the upper classes. Bedford School was one of a number of schools in that town which had a good reputation and were relatively cheap. So parents often resorted to the place in the hope of getting good schooling for their children. Among them there were a good many retired officers from the Indian Army and the Colonial Service. The most prestigious of these – the generals and colonels – tended to retire further west to Cheltenham, which had a similar reputation for its schools but at a rather higher social level. I think that Bedford, a placid little town in the East Midlands, mostly got the majors and the captains.

It was quite remarkable how this concern dominated talk in the town, which was otherwise then just a market town, dealing mainly in produce from the cabbage-strewn plain around it. As one walked down the High Street one would be stopped by anxious parents wanting to know whether the results were out yet for the Lower Fourth's term exams? And what was going to happen about those scholarships . . .? It was all education, education, education. Top of the female sector and corresponding to the boys' Bedford School was the Girls' High School, and at the next level there were Bedford Modern and Bedford Girls' Modern and no doubt plenty of others.

The Headmaster of Bedford School proper was naturally anxious to keep up his school's prime status so in 1944 he had a problem. He could no longer find any properly qualified men to fill his sixth-form posts because they were all at the war. He had therefore decided to take a deep breath and try women. Thus he appointed me to teach the Classical Sixth and another Oxford graduate, Peggy Torrance, for the History Sixth and we duly started our work there.

It is hard to convey the atmosphere of the place. It really does seem like another world. I remember coming into the school hall on the first day before morning assembly, and being surprised at the good behaviour of the boys. Six hundred of them were sitting there in rows, perfectly quiet and still, but as I gradually realized that this was not by chance. Beside every pillar stood a prefect holding a long stick, with which he reached out and whacked the head of any boy who failed to maintain the stillness. Then the Headmaster came in, we all sang a rousing hymn and the day's routine began.

The next surprise came at mid-morning break. At Downe this had been a most useful occasion – a time for finding anybody whom one needed to talk to or, if there was no such need, for relaxing together and recovering from the morning's troubles. And – in spite of the war – there had always been coffee, perhaps not particularly good but perfectly acceptable. The senior common-room at Bedford offered no refreshment whatever and very little talk. Some of the masters just stood, staring into space. Other sat with exercise books before them, grimly continuing to mark. Anybody who did talk did it apologetically in a low voice, rather as though they were at a funeral. Peggy and I looked at each other and exchanged the silent thought, 'These people must be crazy'.

After a day or two we discovered that the quarter-hour break gave us plenty of time to cross the road to a handy milk bar, where we could get not only coffee but a jam tart as well. On the way, too, we could exchange such tips as we had been able to pick up about the customs of the tribe we were supposed to be working with. It would have been useful, of course, if we could have got some of those tips from the inhabitants themselves, but even if they had not been maintaining a general Trappist silence it is not likely that they would have given us any. Nearly all of them avoided speaking to us if they could possibly do so, and got away as soon as they could when they had to. An honourable exception was the master in charge of the Mathematical Sixth – Mr Clarke I think. He introduced himself to us cordially at once and offered to help us in any way he could. We got most of the information that we did collect from him. The Headmaster, who knew that he had to make our work possible, was reasonably helpful if we actually consulted him, but this had to be specially arranged. He couldn't normally be seen without an appointment.

The masters' responses to us probably varied from real misogyny to simple shyness, but I think one trouble – which I never thought of at the time – may have been that these people saw us as a real threat to their livelihood. Many of them were not very well qualified. (Mr Clarke was plainly a real scholar but not all the rest even had degrees, though they all wore gowns.) If this custom of importing educated women were to catch on, they might find themselves in trouble. They may well have thought that the Headmaster – who hadn't been there long and was obviously ambitious – was sacrificing their interests by this innovation, so they may have wanted to show their disapproval by boycotting it.

As time went on and we settled down at Bedford, we met several of these masters outside school because they were friends of our landladies, and in this context they treated us normally, though without particular enthusiasm. My landlady, Mrs Parker, was luckily a real honey, with plenty of friends locally, so we got a good deal of society. Jewel often came down at weekends and took me for long walks along the river Ouse (which was then – and perhaps still is – about the only feature that interrupts the endless expanse of cabbages surrounding Bedford) and she was able to tell me a good deal of local lore to explain the background of the school situation. She also took me to visit the home of her mother and aunts, a classic clamjamfrey of elderly ladies and cats with the cats mainly in charge, and we learned from them a good deal more about Bedford history.

The actual work of teaching was much more straightforward since the boys had none of these grievances and were bright enough. They showed plenty of interest in the books we studied, and it was some time before I discovered that they hadn't actually chosen to do Classics but had simply been directed into it. The class was small – only seven boys – which made it easy and pleasant to teach. (It is possible that the Headmaster may have been finding it harder to direct a lot of pupils that way than it had once been.) When I did ask the boys why they had chosen the subject they simply said they hadn't been asked about it. They were not much interested in what reasons there might have been for or against doing so. I suppose that, in the war, choices like this seemed less important than they might have done normally.

Mostly the boys and I understood each other very well, though I found it rather tiresome to teach them the verse composition which I was bad at myself, and had already concluded was pretty pointless. I only remember a few real misunderstandings. One of these occurred when we were reading Plato's beautiful little epigram addressed to his lover Aster. The point of it is that this word means 'star', so translators sometimes render it by 'Stella', thus avoiding trouble about gender. It didn't occur to me to use this evasion so I said something about 'the man that it's addressed to', and this upset them quite severely. It gave rise to a good deal of embarrassment.

I have no idea what their actual thoughts about homosexuality were, but they didn't seem to have connected them with those heroic characters the Greeks. Since they had already read quite widely in the Classics I don't know how they had managed this, and it never struck me in advance that they might have done it. I suppose it was part of the general tendency to keep thought separate from life, but their previous teachers must surely have colluded with it pretty actively. I don't think that the shock arose merely from hearing a woman mention the matter; they were genuinely surprised. But of course that extra factor made it harder to deal with once the trouble surfaced. Still, we got over it somehow.

The only time when I had anything to do with the teaching in the rest of the school was at termly exams, when I was asked to mark papers written by boys of, I suppose, about thirteen. This was an eye-opener. Out of quite a large class taking Latin, very few seemed to have any idea at all of how different Latin word order is from English. Without this talisman, most of them, confronted with a sentence in Caesar, simply gave up all attempt to make sense of it and translated individual words, throwing them together in the order in which they happened to think of a plausible translation for them. The result often didn't have any English meaning at all.

No doubt this state of things represents a dark tradition that had trickled beneath the surface of gentlemanly scholarship all through the time when Latin and Greek were compulsory parts of education. Such supposed learning must surely have been not just a waste of time but a direct training in *not* thinking – in putting up with meaninglessness rather than trying to find a sense behind it. This entirely undercuts the defence which is rightly given for the learning of languages such as Latin and Greek – namely, that understanding their different structure makes you rethink ideas that you have so far only seen represented in the limited forms of your own language. If you don't grasp that structure you are wasting your time.

This pointlessness was a main reason that got Classics ejected from the main curriculum after the war. Some lurking uneasiness about it may, too, have infected even those who practised it, and it might account for some of the insecurity that Bedford masters felt at the thought of finding themselves in competition with those sinister representatives of the modern world, qualified women.

Altogether, work at Bedford had its pluses and minuses, but I certainly didn't want to stay there for ever. The war was moving towards its end. After the long early period of intense alarm things had gradually eased during 1943 as the Allies began to win battles in North Africa and then invaded Italy, thus fulfilling at last the left-wingers' constant demand to 'start the second front now'. In September the Italian government surrendered and in January 1944 the Allies landed at Anzio. In June of that year came the D-day landing in Normandy. It began to make sense to look towards the future.

Other things too began to turn up. During 1943, Jean Rowntree, now working at the BBC, occasionally asked me to take part in radio discussion programmes. And about this time, or perhaps a bit later, I got, through Donald MacKinnon, an invitation to review a book for the BBC Third Programme. That amazing institution used regularly to put on twenty-minute talks reviewing quite difficult books, and after this first one I did a lot of them, working with a charming and most impressive Russian producer called Aniouta Kallin. The first book that I dealt with there – perhaps while I was still at Bedford – was Bertrand Russell's *Human Knowledge, Its Scope and Limits*, to which, after anxious efforts, I gave the savage and intolerant treatment that comes so naturally to young and very nervous reviewers.

One of Jean Rowntree's commissions, however, was a radio discussion with Gilbert Murray, then Emeritus Professor of Greek at Oxford. I don't remember at all what the discussion was about or how it went. It was probably on something like The Meaning of the Classics in the Modern World. But after it Murray wrote to me saying that he needed a secretary and might I like to take the job? I thought I might and promptly gave in my notice.

When the war with Germany ended I was in London on VE Day (8 May 1945) and it's the only time when I have had the experience of dancing in the streets. I had always wondered vaguely how people did it, but it turns out to be quite easy. Dance music was being broadcast when I came to Trafalgar Square with some friends, and everyone just drifted into concentric circles that went round in alternate directions. After staying there for a time we went to Buckingham Palace and cheered duly there, and then spent the rest of the evening wandering through endless streets filled with that vast and amazingly harmonious gathering. Being in a large crowd that is genuinely joyful and unanimous is a wonderful thing. It doesn't often happen, but this did seem to be the right occasion for it.

I know exactly when I left Bedford because my last memory of it dates from the evening of the day when we heard that Labour had got in with a big majority in the post-war election, and that must have been 26 July 1945. A lot of cheerful people were wandering about Bedford streets on that evening too, mostly celebrating. But in our road things were different. Our opposite neighbour, an extremely dignified old lady, was seen leaning over her front gate with her eyes full of tears. 'I would never have thought', she cried, 'that the forces would have done a thing like that to Churchill, after he'd won the war for them.'

My father Tom Scrutton, answering questions on Christianity on Tower Hill, 1958

Geoff Midgley in 1950

Philippa Foot in the early 1970s

Geoff, me, Martin, Davy and Tom at Runswick Bay, 1959 – Geoff is taking the picture

Mike Brearley, lecturer at Newcastle in the 1970s, captain of the England cricket team in the 1980s

Elizabeth Anscombe in the mid-1940s

6

In Oxford Again, 1945–9

On Boar's Hill

Gilbert Murray was a scholar whose translations of Greek plays made him widely known in the early 1900s. These translations were successful because they were the first versions of these plays into English that could be convincingly acted on a modern stage and they were indeed acted there, becoming very popular for a time. They had a long string of successful West End productions, lasting from the early years of the century into the 1930s, and in many other kinds of theatres as well.

Later fashion turned against these versions because their style of verse belonged to its own epoch, which was the late nineteenth century. But it was still a coherent style – a usable language in which the plays were able to come across and to reach their audience. By showing that this could be done, Murray made it possible for later translators to follow his example, doing it again in different language for their own times. T. S. Eliot savagely denounced Murray's verse, but he did not himself plunge in and demonstrate how he could have done the thing any better.

Of course all translation is a compromise; it can't get things quite right. But at that time it was really important to breach the wall that shut off Greek literature as a private preserve for upper-class men and excluded the wider public, including women. Dr Johnson made this bizarre social function clear when he said, 'Greek, sir, is like lace; every man gets as much of it as he can.' Like *lace* . . .? That's no way to look at poetry.

Murray originally made his translations because, as a young professor teaching large classes in Glasgow, he wanted his pupils to understand and enjoy the plays, rather than just having to endure them. He succeeded roundly in this, and his success expanded to great numbers of people who could read the translations, as well as to those who saw them on the stage. This was what he wanted. As he put it in his first Presidential Address to the Classical Association at the start of the twentieth century, 'The scholar's special duty is to turn the written signs in which old poetry or philosophy is now enshrined back into living thought and feeling. *He must so understand as to relive.*' His successor, E. R. Dodds, in quoting these words, remarks that 'In the Oxford of fifty years ago, this was a revolutionary doctrine. The serious Oxford scholars of that time were mainly engaged in exact textual studies . . . the rest were largely occupied in teaching their pupils to put conventional English verse into more conventional Greek iambics or Latin elegiacs.'

It was Murray's translations of the plays that I had read at Downe when I was preparing for college and they gave me a hugely useful window on Greek thought. Looking at them now, I think the Euripides ones are indeed the least successful because – especially in the choruses – they are the most Swinburnian, the most coloured by late Romantic feeling. The Aeschylus ones are better, but it's the Aristophanes ones – especially the *Frogs* – that are the real triumph. I don't know that anybody since has done that particular job better.

The other thing that Murray was known for was his part in the early efforts to establish the League of Nations and to swing popular opinion behind it once it existed. Throughout the First World War, he was one of the group of people engaged in working out the possibilities for the League and in getting the politicians to take up the plan. Later, as is well known, the distortions that surrounded the Treaty of Versailles weakened the League. It did not finally succeed in controlling power politics. I don't think it is clear just what faults contributed to this failure or what more could have been done to strengthen it. But the effort to build and sustain it was surely a right one.

When Murray asked me to become his secretary, he explained that he was now working partly on translating another play (an incomplete comedy by Menander whose gaps he filled in, calling it *The Arbitration*) and partly on his autobiography, for which he would have to go through his early records. I knew that he had been acquainted with all sorts of interesting people, not just in the learned world but in politics and the theatre too, so I thought this was likely to be intriguing. And indeed it was. The letters were fascinating. There were lots from a range of famous actors and from Bernard Shaw. There was a nice one from Bertrand Russell, thanking the Murrays for congratulating him on his escape from death when his plane fell into the sea, and explaining (what he knew would exasperate Lady Mary Murray) that the reason why he had survived was that he was drinking and smoking in the bar, while his fellow passengers who stayed in their seats all got drowned.

The visits were good too. Sybil Thorndyke, who had been the leading lady in some of his early productions, came to see him and so did Ruth Draper, the princess of one-person dramas. (It was she who devised the famous

Garden-Showing piece that centred on the tragic theme, 'but actually of course you ought to have seen these a fortnight ago . . .') Both were delightful.

In fact, the work was quite as much fun as I expected and Murray was a model employer – wise, considerate and full of fascinating stories. And in many ways the conditions were good. The Murrays lived on Boar's Hill, that handy eminence to the south of Oxford to which distinguished dons then often gravitated upwards when they were getting too old or too grand to remain in the North Oxford mansions kindly built for them by Victorian architects. John Masefield, then Poet Laureate, was Murray's neighbour and Robert Bridges, the previous one, had also lived there. (In one of Evelyn Waugh's novels – I can't remember which – the young hero's streetwise mentor warns him that, for the sake of his career, he must never have anything, but *anything*, to do with Boar's Hill . . .)

The inhabitants, including the Murrays, were indeed not young, but the place was attractive, with plenty of country to walk in, and Murray had the sensible habit of taking several walks during his working day, on which he often asked me to go with him. Twice, too, he took me with him on holiday, once to Malvern, once to a nice place on the coast of South Wales, also taking with him an old friend, Professor J. A. K. Thompson. He still did some work, but not a lot. Mostly the three of us went for long walks and did a good deal of reading aloud. Murray who had the most beautiful voice, read all sorts of things but he particularly liked to read authors like P. G. Wodehouse or Kipling's comic stories such as 'Brugglesmith'. He was a genius at this. On top of the more obvious jokes he could get quite unexpected extra funny effects which always convulsed his audience. He used sometimes to read these books at home too, when he had visitors. But if he did this it was liable to produce a jarring effect. There was a difficulty about it which brings us to the darker side of this way of life. Lady Mary didn't really like it at all.

Isobel Henderson and other people had warned me beforehand that I would soon find out why Murray had never managed to keep any of his secretaries for long, and indeed I did. Lady Mary, like MacKinnon, is one of those fabulous Oxford monsters whom it is hard now to start describing realistically. She is perhaps best seen today in Bernard Shaw's play *Major Barbara*, where she figures as the heroine – the high-minded aristocratic, passionate girl who joins the Salvation Army and insists on marrying the idealistic professor of Greek. Her mother, the Countess of Carlisle, appears there as that outsize battleaxe Lady Britomart. In fact, Isobel told me that when Shaw first wrote the play he simply called it 'Murray's Mother-In Law', and that he arranged to read it, before it was printed, to a gathering of those who were represented in it (including the Murrays) so as to see whether anything needed to be changed.

Nothing was changed for the printing and, forty years later, it seemed to me that not a great deal had changed in actual life. Lady Mary had, in process of time, mutated into her mother, becoming a battleaxe herself, for she came of a formidable line of matriarchs. (I do sometimes have my doubts about this form of government, though so many feminists recommend it.) Her grandmother had been that tremendous old Victorian steam-engine Lady Stanley of Alderney, who so terrified her other grandchild, Bertie Russell, Lady Mary's cousin, in his early life.

Like her mother and grandmother, Lady Mary combined fiercely progressive and high-minded opinions with the serene and total confidence of the aristocrat whom nobody ever opposes. Like them she was a fanatic for temperance. (It was always said – I believe, wrongly, but with symbolic truth – that when Lord Carlisle succeeded to his title, his wife saw to it that all the wine in the cellars at Castle Howard was poured away into the lake.) Though Lady Mary did not actually belong to the Salvation Army, whose discipline she would certainly not have endured, she was a Quaker, a pacifist and, in her own opinion, a communist, though (again) no branch of the Party would ever have been likely to accept her as such. On the ground that Quakers must always be direct and honest, she always said exactly what she thought. ('Gilbert, how you think we can afford to pay those bills, now that you've got this fine new expensive secretary, *I* don't know!')

On the same principle, she often intensively questioned guests who came to the house for the first time, asking them, quite without inhibition, about all the details of their lives. Some newcomers understood this approach at once and responded gamely, after which they got on well with her. But others, understandably, were shattered. In her dealings with the outside world, she was used to ordering things just as she wanted them, so she gave instructions to make them so. Thus, when her daughter-in-law proposed to bring the grandchildren down next day, I was instructed to ring up the dentist and require that appointments should be provided for them at once – other patients naturally being put off till a later date. And again, when Murray was dictating letters to me in his study, in she stumped, banging the floor with her cane, to exclaim, 'Gilbert, you've got to sell out a thousand pounds *now* to send to the starving Hungarians. Now *don't put it off*!'

The thing that made my work most difficult, however, and that put most strain on my digestion, was her passion for interrupting things. She would come in at any time in the middle of whatever was going on and tell me to drive down into Oxford *at once* with a list of complicated commissions, each of which was liable to involve a long message to the tradespeople involved. While she explained these she interrupted herself constantly by thinking of new ones, and ended by hurrying me off, calling out, 'And don't forget, lunch is early!' The car itself didn't help, being an ancient Wolseley that sometimes stalled and had to be restarted with one of those handles that you turn from the front. It did this once at the Carfax traffic-lights, making me hold up the whole queue of cars behind me while I twiddled. Altogether the lifestyle she generated was certainly not soothing.

She sounds awful. And in a way she certainly was. I did not put up with life on Boar's Hill for very long any more than the other secretaries had. Yet she did have real redeeming features. Essentially she was sweet-natured – genuinely fond of people, impulsive, generous, going to all lengths to help those in need and often doing it in the right way rather than the wrong way. She was often apologetic afterwards when she had been particularly fierce. She was genuinely concerned for the starving Hungarians, going to great lengths both to help them herself and to get other people to do so. Democracies need such people. But households don't run the easier for them.

As for the Murrays' marriage, it was surely one of the many that work on the principle of compensation. A man who is almost too reasonable, too averse to friction, marries a woman who will do all his unreasonableness for him free and for nothing, a woman who isn't afraid of shouting and throwing things should that be necessary. Such marriages tend to go a bit too far both ways, but they can be quite successful so long as everybody involved can accept the conventions involved. I think the Murrays did that quite well, and I understood, after a time, that the separate holiday was part of their arrangement. When I hesitated to accept this tempting freebie, Murray explained that he had always gone on holiday like this with a friend and a secretary. I saw then that he really needed a break.

The matter of the reading aloud was quite significant. The trouble was that Lady Mary couldn't actually bear jokes at all because she couldn't understand them. One talks of people not having much sense of humour, but this was something more extreme. Though she sometimes smiled and laughed in quite a genial way, she didn't actually have any sense of what was funny, and it frightened her. She declared that her objection to 'Brugglesmith' arose from Kipling's right-wing politics, but these don't come into the story and were certainly not the point. Her black-and-white straight-up-and-down world-picture simply couldn't accommodate the subversive view from one side that shows things as funny. But to Gilbert – as to me – that angle was a real lifeline.

In his contribution to the memorial volume, Bertrand Russell tells several stories which bring out this difficulty nicely. For instance:

> One day, when the parlourmaid answered my ring at the front door, and I enquired whether Professor Murray and Lady Mary were at home, she replied, 'Well sir, I think they're *probably* in – unless they're out.' It turned out that they were in, and I said, 'Mary, your parlourmaid is of the opinion that the laws of thought should not be applied to empirical material except with great caution.' Mary remarked, 'Oh, what an unkind thing to say!' And Gilbert said, 'I am glad to know that she has such just views'.

Luckily, I did not actually live on Boar's Hill. On returning to Oxford I had found a small attic bedsitter in Park Town, that delectable little bit of 1860s town-planning that provides a classical refuge among North Oxford's imposing Gothic mansions. Park Town consists of two rather grand-looking Regency-style crescents facing each other with a garden between them and then, after a few detached houses, another crescent, less grand but taller, across the end. It was at the top of this that I found my attic, and the place turned out to be very handy. Philippa, now married to Michael Foot (the historian, not the politician) and working as a tutor at Somerville, was settled in no. 16 at the end of one of the grander crescents and in 1948 Iris, returning from graduate work at Cambridge to become a tutor at St Anne's, lodged there with the Foots for a time and then moved to her old undergraduate digs in no. 43, which was one of the detached houses. Thus for a time the sweeping view from my attic window included them all and I soon began to see them a good deal, getting back into the philosophical scene.

This, however, actually turned out to be the last part of my life when I saw much of Iris. I do remember talking then a good deal with her, as well as with Philippa and Elizabeth Anscombe, about Oxford moral philosophy and what should be done about it. Indeed I think that this was when we all hammered out our various thoughts on that topic, a lot of which we later published. But a year after Iris arrived in Oxford I left it myself for Reading, and from then on we never again lived near each other – in fact, after I came to Newcastle we were usually hundreds of miles apart. And there gradually opened up at that time a gap between our outlooks – though never any sort of hostility – partly, no doubt, as a result of my own increasing absorption in my family and also of Iris's total absorption in writing her novels.

After leaving St Anne's in 1952 she quickly became a very full-time author, laying it down that she was not to be interrupted except for carefully arranged afternoon visits. In my occasional trips southwards I usually managed to fit in these visits and when I made them I found her still delightful and affectionate. But she did seem to grow increasingly remote – especially so when she and her husband John lived in the country at Steeple Aston in a house that was surrounded by a wood of rampantly neglected greenery, suggesting a Sleeping Beauty's defence against the world. An extra difficulty for me at this time was that she had completed her odyssey across the political spectrum by supporting and voting for Margaret Thatcher. On visits to her I avoided raising this topic, having been warned about it, but I still managed to upset her on one of them by making some critical remark about the Reverend Ian Paisley, the extreme Protestant leader in Northern Ireland.

This triggered such a sharp response from Iris's still-active Ulster loyalties that I began to wonder whether I might have to stop visiting altogether. But soon after that time Iris and John moved back to Oxford, becoming, I think, more integrated with the world, and she gradually returned to being much more relaxed. The high point of this change for me was an occasion in the early 1990s when I rang her, quite without warning, to ask if I could visit next day and she answered cheerfully, 'Well I'm going to Japan tomorrow afternoon but yes of course, do come in for coffee in the morning, that's lovely'. So I did, and all went well.

To return to the late 1940s. Life at no. 55 Park Town was not luxurious. My room contained a gas-fire and gas-ring, fed with shillings through a meter, and (behind a curtain) some shelves and a jug and basin. One level down, on the floor of the staircase, there was a battered sink with a cold tap, and by going lower still you could find a bathroom with a brown-stained bath and a temperamental geyser – a geyser that ate pennies, took a week to work and gave out far more steam than hot water. (Occasionally, too, other people pinched one's bath before one could get back to it.) You boiled water to wash your smalls in the basin and dried them by draping them over the curtain-rail. But it was heaven to be independent after years in schools and lodgings.

For decor I had, as a bedspread, a huge Chinese flag that my parents had acquired at some internationalist occasion – a pre-Mao flag displaying a big purple dragon with bulging black-and-white eyes on a sulphur-yellow ground – very encouraging. And there was always the wide-ranging view. I lived there quite comfortably and commuted to Boar's Hill either by bike or bus, according to the weather and the state of my energies. This distance gave me some respite from Lady Mary's demands.

Towards the end of my time with the Murrays I found that (not surprisingly) my nervous indigestion was getting worse. I went to my doctor, who suggested that I try some psychotherapy. Far from resenting this idea I thought at once, 'My goodness yes. I'm certainly not going to go on like this – I've got to do something about it.' So I went for six months to a somewhat unorthodox partially Jungian Austrian called Hornik and this worked reasonably well. It was really a matter of getting things rather more in perspective – of not being driven mad by treating things like Lady Mary's tantrums as seriously important. This gradually led me into a more general mid-life crisis where I began to grasp that a lot of alarming things that happened – particularly occasions like lecturing – weren't important at all and would all be forgotten in a hundred years' time. In this way I quite stopped being nervous about public speaking and though – as I've said – this didn't put my digestion entirely right it made it much easier to control.

In the summer of 1947 I had my first holiday abroad since the war, going to France for a fortnight with Iris and an old friend of mine, an architecture student called Tom Greeves, who had been Hugh's chum at Cambridge and had (I think) spent most of the war, as Hugh did, in India. Tom was an entrancing person with an unbridled passion for old buildings and a deep loathing of the Bauhaus ideology – so prevalent at that time – which was trying to tear them down and replace them with something out of the latest *Architectural Review*. A tall, rangy, slow-spoken figure with a tendency to shout things suddenly in an Ulster accent and an infectious laugh, he was a friend of John Betjeman's and later a co-founder with him of the Victorian Society, designed to defend these treasures against the invading hordes. (Tom had a confusing effect on me, incidentally, by making me associate Ulster accents with charm – a notion that can't always be relied on to guide one through life.)

Tom's kind of fervour may sound unnecessary now, when 'heritage' has become accepted – indeed sometimes over-trumpeted – as an important value. It wasn't at all unnecessary then. After the war, the sense that a quite new world must be built was often expressed in simple literal terms in proposals to demolish and replace really splendid buildings – for instance York Railway Station – as a gesture of enlightenment. And a good deal of this was actually done.

These views naturally made difficulties for Tom in his chosen profession. Though he duly went through his training, he never practised much as an architect. Having some private means, he devoted himself all his life to conserving things – buildings of all sorts, not just Victorian ones, and also old musical instruments, about which he knew a great deal. He had a wonderful grasp of the different styles of architecture and design generally and of their historical meaning. He had been explaining these things to me and Hugh as long as I knew him, which was from Hugh's days at Cambridge before the war.

He also illustrated them by making wonderful drawings of imaginary buildings – often ruinous and topped with waving foliage – and still more amazing ones of hypothetical aircraft driven by steam. These were fantasies of what might have been if only that line of invention had been continued – I suppose they were lost descendants of my grandfather's Stanley steam car. Later he took to using these drawings as Christmas cards. Those who received them still treasure them today and I still have three of them on my wall. I'm particularly fond of the Steam Hovercraft, which is sending out tremendous puffs from under it as it rises. He had no interest in exploiting these ideas for public fame, catching the current fashion as he certainly could have done. That simply wasn't his thing.

When Tom visited us in Newcastle soon after my marriage, we took him to the top of the Castle and he pointed out building after building in the city which we would never have noticed on our own, or which we would have dismissed, if we had happened to notice them, as ordinary and rather tiresome. He showed you what was distinctive about a building, bringing out its special point in a way that made you recognize and even like it in a way, so that you could pick this style out again when you saw something similar next time.

This is what Osbert Lancaster also did in his admirable books – *Pillar to Post, Homes Sweet Homes* and the rest. I think it is really an important help for urban living. There is something constantly irritating and worrying about buildings that one cannot see the point of, so it can be a deep relief when you do begin to see it. This was the experience that Collingwood described in his encounters with the Albert Memorial. I have had this trouble myself with a lot of styles and particularly with one that (like the Albert Memorial's) is specially ornate – the style that Osbert Lancaster calls Second Empire Renaissance. It is the grand one with all those whopping mansard roofs and dormer windows, the style that you find at Victoria Station. This kind of building used to exasperate me profoundly before I got some idea of what it was trying to do. It is one of the styles that look particularly gross when they are blown up to several times the size that they were originally intended for, which naturally does happen in modern cities. The name that Lancaster used for it was a real help here, as were many of his other names – Stockbrokers Tudor, Edwardian Baroque, By-Pass Variegated, Wimbledon Transitional, Pont Street Dutch . . .

On our post-war holiday, however, we took an important step towards seeing the point of Victoria Station by having a look at the French Renaissance itself. We went to see the chateaux of the Loire – Blois, Chenonceaux, Azay-Le-Rideau and the rest. Having crossed the channel in the proper way by boat – which of course gives a far better sense of being abroad than flying – we stayed in a small hotel at Tours and trundled around on hired bicycles, or sometimes in buses, seeing these marvels. I had never realized before that the palaces that appeared in good illustrations of fairy stories by people such as Edmond Dulac actually existed in the world and could be seen, pepper-pot pinnacles and all, merely by taking a boat to France. It was a revelation, greatly helped by Tom's pointing out of unexpected details.

The trip was, however, also quite an exercise in logistics. This newly opened enterprise of travelling abroad carried a stern financial condition. Each traveller could take only £50 out of the country. This was more money than it would be today but it was still distinctly limiting. I think the actual planning must have been done by Iris, who had been on the Continent at the end of the war (when she was working for the United Nations Relief and Reconstruction Agency) and probably had some contacts to help her organize it.

In order to protect our £50 we carried huge knapsacks full of boring stores – ryvita, soap, tins of sardines, soup powder, spirit-stove for making tea and so forth – and rigorously rationed our occasions of eating out in restaurants. I think we lunched on snacks and ate out in the evening. Here there was a bit of a clash between Iris, who said she didn't actually mind whether she ate French food or not, and Tom, who decidedly did mind and wasn't going to waste his chances. Once or twice he took off and ate on his own. I thought he had a point, but the idea of running out of money at the end made me so jumpy that I mostly stayed with Iris and the sardines.

Things worked out well in the end and we were able to have a week in a small hotel on the Left Bank after the one at Tours. I had not seen Paris before, any more than the chateaux, and I found it wonderful – bridges, statues, shops, the lot. We also went to see Versailles, which I didn't care for then and still don't. But I recently found a little guidebook to it which we used, all scribbled over with the limericks that we kept making up, each person in turn producing one line. One of them went:

> The citizen Louis XIV
> Built his houses with plenty of dV.
> But this habit resplendent
> Didn't help his descendant
> When the mob shouted, 'Regibus MV!'

In Paris, we had dinner with a lively Belgian couple, friends of Iris's. The husband explained to us the labyrinthine state of Belgian politics, giving an endless list of Belgian political parties. This bewildered me and I eventually asked him which of these parties he would vote for. He exploded with tremendous force. 'I would vote for *none* of them', he shouted. 'I would make a quite new party of my own', and he explained its policies. It was a useful glimpse of the troubles that can arise from different voting systems.

We also went to a fair – I think in Montmartre. Here they had that quite new marvel the Rotor – a large drum in which you could stand against the wall and became gradually stuck to it by centrifugal force as the thing span round at increasing speed. You were supposed to stay fixed there while the floor fell away beneath you, and still to be there when the spinning slowed and the floor finally came back. Citizens who were brave enough to do this didn't have to pay – it was the spectators in the little gallery above, watching and no doubt hoping for a disaster, who paid. Iris, quite typically, volunteered at once to be rotated. Just as typically, Tom and I paid our francs, scuttled upstairs and nervously watched her. Of course it turned out all right. I don't know whether this simple device is still entertaining people or whether they have found out by now that it doesn't go wrong, and thus is not terribly interesting.

At home, as time went on, I gradually became sure that I didn't want to be on Boar's Hill for ever and I began to suspect that perhaps I might think about getting back into philosophy. Murray's autobiography was not finished, but it seemed to be trundling along at a reasonable rate. In fact he never did finish it, but what he had written of it when he died in 1957 was published as a fragment with the title *Gilbert Murray: An Unfinished Autobiography with Contributions by His Friends*. His son-in-law Arnold Toynbee explained in the foreword that, 'when he came to the chapters in which he himself was the central figure, he had a dislike for carrying it on; he felt that writing an autobiography was egotistical'. As for his translations, *The Arbitration* did get published in 1945 and he then started to work on a Sophocles play, *The Wife of Heracles* (*The Trachiniae*), which came out in 1947.

There was really nothing special that I could do for him in this work that another secretary might not do better, so as 1946 went on I began to think about leaving. Just at that point, however a crisis blew up that meant I could not leave until it was resolved.

The Murrays lost their servants. New ones had somehow to be found. But the age of domestic service was almost gone. Few women were now willing to live and work in other people's houses, above all not in places like Boar's Hill that were far away from city centres. What was to be done?

Up till then, the Murrays had kept their large house, Yatscombe, and its frequent guests going on a mix of resident refugees and a few lifelong retainers (now retired and living in the neighbourhood) who came in daily. The retainers understood Lady Mary's way of running things, and anyway they dated from a time when such methods were normal. But their contribution was steadily shrinking now as they grew older. The refugees, for their part, had mostly been too grateful for being saved from a worse fate than Yatscombe to be very critical. Often, too, Lady Mary had helped them in substantial ways. In any case, not many alternatives were open to them while the war lasted and they were willing to put up with working there till it was over. But now it was indeed over and they could go back to their own countries. They did so; hence the crisis.

Attempts to find replacements through informal channels failed, so the Murrays decided that they must advertise. They did this in a periodical called, non-Marxistly enough, *The Lady*, which was seen as sovereign for this purpose. It was supposed to tap a reservoir of people who were not working class but who needed to work and didn't mind doing it domestically, provided that someone else was present to do 'the rough'. These ladies saw themselves as housekeepers and perhaps cooks. But their employers, given the difficulty of persuading anyone else to do the rough, tended to inveigle them into wider roles, so that there was a false basis to this whole market.

Today the same sort of falsity reigns. Most people still don't want to work in someone else's house, so au pairs and various kinds of foreign maids get trapped into situations that they did not bargain for. It's all very unsatisfactory. But for the Murrays, and especially for Lady Mary, it came as a grave culture shock. Lack of servants was something that she could hardly imagine. Much earlier, I had asked her whether it wasn't in some ways difficult to live at Castle Howard, where she had been brought up. She stared at me uncomprehendingly, then drew herself up and said sharply, 'We lived in it exactly as you would live in any other house – there was nothing difficult about it at all'. And, with servants enough, perhaps this was true. But that support was now crumbling.

This remark reminded me at once of the cheerful little poem – which used to be attributed to Pope but now apparently isn't – about the thoughts arising in the visitor's mind after being shown over that other terrific Vanbrugh mansion, Blenheim. It ends:

'Thanks, sir', cried I , ''tis very fine.
But where d'ye sleep? Or where d'ye dine?
I find by all you have been telling
It is a house, but not a dwelling.'

Houses like these are grand and eloquent statements, and among the things that they state there is always the one essential clause, 'We have plenty of servants'. Those were the days.

It so happened that I had come across the tangle of misunderstandings surrounding advertisements in *The Lady* before this when my mother was struggling with the problem of providing for my grandmother's house, Flimwell Grange, during the war, so I wasn't too hopeful about them. But the Yatscombe case turned out to have an extra complication that would never have occurred to me, one that was due to fame. When Dr Gilbert Murray's name appeared in the advertisement asking for two such ladies, half the distressed gentlewomen across the country became excited and decided to apply at once. We had no end of trouble sorting through a crowd of letters and picking out some who should come for interview.

So those chosen ones duly came. Confronted with Lady Mary the shrewder ones among them saw the red light at once and politely withdrew. The real trouble came with the others, the uncertain ones who dithered – said that they would think about it – went away and dithered some more – asked further questions – and sometimes finally said that they would try it for a time. I don't know how many of them actually did this. I have the impression that two or three pairs of eager ladies actually arrived, along with their massive luggage – tried to settle down – grew increasingly bewildered and finally, after some days, gave up, not without tears and recriminations as I finally drove them down to the station. I even moved into Yatscombe myself for a while in order to help out and, if possible, to settle these victims in. When that process repeatedly failed to work, I began to think I was going to be there for ever.

This problem did finally get resolved in a way the details of which I can't now remember. I think the relief of this event must have clouded my memory. From some source – I think not from *The Lady* – a couple of people did somehow appear who were willing to stick at the job. And almost at once after they had done so my own situation changed sharply.

Winter interlude

Towards the end of January 1947 my father rang to say that my mother had fallen on a slippery floor and had broken her thigh. Would I come home at once? Of course I did so. I could see that my leaving would not now be a total disaster for

Yatscombe. It might well lead later to my moving away altogether, as I had been thinking of doing. And I was badly needed at home.

My mother stayed in hospital for about ten days, having her femur pinned and gradually recovering from this operation. She then came home, but she was still in bed for a while and in fact she never did recover totally from the accident. From that time she was increasingly troubled by rheumatoid arthritis, a crippling complaint for which there was then no cure. She had had it slightly before, but it very gradually and steadily became worse later, causing her to shrink and stoop.

Throughout the spring of 1947, then, I stayed at home in Kingston, looking after her and helping generally with the household. That was quite exciting because this was one of the coldest winters on record. Distrusting my own recollections of it as too melodramatic, I have just looked it up on the Internet and checked the Met Office records, which fully bear me out. They call it:

> the remarkable winter of 1947, the snowiest winter since 1814 . . . From 22 January to 17 March . . . snow fell every day somewhere in the UK, with the weather so cold that the snow accumulated. The temperature seldom rose more than a degree or two above freezing . . . Across Britain, drifts of more than 5 metres deep blocked roads and railways . . . The cold, snowy weather continued through February and March. February 1947 was the coldest February on record . . . [it] bore comparison with January 1814 . . . Another unusual feature of February 1947 was the lack of sunshine . . . The severe difficulties caused by the winter of 1947 were aggravated by the fuel and food shortages that remained after the Second World War.

That's just how I remember it. The year 1814 was the famous 'year without a summer' that caused such terrible hardship at the time – an exceptional case that is thought to have been due to a volcanic eruption. I don't know that any special causes were found for the 1947 winter but it certainly did seem exceptional. Ink froze in people's ink-pots, making it impossible to write. Electric fires refused to function because their elements were too cold to start. The accumulating snow meant that there were great hard-packed frozen dirty ridges of it everywhere, especially along the edges of the pavements where it froze in big rough mounds after being thrown off the road. It was really hard to get around on foot and it wasn't possible to bicycle. My mother, with her bad leg, could scarcely get outside at all until conditions eased.

As for the shortages, on top of the lack of food and fuel, years of clothes rationing had left us without much that was warm to wrap up in and there was no central heating. I can't think what it was like in devastated Europe; it was bad enough in Kingston. But what the Met Office doesn't know about is the extra complications produced by living with my father, who was now a specialist in economizing fuel. This was the time when he perfected the art of making a single lump of coal last all day in the dining-room stove ('Don't disturb it, it's doing nicely!'). He objected to my using the gas-fire in my bedroom at all. He didn't seem to feel the cold himself – he just kept his overcoat on all the time in the house and seemed to find that enough. His passion for economizing did, however, have one rather satisfactory result. At one time matches became scarce, so, in order to save using a match in the morning, he took to leaving the kettle on all night on a very low gas. This not only made it easy to make tea in next day but did quite a lot to warm up the kitchen.

After the great freeze came the thaw, with floods all over the country. These didn't do us any harm, but I remember walking by the Thames at Teddington Weir and seeing the river running quite full – going pretty well straight down whole water over the weir. It was all very exciting.

Not doing the B.Phil.

When my mother was better in the summer of 1947 I went back in Oxford to consult with Isobel Henderson and others about finding the best way to do some work in philosophy.

There were two options, much the more obvious being to take the regular course for the B.Phil. This was a graduate degree that had lately been invented, mainly at the instance of Gilbert Ryle, as a general training for young philosophers. Ryle had, I think, understood early in the war that there would be a great expansion of universities when it ended, and he wanted to make sure that plenty of well-educated philosophical graduates were there to work in them.

This course gave a training that was in many ways a good and thorough one. It was examined partly by set papers and partly by dissertation, and it is much respected as a philosophical qualification. The trouble about it is simply that it necessarily reflects the philosophical slant of those running it, and in my time that slant was somewhat narrowly linguistic.

Ryle and the other analytic philosophers of that time were not, of course, full-time logical positivists. They did not confine the scope of philosophy within the limits set by *Language, Truth and Logic*. Indeed, it was quite a favourite exercise among them to attack the crudities of early verificationism. Ayer himself had already begun his long and tortuous withdrawal from his original extreme position. Nevertheless, the area now assigned to philosophy was still one firmly determined by ideology.

Here we again come back to Iris's question. It is indeed important to ask what any particular philosopher is afraid of. It stuck out a mile that what really frightened analytic philosophers of that time was the danger of being thought *weak* – vague, credulous, sentimental, superstitious or simply too wide in their sympathies. Unlike their forebears in William James's time, they were much more afraid of looking weak than they were of missing something unexpected and important. They were not at all afraid (on the other hand) of being thought too narrow. So they were happy to exclude all topics that could expose them to that central danger.

Though religion was the most obvious of these dangerous topics, plenty of others were felt to be just as sinister. For instance, questions about queer phenomena such as telepathy – questions which William James and his colleagues had treated as important empirical issues – were now sharply tabooed as fringe interests, things it would be unscientific even to ask about. Similarly, questions about human motives, such as those raised by Freud and Jung, were viewed with deep suspicion. Motives were held to be factual matters that ought to be left to psychology, but preferably to the kind of psychology that would be sure not to make too much of them. Thus, when Oxford at last introduced psychology into its syllabus (I think some time during the 1950s), a friend of mine, then head of a women's college, said that she was rather worried about this innovation. 'But I dare say', she added, ' it may turn out to be all right, because it's only experimental psychology.'

It was central to this slant that – except for Peter Strawson, who was devoted to large-scale metaphysics – analytic philosophers at that time tended to treat the metaphysical enquiries of the mighty dead with suspicion, disapproval or sometimes outright ridicule. Indeed, they often followed the logical positivist lead by using the term 'metaphysic' itself to mean something outside the range of rational thought, sometimes even actual nonsense – a most confusing usage which was unfortunately encouraged by Karl Popper. Though they were often willing to quarry former philosophers for techniques of argument, they avoided taking their large-scale contentions seriously. Indeed, as time went on, increasing numbers of them objected to studying past philosophy at all. They veered towards the view which I quoted from Ted Honderich earlier, that this stuff was now obsolete and ought to be forgotten. In some people's view – especially in the USA – it was necessary only to read the articles in the recent journals, which were still steadily narrowing the range of topics that they allowed.

In particular, English-speaking moral philosophy at that time was shut off on its own from the rest of thought by a strict orthodoxy based on the notion of the naturalistic fallacy – a radical break between facts and values, which meant that moral thinking could have no intelligible link with reasoning about the natural world. Its reigning prophet was R. M. Hare, who had replaced the wilder forms of the Boo-Hooray theory by prescriptivism, a view of morals which acknowledged a certain amount of reasoning as internal to morality, but still shut it off from any rational connection with other areas of thinking.

Ryle himself eventually became somewhat alarmed by all this. He was actually a cultivated man with a wide philosophical background, indeed, he had originally been a student of Husserl's phenomenology. He was seriously worried, as time went on, at the philistine ignorance of his younger followers. But he could not put the genie back in the bottle.

All this bothered me because this large-scale metaphysics was just what I wanted to look at. I therefore got interested in exploring the other avenue to graduate work, which was to attempt a D.Phil. thesis – a longer affair, which could take up to seven years, concentrated on a particular topic. My first thought was that this topic might be the symbolism of the Cave and the Sun in the seventh book of the *Republic*. In particular, what did Plato mean when he said that the intelligible world was *more real* than the physical one? Can there, as the Idealists thought, be degrees of reality? What (for instance) did Bradley mean by saying that 'the more anything is spiritual, so much the more is it veritably real . . .'? This passage in the *Republic* turned out, however, to have been investigated in far too much detail by too many people, and in reference to too many other controversies, to leave any room for an ill-qualified newcomer.

At this point somebody suggested investigating the neo-Platonists, who had developed this symbolism and expounded Plato's meaning in important ways. I was advised to look at some of them, and at once I liked the look of Plotinus. I could see that he was a shrewd and serious philosopher, and that he was indeed dealing with the problems that interested me.

Plotinus accepted and developed Plato's thought that there is a far vaster and more serious reality lying behind the everyday scene around us. But he also accepted Aristotle's insight that everyday realities must be taken seriously as well. Like Spinoza, he wanted somehow to relate the world of the senses intelligibly to the world of thought, rather than just dismissing it, as Plato did, as ultimately incomprehensible. He wanted to find a wider, more inclusive perspective which could bring together both these aspects of life, showing a continuity between the physical and the spiritual.

He therefore fiercely opposed the Manichees and Gnostics who thought that the physical world was simply evil. Instead he vigorously celebrated its goodness. This world (he said) is excellent at its own level. But that level is only one part of our life and our understanding needs to move far beyond it. This is not a move to alien territory but a move in which we exercise a deeper part of our own nature, since we are ourselves spiritual as well as physical. When we move inwards, we are coming home. We are richly composite beings whose souls already extend through all the levels of reality, and the first step to better understanding of the world around us is to explore this large world within, moving steadily towards its most 'real', most important central areas. As one Plotinus scholar puts it, by this neo-Platonic way of thinking 'philosophy came to seek the cosmos predominantly within the soul'. That soul was correspondingly seen as hugely more complex, more interesting and more philosophically important than it had appeared before.

This idea was not wholly new. Heraclitus had already suggested that our souls – the selves within us – are vaster and far less well known to us than we tend to suppose. So deep (said Heraclitus) is the soul that you could never find its boundaries, however far you might travel . . . But Plotinus took up and developed this suggestion on a quite new scale, making it clear that this self – which reaches far beyond consciousness – is not just one more kind of *object* alongside those that we meet in the physical world, but really is a *subject* – an experiencer – a kind of item that needs a quite different metaphysical treatment. That was why, although Plotinus accepted Plato's view that mathematics and other intellectual disciplines are a necessary part of spiritual development, he was insistent that they are not the whole of it. Because we are such complex beings – because we are not just dedicated calculating machines – we need to pass far beyond such abstract formulations so as to contemplate the world directly, responding to it with the whole of our being.

Much attracted by this seductive candle I fluttered round it for a bit taking advice. Some of this came from E. R. Dodds, the professor whose lectures I had earlier attended and liked. Dodds, a most impressive man, was keen to get attention given to other parts of Greek thought besides its well-trodden highways. He had written a good book called *The Greeks and the Irrational*, aimed at shifting the stereotype which showed Greece as full of sober, orderly characters with a public-school education. He encouraged me to go for Plotinus and agreed to be my supervisor if I did. With his help, I outlined a research topic which was to deal with Plotinus' psychology – his doctrine of the self – and this was duly accepted by the authorities. So in the autumn of 1947 I began to work on it for the D.Phil. degree.

I should say at once that I never finished that thesis. The whole scheme was indeed impossibly ambitious. It quickly turned out that Plotinus, besides his debt to Plato, was involved in controversy with a whole raft of other philosophers from Aristotle down to his own time, which was the third century AD. Some of these philosophers I had never heard of at all; all of them needed a great deal of attention. My knowledge of Greek, though now much improved, was too faltering to deal with the variety of styles and ages that I now encountered, nor did I have enough experience of how to manage libraries.

And Dodds himself, though benevolent, was not a good supervisor because he was shy and remote. In fact, he was an example of the kind of academic who is a first-rate lecturer – perfectly at ease on a platform – but not approachable socially. He was not someone you could easily consult each time that you got lost, as I constantly did, in some tangle about secondary authorities. My own social incompetence, too, which had prevented me from coping properly with Betty Ackroyd at the Ministry of Production, stood in the way of my telling him properly about my difficulties.

So I never finished working on Plotinus. But I haven't the least doubt that I was right to start doing so. I am most grateful to my advisers – particularly to Isobel Henderson – for not pressuring me to take the B.Phil. course, which would have been so obviously the prime career option. What I actually did, besides reading Plotinus himself, which was hugely valuable, was to take part in other courses that were going on. Some of these were on other parts of Greek philosophy – on Plato's later work and on Aristotle's *Metaphysics* and *De Anima* – all of which were exactly the kind of thing that I wanted. But so were the other courses that I went to, such as H. H. Price's, on contemporary philosophy, which was mainly attended by people taking the B.Phil.

Thus I got the benefit of a wide range of discussion on a lot of topics. In particular, I now began to pick up some idea of Wittgenstein's later philosophy – of the thoughts that he later published in 1953 in his *Philosophical Investigations*. Several people who had studied with him at Cambridge, including Peter Geach and Yorick Smithies, were at these classes. But I think it was Elizabeth Anscombe who really made this new approach visible to me. Repeatedly and carefully she spelt out how our thought about language has to be rooted in the complexities of real life, not imposed on it from outside as a calculus derived from axioms.

The special importance of language does not, then, flow from its being a particularly grand isolated phenomenon. It arises because speech is a central human activity, reflecting our whole nature – because language is rooted, in a way that mathematics is not, in the wider structure of our lives. So it leads on to an investigation of our whole nature. She rightly pointed out how Aristotle supports this pluralistic approach in preference to Plato's more reductive and geometry-driven vision, exalting mathematics as the model for all thinking, which has had so much influence on later thought.

At that time, I think many people thought that she deepened our confusion because she was rejecting handy simplifications. But as one got leisure to think it through, her contribution was invaluable. Indeed, altogether I found these discussions enormously useful. They were, however, as I have said, a passing phenomenon, a consequence of the presence in Oxford at that time of people with very diverse views and backgrounds. They weren't going to last.

Some time during the late 1940s Wittgenstein himself came to Oxford to speak to the Jowett Society (the philosophical discussion club). This occasion roused fierce excitement, though we had been warned in advance that it might turn out frustrating. The room, which was not very big, was packed with eager listeners. Wittgenstein, thin, spry and neat in his green pullover, made an impression of volcanic energy, tightly controlled. According to his custom he had refused to prepare a paper himself but had agreed to reply to a short one from somebody else. A heroic character called Oscar Wood accordingly read a brief piece on Descartes's *Cogito*.

Wittgenstein then began to reply. For about five minutes what he said seemed incredibly important and illuminating. But then he started to see difficulties. He hesitated and interrupted himself – 'No no, that isn't it – What should one say? You see, the real difficulty here – Oh no no, it is terrible . . .' dropping his head in his hands and then beating it, and so on. We knew that this was how he habitually went on in his regular classes, but it was distracting for hearers who weren't used to it. I quickly lost the thread and forgot the invaluable thoughts that I had picked up at the beginning. (With hindsight, it might have been best to have left at that point, but we didn't know that.)

Things went on confusingly enough all the evening. I'm sure that some points did become clear, but the only bit I now remember is a row that suddenly developed after an interruption by Professor H. A. Prichard. He was the intuitionist moral philosopher who had dominated the Oxford ethical scene for a long time before the logical positivist dawn. Not surprisingly upset by something that Wittgenstein said about ethics, he loudly denounced it. There followed a strange brief scene in which two people, neither of whom was at all used to being contradicted, sharply contradicted each other. Then Prichard left, and Wittgenstein continued his mining operation on the *Cogito*. At the end of the evening he said unhappily, 'Oh dear, we have not finished this', so somebody suggested that the discussion should go on the next afternoon. He agreed, and we all came back for it, but I never found that it got much clearer.

The extraordinary thing about Wittgenstein is that he succeeded in making crucial things clear in philosophy in spite of his fearful communication difficulties. These difficulties seem to have been more or less of the kind that is now discussed under the heading of Asperger's Syndrome, and though such classifications can be slick and misleading I think the central point does seem right. There was surely a kind of emotional remoteness that shut him off in many ways from those around him. But perhaps it was the terror induced by that very sense of remoteness that made him able to stress our social nature so powerfully. Having been very close to real solipsism he rebounded from it with tremendous violence. Thus he was able to break away from the conviction of individual isolation produced by the *Cogito* and to replant us in our proper soil as social beings.

As for my own life, in these years I also gave tutorials to several undergraduates from Somerville and, I think, some from St Hugh's as well. This was great and I got a lot from them. As it happens, two of the Somerville ones have later become rather celebrated – Anne Warburton, who was later Principal of Lucy Cavendish College at Cambridge, and Carmen Blacker, who became a distinguished Japanese scholar and, I think, reader in Japanese at Cambridge. It was Carmen who supplied me with the best example I have ever met of the diversity of moral views. When I raised the topic of conflicting customs, 'Oh, I see', she said. 'Like, there's a verb in classical Japanese which means *to try out one's new sword on a chance wayfarer*?' I used this one later, with Carmen's permission, in an article with that name which now forms part of my book *Heart and Mind*.

I also occasionally turned an honest penny by doing small odd jobs, one of which was invigilating A-level exams for a small but very upper-class girls' school in the Cotswolds. This school had been disqualified from doing its own invigilating because, the year before, the weather had been particularly fine on the date when the exams were supposed to start, so the headmistress had let the girls go out hunting on that day and do the exams later. (They all had their own horses.) The authorities had found out about this and said that it must not occur again, so I was paid to spend a very comfortable summer week in this idyllic spot, somewhere on the river Windrush. I was interested to see that the set books for one of the English papers included *Tom Jones* and *Clarissa*. 'Do you like these books?' I asked one of the girls afterwards. Astonished, she stared at me and replied at once, 'Oh we don't *read* them'.

Another of these jobs was marking the General Papers for Somerville entrance. For some reason that I can't now recall – probably so that the candidates could be promptly invited for interview – it had to be done in a great hurry and I had to work most of the night. It is the only time in my life that I have tried to do this and I found it fearfully hard. However much black coffee I used, towards three in the morning all the essays looked exactly alike. In fact, writing general essays quickly can be pretty difficult for people who haven't had the kind of practice in doing it I had myself, and this sometimes makes them correspondingly difficult to mark. On these occasions, I think I earned my money.

All this time, however, the question of jobs and careers naturally loomed over us. In the 1940s that topic was less frightening than it often is because universities in Britain were expanding at unusual speed. During the two decades after the war quite a lot of new universities were founded and the older ones were enlarged to take on more students. A serious effort was being made to admit far more people to higher education. Moreover, the newer universities sometimes put together unconventional mixtures of courses which might employ people trained in philosophy in unfamiliar ways. (Most of these bright schemes caved in later because of practical difficulties, but they were still around in the 1940s.)

On the other hand, there were also more graduates to fill these places than there normally would have been, because of the backlog of people returning from the war. As each new job came up, the negotiations about it were anxiously watched. One intriguing thing was to see how the salaries offered reflected the distance that an aspirant lecturer would have to move away from the hub of philosophical civilization in Oxford. When I got a job in Reading – only half an hour's journey away – I was paid £400 a year. Geoff Midgley in Newcastle – five hours away – got £550. (I still have the letter offering him the place at that commencing salary.) And when Tony Flew went to Aberdeen he got £800. I don't know what those who actually got posts in Oxford were paid, but it looks as if it must have been rather modest.

There were, of course, no mixed colleges then in Oxford. But jobs in the women's colleges there did sometimes come up and when they did I naturally put in for them. By good fortune, however, I didn't get them. In 1948 St Anne's very sensibly chose Iris as tutor rather than me and St Hugh's with equal good sense chose Mary Warnock. Sheer luck had again saved me from a mistake that I did not have the sense to avoid. I did not see that I could not possibly have settled to work properly in the steadily narrowing circle of Oxford philosophy and the feuding that went with it. Had I remained there, I would certainly have got out of philosophy altogether.

I remember particularly a meeting of the Jowett – the philosophical discussion club – at which a disciple of J. L. Austin's read a paper on a very small point of linguistic usage. Small though it was, however, that point hardly came up at all in the subsequent discussion. As soon as the speaker had finished, his critics piled in to attack him – not on this supposedly main issue but on a crowd of even smaller linguistic points arising in the course of his argument, places where they thought his wording was mistaken. The game went on for the whole evening and obviously could have gone on for ever. I went away deeply depressed.

I thought of this escape again just now, thanking Providence once more, as I read Colin McGinn's account of what he calls 'the cut and thrust of philosophical debate' encouraged by the teacher of a class that he attended when he arrived in Oxford to do the B.Phil. in 1972:

> Evans was a fierce debater, impatient and uncompromising; as I remarked, he skewered fools gladly (perhaps too gladly). The atmosphere in his class was intimidating and thrilling at the same time. As I was to learn later, *this is fairly characteristic of philosophical debate. It is not the sonorous recitation of vague profundities, but a clashing of analytically honed intellects, with pulsing egos attached to them* . . . . Philosophical discussion can be a kind of intellectual blood-sport, in which egos get bruised and buckled, even impaled. I have seen people white and dry-mouthed before giving a talk to a tough-minded audience, and visibly shaken afterwards . . . In Evans I saw someone with considerable debating skills, and I was no doubt attracted to the kind of power and respect that goes with that. *Plain showing-off is also a feature of philosophical life.*
>
> (p. 63. Emphases mine)

Showing-off is indeed a feature of many kinds of life and of course it is often a harmless one But that is no reason why it should be allowed to take them over. Any situation where a lot of young men are competing to form a dominance hierarchy, will produce cock-fights. But – as Plato pointed out already – these fights are not part of its essence; they are distractions from it. They interfere with philosophical work. 'Tough-minded' is much too polite a word to use for people who go to a meeting, not in order to understand what someone is saying but in order to catch him or her out by picking holes in it.

As McGinn sees it, the only possible alternative to cock-fighting would be bombast, 'the sonorous recitation of vague profundities'. But surely if any other topic were in question, nobody would suppose that the people discussing it were forced to choose between bombast and a boxing match. Philosophy is no different. It can perfectly well be discussed without aggression. No doubt people discussing it will always show off at times, but they can keep their egos under normal control.

McGinn, a strenuous and athletic character himself, clearly enjoys the competitive exercise. That is fine, but why should whole philosophy departments have to do it? Perhaps it could be set up in separate arenas – Departments of Cognitive Poker, or Institutes of One-Upmanship, so as to cultivate it wholeheartedly on its own. In any case, the practice of bullying one's students – which seems to be what McGinn is describing at the beginning of this passage – is not a sport at all; it's a vice.

It is worthwhile to notice how far this competitive conception of philosophy has taken us from the main traditional view of its place in life. That tradition comes out illuminatingly in *Romeo and Juliet*, when Friar Laurence is trying to make Romeo accept the fact that he has been banished:

Friar Laurence.	Thou fond, mad man, hear me but speak a word.
Romeo.	O, thou wilt talk again of banishment!
Friar Laurence.	I'll give thee armour to keep off that word Adversity's sweet milk, philosophy To comfort thee, though thou be banished.
Romeo.	Yet 'banished'? Hang up philosophy Unless philosophy can make a Juliet, Displant a town, reverse a prince's doom, It helps not, it prevails not, talk no more . . .
Friar Laurence.	O then I see that madmen have no ears.
Romeo	How should they, when that wise men have no eyes?
Friar Laurence.	Let me dispute with thee of thy estate –
Romeo	Thou canst not speak of what thou dost not feel!

(Act 2, Sc.3, ll. 54–65)

When Friar Laurence asks for *philosophy* here it may seem that he simply means connected thought – some recognition of a background, some power of thinking beyond the moment, some element of common sense. Even this, however, is more than Romeo can face. He can't endure thought of any kind. He simply *is* his present feeling, a feeling which resents the very possibility of thought.

This does often happen to us. Yet it is odd because our thoughts are not really hostile strangers. As Wordsworth put it, our thoughts are actually 'the representatives of our past feelings', reminders of what we have accepted and felt at other times. The battle is not actually between thought and feeling but between our present feelings and other feelings which have prevailed in life up till now. And the most central area of these conflicts is, of course, within ourselves, not in disputes with outsiders. Most of the time, Romeo and Friar Laurence are both parts of one person. Neither part can be thrown out. They will have to be brought together somehow.

Thus, the idea of Reason and Feeling as distinct forces battling for control of our lives is always a distorted one. Yet it has been a powerful pattern in the European tradition and, in spite of various attacks on it, it still is so today. The name of 'reason' is often given not to thought itself but to a certain set of rather bourgeois motives centring on prudence and social harmony.

These, of course, are the motives that Romeo cannot bear. He sees them as his enemies and rejects them. He sees his situation as a warfare. But seeing it like that makes it look as if there is an incurable division between our central faculties – as if thought simply cannot do business with feeling at all; 'Thou canst not speak of what thou dost not feel.' Yet we all do have to speak of what we do not feel, and to think of it too. The difficulty is how to do this properly, how to bring our warring faculties together.

An unusual consolation

The word *philosophy*, however, may not be being used here in quite that straightforward way. When Shakespeare made Friar Laurence speak of it, he probably did not mean only common sense and discretion but had something more specific in mind. He was thinking of Boethius' book *On the Consolation of Philosophy* and his audience will at once have done the same.

That book was immensely popular and well-loved throughout the Middle Ages and the Renaissance. Endless people, including King Alfred, Chaucer and Queen Elizabeth I, translated it into their own languages. Countless readers used it, not just as a literary text but as a prop and support for life, and found it a good one. Dante set Boethius among the twelve lights in the heaven of the Sun, calling him

> That joy who strips the world's hypocrisies
> Bare to whoever heeds his cogent phrases.

For, along with Cicero's *De Amicitia*, the words of Boethius had provided him with his greatest consolation after the death of Beatrice.

This, in fact, was a consolation that actually did work. It was an owl that could fly even in that profound darkness. It really was adversity's sweet milk, a fact that may have something to do with the circumstances in which Boethius wrote it. He was a distinguished Roman scholar and civil servant under the Emperor Theodoric in the sixth century AD, but he fell from power and was condemned to death. He wrote his book in prison while he was awaiting execution. Eventually, after being cruelly tortured, he was bludgeoned to death at Pavia, the place of his exile. And, since he knew the regime very well, he must have expected exactly that fate.

Yet in that prison he was able to find, and to express, thoughts that not only supported him but have supported many other people, under such burdens. By thinking, he somehow managed to arrive at a mood that was not just courageous but also deeply friendly and benign. He genuinely comforted other people.

The wrong kind of detachment

I think this story is interesting in relation to an incident that Simon Blackburn has described in a recent book. He writes:

> I was once defending the practice of philosophy on a radio programme where one of the other guests was a professional survivor of the Nazi concentration camps. He asked me, fairly aggressively, what use philosophy would have been on a death march? The answer, of course, was not much – no more than literature, art, music, mathematics, or science would be useful at such a time. But consider the ethical environment that made such events possible. Hitler said, 'How lucky it is for rulers that men cannot think'.
>
> (*Being Good*, Oxford University Press, 2001, p. 2)

Of course Blackburn is absolutely right that we need to use good thinking in order to prevent social disasters, not just in order to endure them. But the one use does not exclude the other. Over the ages, people who have actually *used* philosophy – rather than just talked about it – have undoubtedly made it work for both purposes. The *Oxford English Dictionary* is not just being careless when it gives, as the second still-current sense of the word *philosophical*, 'characterised by practical wisdom or philosophy, befitting or characteristic of a philosopher, wise, calm, temperate'. This is indeed one of the commonest meanings of the word.

During the last half of the twentieth century, however, professional philosophers in English-speaking countries were much embarrassed by this usage. They were alarmed by the thought that they might seem to be laying claim to practical virtues, and still more so by the thought that they might seem to be telling other people how to behave. Thus, in 1944 the American philosopher C. L. Stevenson began his book *Ethics and Language* (Yale University Press, 1944) by nervously disclaiming any intention to talk about morals:

> One would not expect a book on scientific method to do the work of science itself, and one must not expect here any conclusions about what conduct is right or wrong. The purpose of an analytical study . . . does not require the analyst, as such, to participate in the enquiry that he analyses. In ethics, any direct enquiry of this kind might have its dangers. It might deprive the analysis of its detachment and distort a relatively neutral study into a plea for some special code of morals . . . The present volume has the limited task of sharpening the tools which others employ.

Stevenson and his colleagues were claiming that it is possible to think about the *forms* of moral language detachedly, without attending to its subject matter or having any views about it. They thought that you can practise and teach clear thinking about ethics without committing yourself in any way to the clashing propositions that worry the (quite separate) people who are actually trying to live. They were also, of course, making an equally dodgy claim about science – suggesting that you can do philosophy of science without committing yourself to any views about the topics that scientists discuss.

That idea of detached clear thinking about practical questions was – itself – surely never very clearly thought through. Form and matter are indissolubly linked here. The moral problems that face us are troublesome just because they arise out of the wider practical concerns of life. Anyone who did not share those concerns would not be likely to be able to grasp them and think clearly about them. But people who do share the concerns will naturally be groping their way towards finding how to resolve them. Those who try to use philosophy on such problems are not claiming a special status as impartial judges, outside the struggle. Nor are they claiming to be wise. What they are doing is *attempting* wisdom – joining in the general search for it – struggling to get nearer to it through the usual mass of difficulties.

Thus Pythagoras, when his followers called him *wise*, is said to have replied that he was not wise but was indeed a lover of wisdom – *philosophos*. That was the origin of the word and it has remained the sense in which the great thinkers of the European tradition have used it. They have not differed about this central point from great thinkers in other traditions, such as the Indian, Chinese or Tibetan. Academics who now want to change their profession into one of pure detached criticism need to find a different name to put on their doors – linguistic engineer, perhaps, or grammatical consultant or conceptual analyst?

I am happy to see that, in the past decade or two, English-speaking philosophers, even at Oxford and Cambridge, seem to be moving out of this ivory tower of pure formalism and back into the marketplace. They are badly needed there, and they will surely find that the move improves their health.

7

At Reading, 1949–50

Dialectical difficulties

For me, however, another option turned up during the summer of 1949. News came of an option which wouldn't have these drawbacks but a whole set of different ones instead. Philippa Foot told me that Professor Herbert Hodges at Reading was looking for an assistant. I put in for this job, promptly got it and started work there in October.

Hodges was an interesting survival, a traditional metaphysician still in business, trying his best to stand firm against what he took to be the flood-tide of positivism. He was not actually old himself, though his ideas were. He was still vigorous and quite capable of doing good philosophy. His department was small, consisting merely of himself and one lecturer, but it was respected and could still confer degrees approved by external examiners from Oxford or Cambridge. Mostly it dealt in joint courses – Philosophy and English, or a language, or some other subject, though a few students did take Philosophy on its own.

Its success flowed largely from the close relations that Hodges maintained with those teaching in the other departments involved, especially with English. The students did not get two quite separate inputs, as they often do with joint degrees. Instead, they could join in discussions about the relations between their two subjects, discussions that were going on already between the people teaching them. These often started over lunch. Because Reading was still a small university, doing much of its work in a cosy Victorian terrace, many of the staff lunched together regularly in the senior common-room. This arrangement – which also worked at Newcastle University when I first went there – made possible a huge amount of effortless communication which now either doesn't happen at all or clogs up people's e-mails. From my teaching room – a small attic in this terrace, furnished with a raucous gas fire – I could go along the corridor at any time to have a word with someone in Classics or English. These two departments were both quite lively. The English Department then included Frank Kermode and the novelist John Wain, as well as a charming English Language lecturer called Mary Salu who had a Roman snail called Virgil.

When I left Oxford, several philosophers, and some other people too, condoled with me on the dreadful prospect of my prospective exile from decent society. This attitude struck me as a fairly awful piece of intellectual snobbery. I certainly did not find that there was any shortage of stimulation in Reading, and in some ways I found its atmosphere liberating. I wrote an article a little later for the *Twentieth Century* about the various universities I had known, in which I remarked on this:

> What did strike me was that it was possible to talk freely. Dons openly admitted that they were interested in subjects other than their own, and were willing to talk about them without looking round to see if the expert was going to confute them. If someone said, 'That's really a biological question,' this did not lead to an anguish-ridden silence, but to finding a biologist at once and asking him about it. Nobody seemed frightened of having their reputation destroyed; nobody considered that a chance question over a coffee-cup demanded an *ex cathedra* pronouncement. The state of being unable to say or write anything for fear that one might get it slightly wrong was not common, and where it existed it was not held in honour. I cannot express how much I liked this. When I had anything to write, I began to be able to write it, and so to work my way past my mistakes.
>
> For Oxford, though it has never managed to stop my mouth, had come very near to freezing up my pen.

Hodges was renowned among the students as an excellent lecturer, giving popular courses on Metaphysics and Aesthetics. He must have made a lot of necessary things clear in these, because the students did absorb them somehow. But, when I asked them to tell me what he had said, I could never get much of an answer. His ideas were Hegelian – that is, he saw the history of thought as a dialectic, a continual progress in which each thesis is contradicted by an antithesis so that a synthesis results, which then becomes the next thesis – and so on. He had written a book on Dilthey, who had developed this approach to the history of thought. He was also much interested in Collingwood's view of history.

Hegelian dialectic can be used in a huge variety of ways and the ways in which Hodges used it often seemed to be sensible. He was perceptive about what philosophers were getting at, and imaginative about seeing where they might need to go. The trouble about him was that he was flatly resolved not to go beyond his Hegelian platform – not to supplement it by looking at any later developments. He regarded the whole of linguistic philosophy as simply a mistake. He thought – very oddly – that it all rested on an error derived from Russell's *Principia Mathematica*, and he secretly nourished the wild hope that one day, when he could get around to it, he would refute that book . . .

It strikes me now that this was a most un-Hegelian line for him to take. Hodges ought surely to have thought of linguistic philosophy as the necessary next step – the proper, overdue antithesis to the Hegelian thesis. He should have set about forging the best parts of the two into the required synthesis, which, in a way, was what the rest of us (who also didn't want to be carried away by the linguistic flood) were trying to do. But Hodges's mind was closed to this possibility. No doubt that was why he now suffered from a painful writer's block. After publishing his book on Dilthey he had never managed to write anything more, though he was always trying to.

This trouble was, I think, connected with a rather unexpected difficulty that he had in dealing with the students. Though he was so eloquent and communicative with them in lectures, personally he was painfully shy. They found him terrifying. He had a far worse form of the same kind of nervousness in these situations that afflicted Dodds. Even in talking to colleagues, Hodges was liable suddenly to stutter and fall silent, staring helplessly at people while his jaw juddered, looking as if something terrible had happened which his interlocutor ought to do something about. And of course it was worse with students.

His previous assistant, Nona Bowring, warned me about this before I arrived in Reading and I found it was quite as bad as she said. In fact, soon after I got there the students came to me in a body and asked me to try to do something about it. So I went to see Hodges and hesitantly raised the subject. 'They seem', I said, getting rather nervous myself, 'to be frightened of you.' He gazed at me for a while, his jaw juddering. 'Are they?' he said. 'Not half as frightened as I am of them!' I don't know what we did about it. I suppose some kind of mutual understanding must have been arrived at. But cosmic terror is never a social asset, and I don't suppose we got rid of the trouble altogether.

Workwise, my chief trouble at Reading was that I had far too much to do. Since there were only two of us we had to carve up rather a large horizon between us. We gave all the students tutorials, which are interesting but time-consuming. I don't remember now just what subjects I actually taught, but I certainly did all the Greek philosophy and the Ethics and a good deal of Kant, which often involved keeping a few pages ahead of the students in particular set books. On the whole, however, these subjects were all right because they were up my street already. What was really awful was a course called First Year Logic.

For some reason connected with the joint courses and the rest of the syllabus, more than three hundred students took this, many of whom took no other philosophy. The text used was a little book on idealist logic. It had a first chapter on traditional Aristotelian logic, after which it went on to say how this wasn't the only important pattern of reasoning, and to explain how the Hegelian dialectic was better. Luckily, Hodges dealt with these later chapters so I was supposed to be doing only the traditional logic. I had naturally learnt about this at Oxford, though somewhat cursorily, as a step on the way to the more up-to-date approaches associated with Frege and Russell. The textbook wasn't very helpful – either to me or to the students – because it regarded traditional logic as a vicious abstraction in any case.

Still, I thought it shouldn't be too hard to explain things like universals and particulars and the workings of the syllogism, so I tried to do this. But – unlike Dodds and Hodges – I was terribly nervous on a platform. I could deal all right with a small class where I soon got to know everybody, but I didn't see at all how to talk to such large numbers. I stumbled on, and after a few weeks a deputation came to me to say, 'We haven't understood anything yet, could you start again?' This I did, and things began to go better. But then there was a different trouble. I thought it might be helpful to use Venn diagrams – circles which overlap, or don't, or are concentric, to illustrate the relations between different propositions. So I did this on the blackboard, and then there came a different delegation saying, 'There are four blind people in the class, could you stop using the blackboard?' Nobody had bothered to tell me about this.

I think the main trouble was that these first-year people didn't actually see the point of logic at all and I should have explained this properly before starting. The idea that the validity of an argument is a standard on its own, an important property quite separate from whether the conclusion is true or not, is one that many people never knowingly encounter and many others find hard to take in if they do stumble on it. They suspect that it is something obscure, pedantic and probably sinister. Further explanation at this stage often helps. But in some people this trouble is just a symptom of a general allergy to philosophy. They should quickly go away and do something else.

While I lived at Reading I still spent a good deal of time in Oxford, seeing friends and trying to work on Plotinus. I was there throughout the summer vacation of 1950, and this is the point at which a character called Geoff Midgley enters this story. He was another philosopher trying to make sense of the relation between older and newer ways of dealing with the subject. After an introductory year at New College he had spent most of the war as a high-grade boffin in the RAF working on research in radar, the development of which was then at its most exciting stage. He did not continue this after the war, but it left him with a reliable understanding of things electrical.

Thus, at a meeting of the Aristotelian Society in the 1980s, when several distinguished philosophers were waiting to speak before a large audience, proceedings could not start because those in charge couldn't get the public-address system to work. Tension mounted till in the end they called out anxiously, 'Is there an electrician in the house?' Kicked by his friends, Geoff eventually rose and walked forward, with one finger held out in front of him, pointing at the microphone. When he reached it he ran this finger along the flex from the microphone till he reached the socket, which was nearby on the wall, and pressed the switch that he found there.

The problem was solved.

After the war he came back to read Modern Greats, in which his philosophy tutor was Isaiah Berlin. (There is a story about this which I have to tell here. Many years later we met Berlin at a conference and, beaming, he stuck out his hand to Geoff, saying, 'You won't remember me, of course. Berlin's the name.' As Geoff said – 'As if anybody could possibly forget him if they tried to!')

Geoff then took the B.Phil. with Ryle as his tutor, qualifying in 1949, and went off, that autumn, to work as philosophy lecturer in Newcastle under Professor John Findlay. I had come across Geoff before that in classes and at some point – I think in the summer of 1949 – another philosopher, Ann Martin, brought him in to visit me in Park Town. The three of us then talked continuously from about eleven in the morning till five, and it later emerged that Geoff thought it was a good idea that I brought out refreshments – I think pork pie and tinned spaghetti – at some point during this session.

Then, in the summer of 1950, we were both back in Oxford working after having taught elsewhere for a year. (I don't remember what Geoff was supposed to be working at, probably beavering up on some of the many unexpected books that John Findlay wanted him to lecture on.) In July we both went to the University of Bristol for the Joint Session, which is the big summer conference that all good philosophers are supposed to attend. One day, after lunch there, when we were all standing about in the sun with our coffee cups, it began to be apparent that one of the biggest bores in the profession was going round trying to find someone to go for a walk with him. Geoff and I looked at one another. Geoff said, 'Yes. Now. Quick!' Dumping the coffee cups we hastily slipped off for a walk across the Clifton suspension bridge. After this one thing led to another, and before the end of that vacation we were engaged.

But there was a problem about which end to live. It is strange to think now that, in that expansive epoch, we could have played it either way. Hodges said that he had been thinking of taking on another lecturer, so would Geoff like to join me at Reading? But we were both sure that Hodges's philosophical policy was a doomed ship and neither of us wanted to go down with it. Newcastle, with John Findlay, another enterprising Wittgensteinian, was a much better bet.

Findlay too then said that he might well expand his department (which indeed he did soon after) and did I want to come on board if he did so? But I was sure, as I've said, that I wanted to be able to have children and that I didn't want not to have time to see them, and Geoff agreed with this view of things. Also I was dead tired after a stressful term at Reading. I really wanted to put my feet up. Luckily this could be managed because I had a small income which had been settled on me when my mother's father died, just enough to make it possible to do without my salary. So, towards the end of the summer vacation we said no to both these ideas and arranged that we should get married at Christmas, after I had served out my notice, so that I could then move to Newcastle.

Before that could happen, however, there were still rocks in the way. A successor had somehow to be found for my Reading job and Hodges, predictably, proved quite unhelpful about looking for one. If he was to choose and appoint a new lecturer he would have to make up his mind, which was something he was finding it increasingly hard to do. In particular, he was terrified that anyone new might introduce seditious ideas derived from Russell.

I rummaged eagerly around myself and managed to produce a number of candidates for the post. Hodges interviewed some of these, but then repeatedly fell into indecision about accepting any one of them. I felt that I was getting back into the situation of trying to find servants for the Murrays. It began to look as if I would never be able to get away.

Eventually, however, Providence intervened by sending along Harry Parkinson, then a promising graduate student with such a passionate interest in Leibniz that Hodges found him entirely reassuring. Harry was appointed and settled comfortably at Reading, where he eventually succeeded Hodges as Professor.

Thus, in December 1950, after getting married in the middle of a snowstorm with Iris as my bridesmaid and having a honeymoon in Paris, Geoff and I were able to settle in Newcastle.

Colin Strang outside the Newcastle philosophy department with a student, 1982

David, Tom and Martin, 1980

Willie Charlton in the early 1970s

Geoff, Jane Heal and Dorothy Emmett, pictured with a student (left), 1986

With Jane Goodall (left), Edinburgh, 1989

January 2001. Photo: Ted Ditchburn, North News and Pictures

8

At Newcastle, 1950–2005

Settling in

We both took to Newcastle at once. It is an ancient city built on hills that rise to the north of the river Tyne, around a castle which was put there by William the Conqueror in order to control both the Scots and the rebellious inhabitants of Gateshead, just across the river. Parts of the city are very old, but its main spread occurred during the Industrial Revolution. Before that time its chief industry had been brewing, but in the nineteenth century it expanded quickly as it pioneered the linked occupations of coal-mining, shipbuilding and other forms of engineering. The city spread widely and its centre was remodelled on classical lines, with fine streets radiating from a high pillar on which stands Lord Grey of the 1832 Reform Bill, the local magnate responsible for that first move towards making Parliament more representative. On one side of Lord Grey's pedestal there is an inscription recording this achievement. On the other side there is a further message, dated a century later, saying that in 1932 the citizens still think that democracy is a good thing.

When we arrived there half a century back, Newcastle was different in some obvious ways from its present self. It was much nicer because there was less traffic, and because the shops on its main streets were still real shops. They had not then been killed by the arrival of shopping centres and supermarkets. On the other hand, a lot of the town was black. Coal dust covered all the older buildings – not with a smeary, patchy coat but with a clear black that sparkled in the sunlight where there were crystals among the coal. (Some people don't seem to have seen these sparkles; I thought them beautiful at once.)

This black, to my mind, was quite impressive, but of course it was the result of something badly wrong – the effect of coal-mining, not just on the miners' health but on everybody else's as well. The memoirs of working-class people of that time show terrible poverty and misery, much of it due to industrial disease. When we arrived, following the war, the general post-war sense that a new world must be built was leading those in charge to direct attention to such things and try to do something about them. And since that time, a great deal has indeed been done, though, as usual, different troubles follow on those that are removed.

The collapse of coal-mining stopped the flow of black dust, leaving us with only the less visible forms of pollution. And that collapse, along with the decline in shipbuilding, also made for a great deal of unemployment, bringing different kinds of misery. As for the handsome buildings, here and in other northern cities they have been washed and look very good. They probably appear now much as they did to their first users. The inhabitants, for their part, don't seem to me to have been profoundly changed. On the whole, they are still as I first found them – remarkably friendly and easy to live with. And the country round is still very beautiful, notably along the Roman Wall and into the Scottish border, and also along the coast. Traffic is getting worse, but it is still nothing like as bad as it is in the south.

Not long after we came, the city fathers, in a fit of modernization, decided to pull down most of the city centre and replace it by a new road scheme. They were stopped, however, after doing only a little of this, by a flood of revelations which surfaced about corruption involving councillors, architects, building contractors and also some grander people, such as Members of Parliament. (The names of Poulson and Profumo may still resound in some memories.) The leader of the City Council went to jail, followed by several of his colleagues, and there were some suicides. Their ambitious scheme then died down. Its traces, however, may still be seen opposite to Earl Grey's pillar, where one of the buildings that used to face it was actually pulled down and replaced by an unspeakable affair faced with pale pink mirrors. There is a well-known danger of such things happening in boroughs where one political party has a longstanding, rock-solid majority, as the Labour Party then had in Newcastle. The price of preventing them is perpetual vigilance.

Today Newcastle is still well known for beer but its chief claim to fame now rests on football. Serious misunderstandings can arise between those of its inhabitants who don't fully grasp the importance of this and those who do. Thus a friend of ours, David Barlow, a composer who worked in the university's music department, was once standing waiting at a bus stop near the football ground in the middle of Saturday afternoon. A passing citizen hailed him, calling out eagerly, 'What's the score?' 'Oh', said David, beaming and pulling out a little book from under his arm, 'actually it's Bartók's second string quartet . . .' I don't know how this conversation ended.

We settled in Jesmond, a tolerably leafy suburb about twenty minutes' walk from the university, which is near the city centre. Jesmond was quite grand in the nineteenth century and is still comfortable, but it is no longer smart, its large houses now mostly sheltering crowds of students and nurses from the nearby hospital. At first we lived in the small flat that Geoff had occupied before I came, which looked out on to a rather nice wooded cemetery. It was pretty convenient except that all its rooms opened off a central sitting room, the floor of which was always covered with the innards of a large and ambitious radio, which Geoff was chronically rebuilding. Having spent so much time during the war on such work he always liked to have something of this kind going on. It took me some time to realize that, unless I interfered, this creativity would always happen in the central living space and would expand until every province was taken over.

Because of these needs and (more urgently) in order to provide room for children, we moved during the late summer of 1950 to a three-storey Victorian semi with a garden. This house looked out behind on the railway, but it was a quiet little railway carrying only small trains to the coast and it turned out later to provide rather good entertainment for those watching from the nursery windows, from which one could call out 'Bye bye Guard . . .' Later again, in 1961, we moved to a slightly larger terrace house not far off, near to Jesmond Dene, which is a fine wooded ravine laid out as a public park, where the children played and where I still walk daily. This splendid place was made and given to the city by Lord Armstrong, the same useful tycoon who founded the Armstrong College – the seed of the University – and provided many other civic benefits. It has to be said that he was also the originator of the Armstrong Whitworth gun, and that his firm eventually became the great armaments combine Vickers Armstrong. But he had a lot of other interests. He did useful pioneering work on things such as hydraulic engines and electric light. And it does strike me that today an armaments tycoon like him would not be so likely to be an active engineer, and would also be much less likely to leave such generous and useful legacies to his native city.

I think that, while we were still in the flat, I did try quite hard to keep on working on Plotinus. But once we started on the house I more or less stopped trying. Apart from the bother of finding and buying it, it had to be furnished, and very little of what we had in the flat was our own. My great-aunt Jeanie, who had recently died, had left me her things, so these needed to be sorted in her Buckinghamshire house and some of them duly sent north. There were also things from my grandmother's house, Flimwell Grange, which my mother was now dismantling, but these too had to be sorted. We always had far too many books, a problem which was partly solved, but only partly, when an uncle of Geoff's gave us some huge metal office bookcases. There was also some decorating to do and the garden needed attention. Altogether, after living with little effort in other people's houses for so long, I found that I was kept pretty busy during that autumn, and after Tommy was born in December 1950 and David followed him in August 1953 I naturally became more so.

*

I had always wanted children and I think that looking after them is really good fun provided that you get some help and have other things to think about to distract you. I never repented having gone in for this occupation. But even with these advantages I did at times get desperately tired. I am very bad at doing without sleep, which makes me so stupid that I don't know what I'm doing. Certainly I found that one husband and three children were quite as much as I could manage. I never felt inclined to branch out on larger numbers of either, as so many people do. At times indeed I found that the confusion overwhelmed me and gave me an uneasy feeling that perhaps I had lost my way – that I wasn't aiming clearly enough in some particular direction. I found it hard not to worry unreasonably about the children themselves. Like a lot of parents now I had no experience of small children, and it took me quite a time to realize that they would not fall to pieces if I took my eyes off them.

I was, however, lucky enough to be able to afford a bit of help with the house and sometimes with the children as well. For a time, when we had two small ones, we tried having an Austrian au pair, but she was a disaster and we never tried another. A rather splendid old lady called Miss George came in daily for a bit, and at another time we had a vague but amiable resident girl called Ruth. But mostly we had ladies in for cleaning during the day and used our attic rooms for student lodgers, who were very helpful and made good babysitters, rather than for resident help.

I can't go into a lot of detail here about our family life or I would never get this book finished. My sons, too, have their own lives to live and they may prefer to write their own memoirs rather than having me do it for them. It is actually quite hard to pick a trail through the jungle of a life experience, and I can only try to make the general course of things intelligible. But there is one factor from this early time that should be mentioned. This was a cottage in the Northumbrian countryside north of Hexham, which we rented cheaply for ten years or so from 1958 along with a half-Hungarian family, the Tordais, who were neighbours living on the other side of the railway and who also had three boys.

This place was quite basic. The only thing laid on in it was water, which came through the floor as well as out of the tap when there was much rain. We used a stinky Calor gas cooker, paraffin lamps and heaters and a chemical loo, all of which, along with furniture and stores, had to be carried up a steep slope – which was why the place was no longer in demand to house a farm labourer. But it stood on the top of a hill looking out over half Northumberland. The boys quickly explored the woodlands around and would simply vanish into them each time when we arrived, coming out only when they wanted to be fed and never, to my recollection, getting into any real trouble. The villagers were friendly and blackberries were abundant. I was able to feed Martin, who was then a baby, sitting in an upstairs window looking out at the distant hills rather than reading novels, as I had done with the older boys when I was reviewing novels for the *New Statesman*. I don't know what difference this has made to his psyche but I don't think it has done him any harm.

For these expeditions we now took the bold step of buying a car – a green second-hand Bedford van, also rather basic. It could seat twelve small people at a pinch or, more comfortably, five ordinary-sized ones and a lot of luggage. It didn't have much power for overtaking and it usually needed to be double-declutched for the gear-change down from second to first, but it went pretty well on the whole and its capaciousness was very useful. Besides taking us to the cottage it carried us all on many journeys south to visit parents and others, and for a lot of holidays, often in cottages in Scotland or Yorkshire, sometimes further afield to Ireland or Wales. We were never bold enough to take it to Europe, though we did have one excellent holiday in Switzerland by public transport.

At first I drove it, since Geoff, who had not learnt to drive in the RAF, said that he thought he was too excitable and would be dangerous at the wheel, but he was fully willing to see to the repairs and maintenance. This bargain suited me all right because I had learnt to drive early and quite enjoyed it, but I hadn't the first idea about mechanical problems. A few years later Geoff decided that he could drive after all and he learnt to do so before the van breathed its last. He then became an excellent driver, greatly enjoying the real cars that we bought to succeed it, and we then began to overtake at speeds that were far more satisfactory to the boys. Later again, when my eyes began to be troublesome, he became the family's only driver.

Journalistic ploys

As for my helpful distractions, during this time I went on doing book-reviewing and also quite a lot of broadcasts, sometimes going to London for these, sometimes doing them from the BBC headquarters in Newcastle, which then lived in a charming house built in Strawberry Hill Gothic, before it moved to its present pink concrete palace. The broadcasts were partly discussions of various kinds, partly book-reviews for the Third Programme, partly talks that I made up on my own.

I have forgotten most of them, but I do remember the first time I was interviewed on television. This was for *Woman's Hour*, which was then a live television show in the afternoon. It took place in a vast hall in Alexandra Palace, a huge dusty chaotic cavern littered with trolleys, arc lights, endless tangles of flex and strange little two-sided plywood booths, lit up and covered with wallpaper. Each booth represented a corner of a room for an interview and the presenter, Jeanne Heal, was supposed to move smoothly on from one of them to another. But when I arrived the whole place was in an uproar; everybody was panicking. When I asked what was wrong I was told, 'They can't start; they can't find Jeanne Heal's eyelashes'. Eventually things did go forward, but I was struck by the thought, which I have seen less and less reason to change as time goes by, that television really is not as good a place for discussion as radio.

It is typical of these occasions that I can't at all remember what I was actually supposed to be talking about on *Woman's Hour*. But I can date the occasion itself to the early summer of 1953. I know it was the time when Tommy, then eighteen months old, was watching, and was much upset because he couldn't get me to respond when he spoke to me on the screen, so Geoff had to take him out. At this time we were staying with my parents, who now lived at Woodford Green, so the family could watch the programme on their telly. We didn't get a telly ourselves till the children forced us to many years later.

I took part in broadcast discussions on all sorts of now forgotten topical subjects. The only series that I clearly remember was one on Sunday evenings called *A Word in Edgeways*. Brian Redhead, who chaired this, avoided the silly habit of insisting on the sharp opposition that wrecks so much broadcast discussion. He quite often left his participants enough time to develop their points intelligibly – a habit that makes them feel much better afterwards than they do when topics have been constantly whisked out of their mouths before they have shaped them. I also continued with book reviews for the Third Programme and sometimes sent in original talks of my own, a number of which appeared afterwards in that very handy magazine *The Listener*. I have incorporated some of these later in my books; two of them, 'Freedom and Heredity' and 'On Trying Out One's New Sword' form part of *Heart and Mind*. I also wrote some articles for *The Twentieth Century*, and other papers.

Aniouta Kallin, who was very friendly, usually accepted my contributions for the Third Programme at once, but I have always remembered that there was one that she rejected with real distaste. I wrote it because I had suddenly been struck by the fact that nearly all the famous philosophers whose lives we know about were lifelong bachelors. Aristotle and Mill are exceptions and there are a few others, but among these exceptions three – Berkeley, Hegel and G. E. Moore – married late, after they had finished their serious philosophical work. None of these philosophers, therefore, had any experience of living with women or children, which is, after all, quite an important aspect of human life.

I wrote an article drawing attention to this statistic and asking whether it might not account for a certain over-abstractness, a certain remoteness from life, in the European philosophical tradition. This suggestion is now something of a commonplace in feminist circles, but it shocked Aniouta deeply. It struck her as a trivial, irrelevant intrusion of domestic matters into intellectual life. So I dropped it.

The books that I reviewed elsewhere at this time were also pretty mixed. I did them for a number of papers, but mostly for the *New Statesman*, whose literary editor, the admirable Janet Adam Smith, took a real interest in her reviewers and went to a lot of trouble to find them suitable fodder. Among the books that I did for her was Colin Wilson's bestseller *The Outsider*, about which I was far too polite because I had such an awful toothache at the time that I simply couldn't trust my impression that it was fairly bogus. On such chances do reputation depend . . .

During the early 1950s however Janet asked me to review novels regularly. My love of stories led me to accept at once and I did enjoy this, but it was a strange sort of life. It meant getting about a dozen books every three weeks, glancing through them to see whether some could be eliminated right away (not many could), and then trying to read the rest fairly enough to say something intelligible about three, or at most four of them, in about 1200 words. Quite often, towards the end of the second week another batch would come along and had to be fitted in somehow.

There were many among them that were exciting. Looking at the crumbling proofs that remain, I see the titles of novels that I well remember by Muriel Spark, Antonia White, Honor Tracy, Patrick White, Mary McCarthy, Jean Cocteau, Margaret Kennedy and Charles Morgan, and there were others by less well-known people that haunt me still. But not all novels are like that and sometimes it takes a deal of effort to remain receptive after the first half-dozen. I was – and still am – really sorry for the novelists who have to force their way through so much brushwood in order to get heard. My next-door neighbour is the novelist Eva Ibbotson, who writes delightful stories that are both funny and romantic, and I can see that it is much harder for her to write than it is for me. The things that I write about are unmistakably *there*, out in the world to be looked at, while she has to spin much more of hers out of her own innards.

I don't think I could have done this stint of fiction-processing if I hadn't, at that time, been spending quite a lot of time feeding babies. This sedentary occupation combines very well with reading novels, especially at night. I think that both Tommy and David must have received a fair infusion of stories in their blood. By the time that Martin arrived in 1957, however, I had (as I say) left the novel circus and taken to something less exhausting, namely reviewing children's books.

These too arrived from the *New Statesman* by the cartload, but they were very much easier to look through and they could then, quite properly, be passed on to more appropriate critics, both in our own household and in those of their friends, for a well-qualified opinion. There were lots of good ones. We acquired Dr Seuss's *Ten Apples Up On Top*, and some Orlando books and the Moomins and plenty of others, and many of the picture books were delightful even when their texts were poor. But there was, of course, after a time a general effect of 'too much – too much'. One can't go on doing these things for ever.

Some time in the late 1950s I varied these occupations by writing a novel myself. It was called *Wintersault* and was a mild piece of science fiction about hibernation – the population took to hibernating, which caused problems; what should be done about them? Several publishers considered *Wintersault*. Diana

Athill read it for André Deutsch and liked it and it looked for a time as if they were actually going to take it, but they didn't and I ceased bothering about it. I think the real trouble was one that afflicts a lot of science fiction – the idea was good enough for a short story but it hadn't enough steam for a whole book. Other things had to be brought in and they weren't strong enough to carry it through.

Though I enjoyed my long stint of novel-reviewing, I think that this prolonged feast of stories may have contributed to my eventually becoming somewhat sated with fiction. As I've said, I began to find that I could sometimes live without novels, and indeed that I could live without some of them – even ones which other people admired and thought important – very easily. As I've mentioned, this does happen to quite a lot of people as they grow older, but it may have been unlucky for me because it was probably the reason I was not able to enjoy most of Iris Murdoch's novels when they came out.

This was not an absolute block. I liked *Under the Net* very much, enjoying the way the narrator, Jake, keeps desperately looking for the person who he thinks will solve his problems when he really needs to deal with them himself. And I really liked *The Bell*. I love the sympathetic way in which it deals with the difficulties of this set of people trying desperately, against the odds, to fit themselves together so as to form a religious community. Glancing at it again now just to see how this works out, I promptly become involved once more in their problems. I thought it was all profoundly humane and delightful. But after *The Bell*, Iris never seemed to me to take her people quite seriously. My impression – and of course I'm just trying to explain what it was, not claiming any critical authority – was that she was somehow looking down from above at their struggles and repeatedly lobbing down bizarre challenges, just to see what they would do. Thus, I was fascinated by the first part of *The Red and the Green*, where she introduced a tribe of people quite new to me – shabby genteel aunties in a Dublin suburb. I wanted to go on hearing a lot more about their intriguing lifestyle, but then it was suddenly cut across by some rather implausible-looking incest. At that point for me the whole thing just collapsed and I thought 'not *again*?'

She seemed to me to keep using incest or some other scandal to break up one pattern after another as it was forming. And incest in particular appeared to have a special significance for her that I don't quite understand. I remember that once, when I mentioned my brother, she said, 'Oh I do wish I'd had a brother. I'd have had a tremendous incestuous affair with him.' I wanted to say, 'But that's not how it mostly works . . .' But there was a dream there that my comments couldn't reach. Because she didn't have siblings I suppose she felt a kind of need there that could never be remedied.

Newcastle University

Meanwhile Geoff was busy at the university and I also saw a good deal of it myself. Indeed as time went on I gradually inched myself on to its staff. As the student body expanded, the Philosophy Department burgeoned with it, acquiring two more full-time lecturers. And some time – I think in 1964 – Karl Britton, who by then had succeeded Findlay, asked me if I would like to work there half-time.

This was beautiful timing for me. Tommy was now twelve and moreover he was settled at boarding school, at the Quaker school at Great Ayton in North Yorkshire. He had been troubled with quite bad asthma, and the doctors had advised that he should go to school in the country. Since David was now ten and Martin was six it seemed quite possible to fit in half-time work while they were at school. Actually half-time proved, as it always does, to be something more like three-quarters and I remember repeatedly getting desperate when I was trying to get away in the afternoon to get the boys' tea, and students kept coming in with problems. But on the whole things didn't work out too badly. And some six years later, when life had got easier again, my half-time post was upgraded to full-time.

Newcastle University itself is one of those English provincial universities that were founded during the nineteenth century to meet the urgent educational needs of the new industries, especially by teaching science, which the older universities were still neglecting. It grew from a union of two entities – the thriving Medical School, founded in 1828, and the Armstrong College, founded by the inventor and industrialist Lord Armstrong in 1871, chiefly to instruct his engineers but also to give his fellow citizens a wider education. These two were combined in 1935 under the name of King's College as part of the University of Durham, and this was still its status when we first arrived. But by that time King's College was larger than the rest of Durham University put together, so the tail was beginning to wag the dog, and the kind of friction that afflicts such unions was becoming troublesome. In 1962 Newcastle became an independent university.

King's College functioned in a way that now seems remarkably domestic and cosy, in a network of Victorian terraces round a central core of official buildings. The Philosophy Department was a tall narrow four-storey terrace house in a cul-de-sac called Eldon Place. The boiler room in the basement was a common-room for the students with an appropriate notice on the door saying THE CAVE. This was recognized as being an essential part of the teaching equipment – a place where, along with other topics, philosophical questions could be pursued at proper length, both by students and by any staff that they invited in. Both Geoff and the Psychology lecturer David Russell spent a lot of time there, and when the department finally moved away into purpose-built quarters in the main building in the 1960s, its then head, Karl Britton, asked for a similar students' common-room to be included in its territory. The University Grants Committee refused, saying sharply that this was an unnecessary luxury. So Karl put in instead for an extra lecture room, and wrote the name CAVE (now in Greek, SPELAION, in case spies from the authorities objected) on its door. It remained central to the working of the department.

This move to larger quarters certainly improved things because it increased variety. The numbers of students in each year grew at that point from about five to twenty, half of whom were taking joint honours degrees – Philosophy with English, Politics, Psychology or (rather later) Religious Studies, all of which brought in other topics. A number of students taking the three-subject general degree also came to our classes, as well as others who took Philosophy as subsidiary to other main subjects. And while the earlier department had mainly been populated by argumentative males with large egos, the later one always had a sex ratio of about fifty–fifty, with a correspondingly wider range of lively characters.

In Eldon Place the English Department occupied a similar terrace house next door to ours and a number of others were sprinkled along the street. The remaining houses there mostly belonged to professors or other university officials, which made their lives easier, but also provided plenty of opportunity for mutual observation and scandal. ('Do you know, she's been down to the pub *again* . . .?') At the bottom, next to the excellent fish shop, was the university bookshop, a startlingly incompetent affair that never managed to get enough textbooks for the students, however much time it was given. The only thing that interested its owner was the fear of selling something indecent. I once saw a notice pinned up by the sales desk that read, 'Under no circumstances may any orders be taken for Frank Harris's *My Life And Loves*'. These qualms may have had something to do with alarm about his other neighbour, a pub called The Dun Cow, which gave the authorities headaches because it was a meeting place for the local tarts. Eldon Place has of course now been pulled down and duly replaced by chunks of standard concrete.

The Philosophy Department

When we arrived, the Newcastle Philosophy Department was twice the size of the Reading one, having a full staff of four. Besides Geoff and John Findlay, there was a lecturer in Psychology, a delightful Welshman called David Russell who had started life as a coal-miner and had taught himself all that he needed to know and a great deal more. He was the seed from which a separate department of Psychology would eventually spring.

And then there was Mr Rayner, an astonishingly dull Scotsman. He taught Ethics and had been in the department a long while. Indeed he had been left in charge of it for a time after the previous professor left and had fully expected to get the chair himself. It went, however, to John Findlay, who was a good deal younger than he was, and the situation was not helped by Findlay's being a campaigning atheist – so vehement a fighter that he could scarcely admit that Thomas Aquinas was a philosopher at all. ('That piddling little Popish priest – going about reconciling everything with everything . . .!') Indeed, Findlay had written an article in which he skilfully stood the ontological argument for God's existence on its head, using it to prove that God could *not* exist. Gilbert Ryle warned him that this article might have 'chair-losing properties', so he delayed publishing it until after he had been appointed professor at Newcastle. But it came out soon after.

At first, it looked as if this was all that we needed to know about Mr Rayner, but it wasn't. Gradually it emerged that he believed himself to be the son of King Edward VII and Queen Alexandra. Did this mean (people cautiously enquired) that he was a natural son, born before their marriage? That was never explained, and the dates didn't seem to fit. What did emerge was that his existence was a grave embarrassment to the royal family, so they were very anxious to keep him quiet. Their agents ('not, of course, the queen herself, I do not mean to suggest that, but people concerned for her position . . .') were therefore quietly poisoning him in a way that confused his mind and prevented him from becoming famous. 'Certain members of this university – I am sure from the best of motives – have been putting various substances in my food . . .' At one time he changed his name by deed poll from Rayner to Windsor; later still he had an actual breakdown and was hospitalized for a while. When Findlay left and was succeeded by the non-atheistic Karl Britton his relations with his colleagues became slightly less fraught, but they never became easy.

Altogether, Geoff's situation in the department wasn't easy and I was quite glad not to be directly involved there myself. Not only did he have to mediate between irreconcilables but even John Findlay on his own would not have been an easy colleague. Findlay was a convinced and fully trained linguistic philosopher who had studied for a time with Wittgenstein in Cambridge, but he prided himself on never going with the current vogue. Since the current vogue told people to study only contemporary philosophy (the latest articles in the journals), Findlay, years ahead of the fashion, insisted on reviving past philosophers whom nobody had heard of for years.

He sometimes even talked of studying Hegel, though I think the difficulties of doing that stopped him from ever actually putting him on the syllabus. But he also particularly liked early twentieth-century proponents of axiological ethics such as Max Scheler and Nicolai Hartmann. He therefore directed Geoff to get these up and lecture on them. (I am not sure how this was supposed to relate to Mr Rayner's Ethics courses – perhaps Rayner was sent off to teach the empiricists.)

Geoff, feeling somewhat bewildered, asked what it was that made Hartmann so interesting. 'Oh', said Findlay, 'you know, he talks about wonderful things like knightly virtue. You'll see.' So Geoff did get up these sages and he did his best with them. But just as he was beginning to see the point of them, Findlay would come up with a different set of prophets for him to propound for the next term – and another the term after. This was very distracting, and of course it stood in the way of Geoff's pursuing his own interests. All the same, he managed at that time to work out certain original ideas about language which he expressed in two very good articles, suggesting what was then a new idea, that the rules underlying language are *constitutive rules*[3] – patterns on which it develops, rather than regulative ones – laws which have to be obeyed. This idea caught on and it has since been largely taken for granted. I don't think, however, that people remember him as its inventor.

In the late 1950s, when Mr Rayner retired, the department gained another young lecturer, an engaging character called Colin Strang. Colin kept the inhabitants of Eldon Place on their toes by regularly taking his ancient car to bits on the pavement every Sunday, helped by a large and clumsy dog. Colin was also famous for always tapping his cigarette ash carefully into the turn-ups of his trousers. Like Geoff, he had been taking the Oxford B.Phil. course and he had absorbed its message more wholeheartedly than Geoff did. Though he was no naive logical positivist, he liked the simplicities of that way of thought and often supported them. Thus, a student who felt that he was beginning to get the hang of the place once said, 'I've got it now! Mr Midgley's the one who always thinks that things are more complicated than they look, and Mr Strang's the one who always thinks they are simpler.' These are the twin poles of empiricist thinking that I mentioned earlier, and both of them are equally necessary.

Near to Eldon Place was the senior common-room where staff often met for lunch – a habit as useful here as it had been at Reading. All sorts of dons used to meet there daily and talk about all sorts of things. Bill Elliot, the Professor of Law, was a most useful person whom we used to consult about every kind of topic. And the Rector of the College, Lord Eustace Percy, who used to lunch there most days, was also very good value. He made a point of constantly sitting next to different people and particularly of getting to know the newest and youngest staff, whose names and needs he would then remember when he had occasion to think about them afterwards. Nothing could have been more unlike the distant executive hierarchy of today.

The senior common-room was the focus for a great deal of other socializing, an important part of which a lively Staff Dramatic Society. Geoff, who was a born actor, had already made a hit in the year before I arrived in the Shaw skit *Passion, Poison and Petrifaction*, and he went on to play leads in a whole string of further plays – *Uncle Vanya*, Dryden's *Love for Love*, Ben Jonson's *The Silent Woman*. I didn't

[3] 'Linguistic Rules and Language Habits', *Supplementary Volume of the Aristotelian Society* XXIX, 1955, pp. 185–213, and 'Linguistic Rules', *Proceedings of the Aristotelian Society*, June 1959, pp. 271–90.

act in these (nor did I want to), but I did enjoy being involved in the stage management. Findlay was a rather temperamental but effective producer.

Writing about beasts and other things

Besides these various goings-on, at this time I was reading another kind of book, apart from those that I had to review, just for my own satisfaction – books about animal behaviour. As I've said, I first got interested in this when I read Konrad Lorenz's little book *King Solomon's Ring*, which came out in English translation in 1952 and was at once hugely successful. Everybody discussed it. My parents soon told me about it and I got it at once. Along with the rest of its readers I was hugely struck by a point which is now accepted as a commonplace. The lives of other animals are far more like our own than we have supposed and are therefore far more intelligible to us. We are much more continuous with them than we have traditionally thought. This means that we are more at home in the world than we imagined. We are not uneasy colonists trying to control something alien to us, but natives who can fit into the world around us provided that we attend to it and take it seriously.

Lorenz and his colleague Tinbergen, the inventors of modern ethology, provided concepts which I thought at once could be used, without distortion, to describe both the behaviour of humans and that of other creatures in terms that could be extraordinarily fertile for further thought. And it seemed to me that they themselves mostly used these concepts in a careful and sophisticated way. But of course not everybody else did. Robert Ardrey in *The Territorial Imperative* and Desmond Morris in *The Naked Ape* (both bestsellers, both published in 1967) made simple comparisons that suggested sensational, one-sided views of human life, and so did plenty of other writers. This naturally provoked a backlash in favour of what is now called 'human exceptionalism' – the idea that no such comparisons are valid at all because culture makes human life entirely different from that of other species.

Morris's and Ardrey's approach to these problems did indeed strike me as too naive and melodramatic. I was sure that species could be compared sensibly without these dramas. But the first thing I wanted to do was to read more ethology, to see how these ideas worked out in practice. David Russell, who was already very interested in these things, helped me a lot here. He lent me some books to start on, and gave me good advice about others. Then for several years I just raided the libraries, going to the appropriate shelves and taking out books on every sort of creature from aardvarks to zebras – ants, red deer, lemmings, baboons or whatever. Naturally I quickly happened on the writings of Jane Goodall, whose quiet, thoughtful approach delighted me. It seemed to provide exactly the counterbalance that was needed to Morris's and Ardrey's propagandist angle. I still think she is quite exceptionally sound on the delicate question of how to think about our own species as what it actually is – one among others. In later years I was lucky enough to run across her several times as she rushed to and fro in her ceaseless efforts on behalf of her chimpanzees. We have found each other's views deeply helpful and we meet again on the rare occasions when we get the chance. Though I see her so seldom, I still think of her as one of my close friends.

As I read these ethological studies, I got interested in the concepts of evolution that lay behind them. I began to read books about it by writers such as Ernst Mayr and Theodosius Dobzhansky. This led me on to think about the wider difficulties that infest the idea of the nature of any species, and especially the idea of human nature. I found it very helpful that I had at that time so much animal behaviour going on all around me, upstairs, in the garden and on the hearthrug. Small children are so literally and unmistakably both animals and human beings that they show up the absurdity of refusing to bring these two notions together.

Then, some time in the late 1960s, David Russell, who did a lot of extra-mural lecturing, suggested that I should run a course on animal behaviour for the adult-education department of the university. I did this, and it was one of the most helpful experiences I have ever had. The great advantage of adult students is that they're there only because they're interested, and they find it easier to say what they think than younger students do. Everybody saw the wide relevance of our subject, and everybody had something thought-provoking to say about it. I acknowledged their help in the introduction to *Beast and Man*, remarking that teaching an adult class is 'a method I vigorously recommend to anyone who wants to get an impossible bundle of questions under control'. Spurred on by these people, I began to bring the thoughts that arose from my recent readings in ethology together with the ideas that I had previously developed about other areas of philosophy. I even began to think that I would like to write something about this. But how on earth was I to find the time to do this?

When I had written *Wintersault* that had not been too hard because I had not been doing outside work. I could write while the children were at school. But things were different now. Family life, along with full-time work, seemed to be continuous; there were no breaks. And then once more Providence took a hand. In 1962, as the university went on expanding, two new lecturers joined our department. Both were excellent value. One was Mike Brearley, who was then a lively philosopher though he is better known for having later captained England at cricket with great distinction between 1976 and 1983. We liked Mike very much. But the one that we became closest to was the other, Willie Charlton, who taught aesthetics and Greek philosophy. Willie and his wife Ann quickly became our close friends and we often visited them at their home – a big attractive eighteenth-century house called Lee Hall in the wilds of Northumberland, to the north of Hexham. Then, when they were going away for a time, the Charltons said that they did not want to leave their house empty. Would we like to come and stay there for a few weeks?

This was wonderful from many points of view but in regard to my starting writing it was a godsend. Willie, who is a real scholar, had an upstairs library – a big, light, airy room full of books and supplied with every convenience for using them. So I took to working there in the early mornings – a time which could be made to last as long as I needed, since the boys were now teenagers and did not willingly get up much before midday.

In theory I could have made the same kind of start at home, but in fact, at that point, having this new and very encouraging place made all the difference. After I had once begun to write there, I found I could do it in other places as well, though I still found that the early morning was the best time for it. (Late evening, which is the obvious alternative, is hopeless for me since I can't do anything sensible late at night.) However, after writing in the mornings in this way for a bit I found that I could also do it at odd times in the day, without worrying too much about being interrupted. This was just as well since my life was then rather full of interruptions.

And in the end, I really took to this schedule. Even if no one interrupts me, I now actually prefer to interrupt myself regularly and do something else for a time because I find that, when I get back, I can see where things are going wrong better than I would have done if I hadn't stopped. If I have to write continuously I am liable to get off course, running on in what turns out to be a wrong direction, and can't see why this is happening. This is one reason why my heart sinks when someone from a newspaper rings me at mid-morning to ask for my thoughts on the latest news item by five – or at latest six – the same afternoon. (Because of my book *Wickedness* they do this particularly when someone has committed an appalling crime, but they do it about other things too.) If I feel strongly on the matter I agree to try, but I know I don't do it well, because I need more time to let the dust settle and check on mistakes as they gradually develop. So I often refuse.

The first article that I managed to write in the Lee Hall library was 'Is "Moral" a Dirty Word?' which appeared in the journal *Philosophy* (Vol. 47, 1972) and is also now in *Heart and Mind*. In this I attacked the various narrowings that afflict the concept of morality and tried to connect the specialized ways in which people use this concept with the everyday senses. This was something that I had been thinking about for a long time, so I felt more confident about it than I did about my more recent thoughts on ethology.

Once this article had been accepted, however, I thought that I might give these ideas a try as well. So I wrote a piece called 'The Concept of Beastliness' about the way in which we compare ourselves with other animals. This too appeared in *Philosophy* during 1973 and it caught the attention of Max Black, the distinguished philosopher of language at Cornell University. He wrote to Karl Britton to ask about its author and, after a bit of correspondence, invited me to visit Cornell and introduce some discussions about the meaning of the species barrier at a series of interdisciplinary seminars for the Program on Science, Technology and Society there.

Early in 1976 I did this, and I have to say that I have seldom worked so hard. The discussions went on for the best part of a week, involving every kind of specialist – anthropologists, biologists, zoologists, literary critics, theologians and Old Uncle Tom Cobbleigh and all. In fact, perhaps the only department in sight that ignored these occasions completely may have been the Cornell philosophers, whom I only saw once when Max took me to a meeting of theirs at the end of the week. The Program for Science Technology and Society was very good at being interdisciplinary and again – as with my adult class, though of course at a very different level – there was the advantage that people don't take part in these mixed goings-on at all unless they are really interested. I made many good friends at Cornell, notably Max Black and his wife, with whom I kept in touch until he died.

After this visit, the Cornell University Press asked me to write a book on the subject. So I sat down and wrote it, and I was much helped in doing so by the weather. The summer of 1976 was amazingly fine and warm, so I could sit out in the garden writing for a good deal of the time whenever I didn't have to be somewhere else. During a great deal of the summer I did this and, some time in the autumn, I sent my typescript in to the Press.

They, however, wrote back saying politely, 'This draft is very nice, but now would you put in the sociobiology?' That word was then quite new to me. But I soon found out that in 1975, while I was beavering away on my own, Edward O. Wilson at Harvard had put out a volume the size of a paving stone with this name. That volume was now a best-seller, causing riots in universities all over the United States and inspiring protesters to pour jugs of cold water over Wilson at meetings. So I sat down and worked away at it, cursing away as I tried to fit my thoughts about sociobiology into what I had already written.

My book undoubtedly sold better because it dealt directly with this urgent and fashionable topic. And I think that, in the end, my alterations to it made reasonable sense. But the need to follow up points that had interested Wilson still seemed to distort my message, distracting the reader from what I had meant to be the central topic. This was the meaning of rationality itself – the fact that *reason* can't mean just deductive logic but must cover what makes sense for beings who have a certain sort of emotional nature. This is still dealt with in Part IV of the book, but it doesn't stand out as it did in the first draft.

Another trouble was that the Cornell University Press, ever keen to be scholarly, sent my second draft round to a dozen specialists in various subjects asking if they had any suggestions to make. They should surely have known that no academic who is offered the chance to do this is going to miss the opportunity to think up some criticism or other. The typescript came back stuck all over with little bit of yellow paper asking me to make things clearer. At this point a more experienced author would have told the Press to go and chase itself, but it didn't strike me that I could do that. Instead I carefully answered all their queries. This made the book longer than it ought to be. I don't know whether it made it any clearer.

Then there was the title. I had meant to call the book simply *Beastliness*. But the Press told me I couldn't do this – in America this word was not a joke, as it is in England, but meant simply bestiality as a vice. They suggested *Beast and Man*. I think I already had my suspicions then that the word 'man' might be going to prove an embarrassment, which indeed it has since done. But I was too exhausted to make a fuss about it. The other drawback, which I didn't foresee, is that – significantly – people very often think that it is called *Man and Beast*, which must cause them a difficulty if they try to look it up in an alphabetical list.

The Cornell Press finally brought the book out in 1978 and it got a reasonably favourable reception. By then, people were getting sick of the noisy clash between extremes that had long been going on in the sociobiology debate. They were ready for a thoughtful synthesis. On the one side, Wilson and his supporters were shouting that there is indeed something called Human Nature, but it is basically quite simple and is best described in terms of selfishness. The proper way to understand it (they said) is through biology, mainly by studying the genome. On the other side, many humanists and social scientists were still saying – as their predecessors had often done – that there is no such thing as Human Nature at all; we are entirely the products of our culture.

My idea, by contrast, was that we certainly do have a nature. We cannot be originally blank paper. But this nature is quite complex and our tendency to form cultures is just a part of it. So, in trying to understand ourselves, we must use many different ways of thinking to match the many different kinds of question that we want to ask about our nature. No academic discipline has a monopoly here. They all have to help one another.

In this way, I was trying to bring back the notion of Human Nature itself – which had been badly discredited by ideological misuses for various ends – to the central place that I thought it ought to hold in our thinking. I am sure that this notion, which was well developed in our tradition by philosophers such as Aristotle and Bishop Butler, is an essential tool, not only for thinking about morals but more generally for a reasonably balanced view of the world. We have to clear it of the distortions imposed on it by various political and moral agendas and bring it back into normal use. Of course we ourselves can never be unbiased in doing this – we always have agendas of our own – but we need to become aware of them and make them explicit. *Beast and Man* outlined this project, and the book remains, in a way, the trunk out of which all my various later ideas have branched.

I will look briefly at these branches presently, but it may be useful to say something first about the way in which they have grown. My habit has always been, if possible, to develop what I write out of a previously successful talk, using the suggestions that have begun to develop in discussion with an actual audience, rather than writing an article to be printed in a journal and then reading it out at a meeting. And in preparing the talk in the first place I would first look for a subject that I myself thought was really important, and then, in working on it, I would try to make the reasons for its importance clear at once to people hearing about it for the first time. This means sticking as close as possible to everyday language, not in the interests of dumbing-down but so as to show how the topic arises out of its context.

Once I have prepared the talk, I then use it, if I can, for a number of different audiences. I start to write it down only when I am fairly satisfied that the point of it is getting over to those who hear it, and have digested their comments. If, at that stage, there still seems to be plenty more to be said on the subject, I may start to expand it till – often by joining itself to several other related talks – it eventually turns into a book.

I am not claiming, of course, to have invented this habit. No doubt plenty of other people work in this way. But it is the opposite to the method that is almost forced on many academics today, where a paper must be written primarily to get printed as a reply to existing articles in the journals. It is read out to a live audience only as a kind of necessary checking process, to get certain obvious objections out of the way before it goes to the journal's referees. After that – with luck – it may hope to achieve the real point of its existence, which is to get printed, whether or not anyone then has the time to read it. At a meeting, papers composed on these principles can be recognized at once when their authors start to read them out and they don't have an encouraging effect on their audience.

An example of the difference this approach makes may be helpful. In the early 1980s the Forum for Science and Religion (an admirable concern, which I later chaired for a while) asked me to speak at a conference on 'Evolution and Religion'. Yes, thought I, but what about evolution *as* a religion . . .? So I talked about that, and it went down well. I later spoke about it to other audiences, who all made such good suggestions about it that in the end it grew into a book with that title. Then, as time went on, I came across yet more astonishing material about quasi-scientific myths and ideologies which I also spoke about and then discussed in another book, called *Science as Salvation*. The ideas behind these two books, ideas which still seem to me quite important, would certainly never have struck me if I had simply been keeping my eye on the controversies that were running at the time.

After *Beast and Man* my main line of thinking about human nature went ahead through *Heart and Mind* – which is chiefly about the contrast between Feeling and Reason – and then through *Wickedness* and *Can't We Make Moral Judgments?* which both try to understand the nastier parts of our nature, on to *The Ethical Primate*, which is chiefly about the nature of human freedom.

One side branch from this main line has dealt with the strange myths and symbols which I sometimes encountered, rather to my surprise, when I read supposedly scientific books about topics such as evolution. This branch runs through the two books just mentioned – *Evolution as a Religion* and *Science as Salvation* – and goes on through *Science and Poetry* and *The Myths We Live By*, which both explore the positive uses of our imagination as well as its dangers.

Another side branch investigates the notion of philosophy itself and how it relates to the search for wisdom, which is its traditional topic. The books on this branch are *Wisdom, Information and Wonder* and *Utopias, Dolphins and Computers*. This last is actually a book about 'applied philosophy' – how we should apply philosophy to practical problems. But in order to persuade people to read it I decided to give it a more cheerful title than *Applied Philosophy* by drawing on the topics of some of the chapters in it – Utopias, etc. This caused trouble when it was translated into Spanish. The translator wrote in some distress, telling me that he did not think Spanish readers were actually much interested in computers. Would I mind, therefore, if he called the book *Delfines, sexo y utopias*? I worried about this a bit, but I finally decided that, as the book did indeed, like so many books, contain some discussions of sex, this would not be too misleading. I let him go ahead.

There are also two books that are more directly concerned with ethics – with how we ought to behave as well as with how we ought to think. *Animals and Why They Matter* deals with the moral aspect of our relation to other species. As soon as I formed the views about animals that I expressed in *Beast and Man* I knew that I ought to write something about this. On the practical side, I did do a good deal of campaigning on behalf of animals – for instance I served for some years on the RSPCA's committee on animal experimentation, and for a time I chaired it. I also wrote articles and letters to the papers on particular issues. But other things kept distracting me from writing at length on the matter. So I was glad when, in 1980, Ted Honderich asked me to write a book about animals for a series that he was editing. It was published as a Penguin paperback which came out in 1981.

Another topic that I always meant to get around to was feminism. Here too a commission finally made me do it, though the results were less fortunate. In 1982 the Social Democratic Party, then launching itself as a separate ginger group that hoped to reform the Labour Party, started commissioning books and it asked me to write something on women. I agreed to do this along with my friend Judith Hughes who, being twenty years younger than me, was much better qualified than I was to discuss contemporary difficulties. She had originally been one of our students and she went on to become a most interesting philosopher – at one time she taught for us in the Department.

Judith and I wrote what I still think was a rather shrewd diagnosis, centring on the difficulties that afflict the attempt to combine the two central ideals of feminism – equality and sisterhood. This combination, we said, is tricky because one of these ideals (equality) points towards trying to be like men while the other (sisterhood) points away from doing so. On practical matters, our chief suggestion was the need for much fuller development of part-time work, to help women (and indeed men) to bridge the gap between full-time domesticity and full-time paid employment. I still think this development is essential, and I haven't seen much progress towards it since our book *Women's Choices* came out.

However, by the time when it appeared in 1983, the SDP was already in serious trouble and was becoming quite unpopular. This was probably one reason why the book got practically no reviews and very little attention, though the fact that it wasn't extreme or melodramatic won't have helped either. It did sell for a time and quite a lot of people found it helpful. But it died a natural death and it is now the only one of my books that is not in print.

Family movements; Geoff's activities

While I wrote these various books I also went to no end of conferences, many of them abroad, and I did a fair amount of journalism, mainly reviewing. But before chasing up these activities it will be best catch up with the family story.

Until 1971 we lived very comfortably in our three-storey house near Jesmond Dene, which we had moved into in 1961. We mostly used its top floor for student lodgers, who babysat for us and many of whom remained our friends for long afterwards. The wife of one of these, Maureen King, who had a baby while she was there, managed to see the notes of the midwife who attended her and she says that they were headed, 'Academic Squalor'. This will certainly have been a good description of both households, but on the whole the arrangement worked well.

In 1971 however my mother died and we invited my father to come and live with us and take over the top flat. We altered it in various ways to accommodate him, and he lived there for some months, but it wasn't a very good arrangement. There were too many stairs and he didn't have a separate bathroom. So, when the larger house at the end of the terrace came up for sale we all went to look at it.

This house turned out to be surprisingly suitable, being already divided – it had a separate downstairs flat – and having plenty of room upstairs for our family. So we bought it for £7000, a price which then seemed terribly high, though my father helped us with it. (Today it seems absurdly small; I suppose it might just about buy you a second-hand toolshed in a London suburb.) My father, however, moved into his flat and lived there quite successfully for a time, after which, with his usual enterprise, he decided to get married again. His bride was a very nice widow whom he had long known and who had fortunately not moved out of the big family house in which she lived at Teddington. This is close to Kingston, so it took him back to people and places that he knew well. They lived together very happily there until he died, rather suddenly, six years later.

His marriage left us with the downstairs flat, which we let to a succession of tenants over the next years. I always found this letting troublesome to look after and I certainly wasn't tempted, as so many people now seem to be, to become involved any further in property management. Then, in 1989, we found that a change in the law had made it possible to sell part of a house on its own. So we sold the upper two floors that we had been living in and moved into the downstairs flat ourselves. It was now quite big enough for us and we had had enough of running up and down stairs. Besides, the flat has the lion's share of the garden. I still live there today.

Meanwhile, during the 1960s, the Midgley household's artistic interests had been shifting from drama to music. The Staff Dramatic Society had gradually declined as the university's wider social life fell off. At the same time, Geoff began to take an interest in my Herwiga tenor recorder, which I had played with various consorts in Oxford, and he wanted to look into the matter further. We found other people who played recorders and quickly bought, and began to play, the whole set, including a rather impressive bass. This led to involvement in other kinds of chamber music and made Geoff remember that he had always wanted to play the oboe. He got one, took lessons and soon became deeply involved with it. He played in various local orchestras and started to go to Edinburgh regularly for lessons with Evelyn Rothwell, who later said that he was the best non-professional oboist she had known. For a long time he played first oboe in the University Orchestra. When that orchestra brought in outside soloists for works like the Bach Passion music, he regularly played second oboe while Leon Goossens played first and he got to know him well. He asked Goossens one time whether he still got nervous. Goossens said, 'Yes – you have no idea how, once you're supposed to be famous, people watch for you to make mistakes.'

The oboe is a most demanding instrument. On top of a great deal of practice, it needs incessant attention to its reeds, which never satisfy the player and need constant work to adjust them. Geoff worked at it like a demon. And it was not the only thing that occupied him at this time. A little later he also began to take a serious interest in computers. I suppose it was some time in the late 1950s or early 1960s that the university Physics Department managed to get one of these new machines and proudly showed it off to all comers. As he was being led round the impressive gleaming array of metal cupboards, shown the programs and told how the thing worked, Geoff frowned and said, 'Yes, I see. But wouldn't it be quicker to do it like this?' It turned out that indeed it was – a great deal quicker, several thousand times quicker in fact, and this was the beginning of a deep association.

He took to these machines like a duck to water and occupied himself with them a great deal from then on, partly using them for his own logic and partly for other projects in the rest of the university or in the hospital, where he worked at one point on a device for allowing paralysed people to operate a keyboard. For a long time our house was festooned with reels of the yellow, blue and white punched-tape which computers used to eat at that time. (It came in quite handy for Christmas decorations.) One way and another, our three sons all learned these skills very early, just as they also picked up a good deal of philosophy which they all quite liked, though only David wanted to go in for this professionally. They took the electronic culture for granted and have made their livings by it for much of their adult lives. Thus they can usually rescue me when my word-processor gets the better of me, which happens all too often because I depended on Geoff for so long that I am still not very spry at controlling it.

Geoff greatly enjoyed this whole activity. But he got very annoyed when people showed awe at the computers themselves, for instance by calling them intelligent machines. 'Nonsense!' he would groan. 'They're not intelligent. They're STUPID! You've no idea how stupid they are. They're THICK!' He thought them most useful tools for lighting up the deep caverns of logic that he was always exploring, and also sometimes useful for everyday purposes. But they could only be useful (he said) when the people in charge of them were asking exactly the right questions, and this was rare. That (he explained) was why, much of the time, a computer was just a device which, if you worked on it for three months, would do in ten minutes what would otherwise have taken you a week.

He really hated Microsoft.

Where, you may wonder, did Geoff get the time to do these things? The answer is that he had stopped trying to write philosophical articles. It was not that he had lost interest in philosophy. Far from that, philosophy interested him more than ever. He taught it, talked it, read it and thought it all the time, whatever else he was doing. But he had indeed lost interest in the journals, which often seemed to him to be going round in circles. He greatly preferred reading and rereading and worrying about Kant and Wittgenstein and talking about their problems with other people to answering the recent articles. So he did most of his philosophizing in the department.

Plato, though he wrote quite a number of books himself, said some things about book-writing which rather support Geoff's view of the matter. In the *Phaedrus* he shows Socrates – who indeed didn't write books and may well have held this view of them – as saying:

> The fact is, Phaedrus, that writing involves a similar disadvantage to painting. The productions of painting look like living beings, but if you ask them a question they maintain a solemn silence. The same holds true of written words: you might suppose that they understand what they are saying, but if you ask them what they mean by anything they simply return the same answer over and over again. Besides, once a thing is committed to writing it

circulates equally among those who understand the subject and those who have no business with it; a writing cannot distinguish between suitable and unsuitable readers. It is quite incapable of defending or helping itself.

(p. 275)

In his Seventh Letter (section 344) Plato put the point still more strongly in his own person, saying that books are bound to be misleading. It is only in living dialogue, 'when questions and answers are exchanged in good faith and without malice that finally, when human capacity is stretched to its limit, a spark of understanding and intelligence flashes out and illuminates the subject at issue'.

Clearly Plato didn't always feel like this, since he went on writing books all his life. Still, in an age when we are swimming in print, both on paper and on screens, all the time we can see that he does have a point. As for Geoff, I think that it is really a great pity that he didn't make the effort to attend to recent philosophizings more and to say why those circles weren't necessary. He probably would have done that if Karl Britton, now head of our department, had put a bit of pressure on him to do it, as Findlay had done. Karl, however, rather shared Geoff's views on the matter. Though he was a very able philosopher himself and did publish the required articles, he had been powerfully influenced by his time in Wittgenstein's class at Cambridge. Wittgenstein thought highly of Karl and told him sternly, as he always did tell people he thought highly of, that he must on no account take up philosophy as a profession. (Wittgenstein didn't actually want anyone to do philosophy except himself, and he, of course, mostly did it, as Socrates did, by word of mouth, not by publishing articles.)

Karl rightly defied this ban. He philosophized well himself and on the whole he ran the department very well too. He wrote interesting things about John Stuart Mill, and also a delightful little book called *Philosophy and the Meaning of Life*, which has helped a lot of people both inside and outside the subject – or, as Karl himself put it once in a talk, 'both those just launched on philosophy and those who are already at sea'. But he remained a worried man, always prone to guilt, inner uncertainty and gastric ulcers, which occasionally made him jumpy. At times Geoff's forthrightness got him down. What is remarkable, and I think does Karl enormous credit, is that, though he was a quiet man whose approach was quite different from Geoff's, he took the trouble to get Geoff (and indeed myself as well) promoted to the status of Senior Lecturer. I think that must have been quite hard even then, and is unimaginable today for people who did not have to their name the longest possible string of publications.

What, meanwhile, was Geoff actually doing in the department? I want to show just what did occupy him because it's the sort of thing which today's climate in universities – and indeed in schools – seems deliberately arranged to prevent. Administrators now see teaching as a minor activity, essentially just a form of transport for information, a process of dropping ready-made material (updated by the latest research) into holes already prepared to receive it. Research itself is believed to be the only source of new thought.

In the physical sciences a lot of teaching has indeed long been of this simple transmissive kind. That is why so few students now want to specialize in these subjects. But it isn't any more appropriate in science than it is anywhere else. This is the approach that has caused the 'public understanding of science' to sink to a level that is causing real alarm. In the humanities, it is much harder to teach in that remote way. But if you decide to do it it can be done, and increasingly the idea that this kind of impersonal teaching is more 'scientific' has caused the habit to spread, especially in universities, along with the exaltation of research and the demand for endless publications.

That is not how Geoff taught. At this point I must simply quote from some of the tributes that came in about him after his death in 1997. This is tricky because of course all obituaries tend to look alike. But I shall pick a few from the great pile of articles and letters that were sent then because they seem to make distinctive points that are worth noticing. Here is part of an obituary from the *Guardian*, written by our colleague Willie Charlton:

> In Geoffrey Midgley, who has died aged 75, philosophy has lost not just one of its most colourful exponents but a much more distinguished and influential one than his publications might suggest. In appearance somewhat like a Rabelaisian version of Michael Foot (with whose politics he was in warm sympathy) he had an explosive laugh, frequent bursts of which indicated to people far beyond the bounds of his department of philosophy that business there was proceeding as usual. Yet *that business was entirely serious* . . . His contribution to the emergence of the new analytical philosophy was two long papers articulating the central concept of a linguistic rule – work which laid the foundation on which contemporary philosophers such as John Searle have been able to build an intelligible account of language. He was, however, set slightly apart from other Oxford philosophers of the time by his deep respect for such then unfashionable metaphysical thinkers as Aquinas and Aristotle. And by a strong conviction that philosophy was not just a game with words . . .
>
> In 1949 he went to Newcastle and began what was to be *his main work for philosophy*, building up a model of what a small department in a non-collegiate university should be. Every day he managed to spend several hours in informal discussion with students, while his unselfconscious way of combining old-fashioned good manners with the politics of the radical left helped to prevent barriers from arising between students of different backgrounds.

> He also managed to convince them, and this was excellent for morale, that philosophy was the best of all academic subjects. *He taught formal and philosophical logic more efficiently than I have seen it taught anywhere else, and, at the same time, in his informal sessions, showed that every question has a philosophical angle* . . . Midgley published nothing after his first seminal articles, and thought that since philosophers are not, like scientists or historians, trying to discover new facts, publication was not an essential part of philosophical work. That centred on teaching, not just as a way of passing on tradition, but as a constant shared revision of the ideas by which we live . . . When Midgley retired in 1986 there were twenty applications for every place in his department. (Emphases mine.)

David McNaughton, a student of ours who later became Professor of Philosophy at Keele, wrote in the *Independent*:

> Midgley's engagement with philosophy was both immediate and intense. Most lecturers rehearse doctrines and arguments to their audience, but Geoff Midgley engaged in philosophical thought before our eyes. Bounding into the lecture theatre with an air of boyish enthusiasm, longish white locks bobbing, no notes in sight, he would plunge into some philosophical problem without preliminaries. What made it so gripping for the audience was the freshness of the performance. There was no feeling of going over old ground . . . each lecture was for Midgley a new experience, a fresh attempt to get to grips with something that puzzled him . . . Midgley published nothing after those two papers (although often urged to do so by his students). He devoted himself instead to making the department a model of what a philosophy department should be; a centre of uninhibited intellectual enquiry and ceaseless discussion.
>
> Tutorials were conducted in his room, which was dominated by a large table, on which assorted items, reflecting his many interests, were piled to an alarming height. From time to time he would leap up and plunge into the tottering edifice to pull out some plum: a quotation, a paragraph from a book, a letter from someone. He would adopt a similar approach to the contents of his own mind, searching for some gem which would illuminate the whole discussion and producing it triumphantly for our edification. *He showed that one can be utterly serious while roaring with laughter at the same time.*

Letters from past students fill in all sorts of backgrounds to this. Here are bits from some of them:

> I don't think I can name another person who has had so much effect – certainly not such a beneficial one – on my mind, the way I think, and therefore my life. More than anyone, he helped me win through my struggle with the ferocious indoctrination in Catholicism which was my upbringing;

no one who has not experienced that straitjacket can imagine the liberation of getting away from it. Not that that was all, of course. Philosophy is much, much more.

He made Logic fun. I'm sure that I would not have opted to take Logic for a second year otherwise. I took several friends who were studying other subjects (even at other universities!) to Geoff's lectures for the pleasure of them . . . One of the great things about the philosophy department as Newcastle, with its 'Cave', was that it was small enough to be personal. I'm sure many students have happy memories of sitting there listening to one of Geoff's many anecdotes, which he seemed able to produce on cue to illustrate whatever point had come up in conversation.

All my memories of Geoff are filled with that enthusiasm and infectious exuberance which I'm sure everyone else remembers too. I suppose there were times when I sensed a darker, more depressive side (perhaps because I was struggling with my own at the time) but I don't think any of us really knew anything of that . . . There was this remarkable knack of ending each session on a problematic note, so you just had to come along next time to discover the resolution.

I have such happy memories of him – as, for instance, his illustrating some point about the nature of mistakes by showing us that he couldn't fall accidentally out of his window into the quad on purpose, his mixture of mysteriousness and broad grins when our degree results were almost due but couldn't be given to us, and so on . . .

I have never known anyone who poured out the riches of his intelligence in such profusion, with no thought of academic amour-propre or status, to any one who wanted to talk. How many times, also, have I made some point hesitatingly or feebly – to have it rephrased by him, polished, made cogent and strong, so that I thought, gosh, did I say that? Nothing can erase Geoff's influence on thousands of students.

It must have taken considerable acting skills to seize on ancient philosophical problems with such a bull-terrier-like intensity, as if the truth was about to be shaken out at last . . . [thus], in a lecture on Wittgenstein, 'The builder says, "Bring those bricks". The other chap brings them, and that's meaning.' Then a cunning glance at his student audience . . . Perhaps the inherent *anarchy* of philosophy is what makes this wonderful subject so unpopular with the powers that be. Philosophy teaches people to think – and that's dangerous.

Of course the student who detected a darker, more depressive side was right. Nobody exuberates as effectively as Geoff did without going down as far as they come up. He said to me quite soon after we met, 'You see, I'm really a manic-depressive. You shouldn't worry if I don't seem to be very happy; that's not to be expected'. But – unlike some depressives – he never took the gloomy side out in his teaching.

He used to illustrate the inner switchback effect by a story about his landlady when he first came to Newcastle. One day he was having a cup of tea with her and they were looking at the newspaper, which was full of dismal stories about the Cold War and the hydrogen bomb. Totally plunged in gloom, he exclaimed, 'The world is too horrible! If we had a button we could press that would finally blow the whole thing up, which of us would be able to help pressing it?' 'Oh, I wouldn't', said she. 'I'm terrified of electric things.' This, he reported, thoroughly cheered him up and restored his faith in human nature.

Of course the tributes that I have been quoting are not unique. Past students have always acknowledged debts like this to their teachers. Indeed most lives of successful people mention some such experience and probably the administrators who devise the current schemes had such influential teachers themselves in their time. No doubt they don't mean to obstruct this kind of influence now. But the patterns they are imposing on schools and universities make it terribly hard for the thing to work. Today's academics, harassed by insecurity of tenure, short contracts and the need to apply for future positions – preoccupied by league tables, impending assessments and grant applications – frequently asked to write long reports whose purpose is often mysterious – constantly needing to keep up their flood of publications – cannot possibly give students the kind of whole-hearted attention that they used to get from teachers like Geoff.

If the administrators were told this, they might, of course, just sigh and say that it can't be helped. Old-fashioned personal attention is, they would say, a luxury, an optional extra that the busy modern age can't afford. But the remarks that I have emphasized in Willie's and David's articles show how wrong that is. Geoff's jokes weren't a distraction or a substitute for real thinking. They were the punch that brought it home. The cheerful logic classes were a sign not of skiving but of logic taught effectively. One reason for this may have been that they went right back to essentials. As a student once said to Geoff, 'You are now answering questions which I was put in detention for asking in a maths lesson when I was thirteen'. It all made things make sense.

A colleague from a much larger and grander department, who had shared in our examining, remarked on this after Geoff's death. He wrote:

> He was able to make students feel at ease and to give them confidence in territory that generally scares them into immobility. Geoff brought out the

best in his pupils and got results of a kind that were not being achieved at all in my own department, whose star-studded (as they thought) logicians were constantly reducing their charges to nervous wrecks.

How did it all work out later? Well, our students got perfectly satisfactory degrees and went on, like others, to all sorts of careers or non-careers as they chose (including teaching philosophy). Many became our lasting friends. Many surfaced again years later with the most amazing stories, often saying things like 'You see, that's when I really began to see how useful philosophy is'.

Darker weather; survival strategies

In this way things went on quite cheerfully during the 1970s. In 1971 Mike Brearley went off to captain Middlesex at cricket, and five years later he became captain of the England team. He held that position with great distinction for most of seven years, including a particularly exciting win over Australia against heavy odds in 1981. When he finally retired he wrote an excellent book about the problems of the post called *The Art of Captaincy*.

We were all very sad to lose Mike. But we knew that for some time he had been torn, as people are who are very good at two things, trying to divide his life between them. Eventually cricket had won. I remember a lecturer in another department being much shocked that any academic should make such a choice, but certainly none of his immediate colleagues felt like that about it. We saw his point entirely. We consoled ourselves by taking in Jane Heal, a lively young philosopher of language. Jane had all sorts of good effects and she greatly improved our sex ratio, shifting it from 1 in 6 to 1 in 3. She left us ten years later, thus saddening us further, to go to a post at St John's College, Cambridge, where she is still busy and thriving today. She soon served as President of her college and she is now a professor there.

As for me, I was getting increasingly busy, and I was at last publishing things where other philosophers could see them. During that decade three of my articles (besides the two already mentioned) appeared in *Philosophy*, a hospitable journal which has always liked to print things that are of wider interest.[4] Two more appeared in the *Supplementary Volumes of the Proceedings of the Aristotelian Society*.[5]

These articles, along with my journalism, led to my getting invited to talk in all sorts of places, both inside and outside universities. In particular I was (and still am) often asked to speak at interdisciplinary conferences where people were

[4] 'The Game Game' in 1974, 'The Objection to Systematic Humbug' in 1978 and 'Gene-Juggling' in 1979.

[5] The Neutrality of the Moral Philosopher' in 1974 and 'The Absence of a Gap Between Facts and Values' in 1980.

trying to sort out the relations between different ways of thinking, notably between science and the humanities. I found myself involved in a lot of places, as I had been at Cornell, with a bewildering mix of people from different backgrounds, talking different languages but genuinely trying to understand one another. This is much harder than it looks, but if the learned world is not to split apart into a batch of mutually unintelligible specialisms it does seem that we must try to manage it.

When *Beast and Man* came out in 1978 the flow of invitations increased. They began coming from America and Europe as well as from Britain, and I accepted quite a lot of them. These meetings were often very good value, but – not very surprisingly – towards the end of the 1970s I found that I was really beginning to get extremely tired. Just at that time, too, universities began to bring in arrangements for letting members of staff retire at sixty without losing their pension rights. In 1980 I decided that it was sensible to take advantage of this and to go before I got completely exhausted.

The relief of retiring was enormous. I had been desperately tired, and in particular I heaved a great sigh of pleasure at no longer being involved in administration. I am really bad at this, and I had been haunted all along by the fear that some day I would mess up spectacularly. I would put students in for the wrong course, I would find that they hadn't got their exam forms, or their references or their testimonials, or I would fail to cope with one of the alarming emergencies about them that so often surfaced, usually at the end of the afternoon just when I was hoping to go home to get tea for the children.

A small example of these crises floats up in my mind. One afternoon I was suddenly rung by the Vice-Chancellor's secretary, who told me in an awed and hesitant voice a story that she clearly found incredible. It seemed that a girl to whom I was tutor had actually come up to the Vice-Chancellor after a degree-giving ceremony and had cheerfully invited him to a party next Saturday, saying, as she turned away, 'Bring a bottle!'

Was this girl (the secretary delicately enquired) perhaps mentally somewhat unhinged, not fully responsible for her actions? If that was the case, the V-C (who was an eminent medic) would of course be understanding about it. He would gladly arrange an emergency appointment for her at once in the psychiatric department at the hospital . . . Meanwhile, would I please discuss the matter *at once* with the head of my department and report back quickly on what action we were taking to deal with the emergency?

It took us some time to get hold of the girl, and a great deal longer to calm down the administration. We had somehow to break it to them that the girl's friends had simply bet her that she wouldn't dare to do this, and that she (being full of the initiative and enterprise that young people are urged to show) had promptly gone off and done it. Eventually the matter was allowed to lapse somehow without any of us actually getting psychiatric assistance. But it was clear that one more black mark, and a heavy one, had been added to the score that was already piling up against the Philosophy Department.

This brings us to the gloomy topic that occupied us during most of the 1980s – the storm clouds already gathering over British universities, the factors that were destined to close our department, along with six other philosophy departments in the country, by the end of the decade. When I took the decision to leave, it never struck me that there was anything sinister about the new scheme that allowed my early retirement. Only gradually did it emerge during the 1980s that this was the first step in a political campaign, rapidly developed by Margaret Thatcher, to pare down public support for the universities, to cut off their less profitable branches and, so far as possible, to force them to pay for themselves. If I had suspected then how these things were going to work out, perhaps I might have felt that I ought to stay to try and help in resisting them. But I couldn't have made any difference to the outcome.

I can't discuss here the wider political and economic background of this campaign. This is my own story and I must just report how things looked to us from the receiving end. It soon became clear to us that, increasingly often, people who retired, whether early or otherwise, were simply not being replaced. Posts, even obviously crucial posts, were being left empty. After a time this made it possible for the university administration to claim that the department involved had now become weak and ineffectual, that in fact it was already too small to be much use and had better be closed. When they were asked why this would be better than restoring it to its former strength, the authorities replied that small departments were anyway feeble and inefficient. The proper system would be to have just a few 'centres of excellence' for every subject – a series of large specialized departments, each in its own university, each engaged in top-level 'cutting-edge research' and therefore qualified to monopolize the study in question.

This idea always seemed to us to be pure fantasy. It obviously ignored the teaching angle altogether, disregarding the fact that students usually need to study more than one subject, often several more, whether as subsidiaries, or in joint and general degrees, or when they want to change courses. This neglect was probably deliberate because the idea was that teaching did not much matter anyway. Attention was now to be concentrated on prestigious research, preferably directed towards Nobel Prizes and resulting in dazzling new technology. But this made no sense there either. Apart from the occasional need to share expensive machines such as cyclotrons, researchers don't necessarily get on any better in huge monocultures than they do in mixed environments. Researchers, as well as students, often need to talk to people from other backgrounds, and that talk is often the source of crucial new ideas. In fact, they often need to get ideas by teaching – that is, by talking to students.

In fact, the whole habit of dividing academic study into fixed disciplines is much more a matter of administrative convenience than of intellectual necessity.

The ways in which subjects are divided often change and original thinkers constantly move between them. The demand for strict monoculture does not come from the scholars (though any set of academics who are told that they constitute a centre of excellence will probably not reject the idea). The real demand for segregation comes from the administrators and, above all, from the accountants.

It is much more troublesome – and therefore more expensive – to administer a mix of varying and relatively independent entities than a few homogeneous groupings that work as coherent empires. The principle here is actually much the same one that is followed in foreign policy, where big nations (however much they say they want democracy) always like to encourage strong governments rather than continuing debates in the small nations that they have to deal with. And in universities the administrative tail is now so heavy that it regularly wags the rest of the academic dog, so this preference has become crucial.

That was how the process that began in the 1980s looked to us at the time, and, though I can't say much about its wider background, perhaps it is just worth while to glance at how it seems to be working out today. Here, then, are a few extracts from a leading article about it by John Crace in the *Guardian*'s Education Supplement for 23 March 2004:

> To most observers, higher education is already effectively a free market. Every university has the right to choose what courses it offers, *every department has become a cost-centre in its own right*. University competes with university for students, and supply and demand largely determine a department's survival . . . [Among many other closures] this year, Durham rubber-stamped the closure of its prestigious department of East Asian Studies, along with linguistics and European Studies, while *its Institute for Middle Eastern and Islamic Studies kissed goodbye to its undergraduate intake* . . . A combination of market forces and a strict funding regime inevitably determines the delivery of higher education . . . [As a Vice-Chancellor puts it,] 'We need to focus on areas of research and teaching where we have critical mass . . . [*chemistry*] *is now too small to have critical mass*' . . . [A critic comments] 'Departments can see which are in surplus and which are in deficit. Those in surplus, typically cheap-to-teach subjects such a law, business studies, English and history, have the power, as big departments, to demand all the resources they are "earning". *There is no scope for the old cross-subsidization*' . . . Modern languages and some humanities subjects are regularly under the cosh, but perhaps *the two biggest losers have been physics and chemistry* . . . [Physics departments have declined] by over 30% since 1994 . . . East Anglia is now a virtual physics desert . . . Chemistry is now crashing on the same rocks. There are currently between 35 and 40 departments in the UK, but the Royal Society of Chemistry is predicting

> that at best 20, and at worst six, will remain in 10 years time . . . Chemistry is an expensive subject to teach . . . There is a tremendous demand for chemistry graduates in some areas of the country, but the recruits just aren't there. (Emphases mine.)

How, we may ask, can anybody have chosen the present moment to cut down on Middle Eastern and Islamic Studies? And again, who would have thought, a couple of decades back, that those two apparently secure scientific empires named at the end would soon face this fate, that they would be the ones deemed not to have this mysterious quality of *critical mass* (anglice, profitability)?

But that is what has happened. Newcastle University's grand Physics Building, once the pride of the place, once housing the department where the cosmologist Paul Davies was a professor, a building designed by Basil Spence and duly opened with much civic pomp in the 1970s, is not called the Physics Building any longer. There are a few physicists still left there, but they are expected to move to Durham shortly. Then there won't be a physics department. 'You can't have a university without a physics department!', people say incredulously, just as they used to say, 'But you surely can't have a university without a philosophy department?'

Such notions are gone. In the 1980s, the talk about centres of excellence was supposed to meet this difficulty by arranging that every subject would be safe. Each was to find its own monocultural home. All the physics would be done at Cambridge or perhaps at Manchester, all the Naval Architecture at Newcastle, all the Philosophy, no doubt, at Oxford, and so on . . . But the new idea of treating each individual department as a cost centre in its own right, a distinct entity which must have financial 'critical mass' to compete with all the others – a firm that must show more profit than they do on the balance sheet of its own university – rules out any such provision.

This principle of avoiding cross-subsidization – of enforcing stark competition between the mutually dependent elements in an organic whole – is an extremely strange one. Nobody seems to have heard of symbiosis. If local town councils took up this idea, they would presumably set up contests like this between their own departments. They would reason that they should always favour the activities that bring in the most money, such as tax-collection and the sale of school playing-fields, and should run down those tiresome elements that only seem to spend the stuff, such as education and the police . . . This might lead to unpopular results. But it is just an example of the well-known paradox of liberty – namely, that if everybody is free to do exactly what they want separately the effects are sometimes ones which nobody at all would ever have dreamed of wanting. And such effects can be very hard to reverse.

It is clear in hindsight that the decision to transform the universities had been taken long before Mrs Thatcher's government actually took power in 1979, and that this was always intended to involve widespread destruction of small departments. If that decision could have been declared from the start the people concerned would have been saved a lot of misery, but of course it wasn't. The façade of consultation was strenuously kept up. Academic staff were forced to waste endless time composing reports and discussing suggested alternative schemes. At first the burden of doing this fell mainly on Colin Strang, who had succeeded Karl as Professor in 1975. But in 1984 Colin himself retired and was not replaced as professor; his post, like so many others, was left empty. This reduced the department's staff from six to five – a dangerously low level – and left Geoff to function as Head of Department without holding a chair. This was then rather a rare arrangement and it always weakened a department's status.

Geoff therefore had to contend, for two horrible years, with the responsibility for conducting nominal negotiations for survival that were pretty obviously doomed to fail. He kept his head and dealt with them soberly and carefully, making the most of each opportunity that seemed to offer, until his own retirement in 1986. But this painful process exhausted him deeply and threw him into a depression that lasted over much of the next three years. This was before the days when everybody had to take anti-depressants, and anyway he didn't go much for doctors. The therapy that he mostly used for it was to lie on the floor playing endless games of patience in front of a Western blaring away on the television. I remember his doing a great deal of this during the time before we moved downstairs in 1989.

Readers will perhaps have noticed that I myself (by contrast) rather like to make the best of things. Usually, indeed, I am a bit of a Pollyanna. Geoff, who preferred to make the worst of them, thought I was far too much of one. But there is no way of making the best of these years. It was a very bad time. Being retired, I was mostly just an appalled spectator as our own department went under and other departments were massacred nationwide. But I wrote letters to the papers about it and also some articles, and in the summer of 1986 I took the less usual step of writing a personal letter to all the distinguished philosophers I could think of saying 'do please do something about this destruction'.

My first idea was that they ought to be writing to *The Times* (which was then – though it is not now – still the natural forum for serious and urgent views). The only person who actually did this was A. J. Ayer, whose admirable letter of protest appeared in *The Times* for 12 August 1986. There is, however, something faintly ironic about this, since Ayer's own book *Language, Truth and Logic* had actually been a strong source of the contempt for philosophy that was now being so widely shown. But Ayer had long moved away from that simple position. Isaiah Berlin replied sympathetically but said he was too old and ill to take up the matter. Various other people said they would take various steps and no doubt they did so. But what I found most striking was the response from a couple of eminent philosophers at Oxford. They both said that they really did not see the need for all these philosophy departments. In their view philosophy was no use unless it was done well and (by implication, though this was not spelt out) most of these departments were surely doing it incompetently, so they did not need to be preserved. In short, they apparently endorsed the government's destructive notion that 'centres of excellence' were enough – an attitude that I still find appalling.

Apart from this worry, during the 1980s I went on doing the things that I had always done – reading and writing books and articles, talking to all sorts of people, going to conferences, visiting friends and sons, going swimming, drawing and painting, cooking meals, gardening, looking after cats, playing Scrabble. Some time in this decade I acquired my only police record, getting arrested for obstruction at an anti-nuclear demonstration sitting down outside the American base at Upper Heyford in Oxfordshire. I had meant to go on from this event to visit Iris, who then lived nearby at Steeple Aston, but instead I found myself taken off in a bus along with a lot of other people to Banbury Police Station. I was bailed there and later tried in a very reasonable court which allowed each defendant to say why we had thought it right to make the protest. The court imposed a small fine which I paid, not feeling inclined to make a bigger issue of it by going to prison.

I do not know why the law should have decided to arrest me at the Upper Heyford demo rather than at one of the others that I had attended over the years. I particularly remember one anti-apartheid procession in Newcastle where I did worry a bit about this because Tommy and David, then eleven and nine, had decided to come on it with me and I wasn't sure how this would work out. In fact they got into a very friendly conversation at once with one of the policemen in charge of us and things went well. I don't overestimate the effect that these protests have, but I think they are still worth making. My back won't stand them now, however, so I have given them up.

There was something rather quaint about intending to combine a visit to Iris with that anti-nuclear protest, because this was the time when she was in full reaction against the politics of her youth and was currently voting for Mrs Thatcher.

This was also the time when I began to take a serious interest in the concept of Gaia. I thought this was a very sensible idea when I first heard about it in the early 1970s by reading James Lovelock's book *Gaia: A New Look at Life on Earth*. But as time went on, I saw more and more that it was needed as a complement to my own views on life and evolution. By stressing our total dependence and involvement in the world around us, Gaian thinking roundly shows up the unreality of our recent view of ourselves as independent observers, almost supernatural beings, detached and secure exploiters of God-given natural resources. Some time in the 1980s I met James Lovelock at a conference and we went on to have a lot of discussions, from which he and his wife Sandy have become my fast friends. It was about this time that I wrote one of my few poems – being struck by the strange shape and name of a hill that stands opposite to a friend's house in Grasmere:

Stone Arthur
On a hill above Grasmere, Arthur lies,
Stone nose pointing up, stone feet trailing down the hillside.
At first you don't see him,
You see only jagged rocks,
But then suddenly he's there, he was always there
And people say, 'Of course. Didn't you know?
That hill's Stone Arthur'.

It takes time to see what you aren't looking for
So perhaps we shall have to look more carefully
But when we do, surely that
Is the earth?

Gaian theory has had an interesting career. Though scientists at first treated it as mere fantasy now, after three decades, its scientific aspects have finally become respectable. They have followed the usual course from being treated with dark suspicion to being taken for granted as obvious. Thus there are now many Departments of Earth Science in which the co-operation between biology and geology, which Gaian thinking requires but which was once quite unheard of, goes on all the time.

Scientists, however, are still very shy of acknowledging the source of these ideas by attaching the name Gaia to this approach. They rightly suspect that this might call on them to think about matters that they usually avoid, so they still tend to dismiss the name as something irrelevant, an effete and Californian extra. Other people too often still find the wider philosophical implications of the idea – the effect of it on our conception of ourselves and the cosmos – hard to grasp. This was why I discussed it at some length in the last part of *Science and Poetry*, and also wrote a pamphlet, which was published by Demos, called *Gaia: The Next Big Idea*. There is a lot more work to do here and I shall probably turn to it again.

Domestically, as I have said, Geoff and I finally moved downstairs in 1989. We no longer needed the space of the two upper floors and we were getting tired of running up and down. The sale of the top part financed alterations down below, producing a big comfortable flat with a garden. In the process the door that had formerly connected the two parts of the house was blocked up, a change of which our two cats strongly disapproved. For a long time they sat ostentatiously in front of the new bit of wall, one on each side, looking round reproachfully at us and waiting patiently for us to open it.

But in the end they gave in and, apart from this, on the whole the move was certainly a success. It greatly helped Geoff in coming out of his depression, which he was now beginning to do. I don't remember his playing patience on the floor in front of the television after we got downstairs. Indeed, one of the first things that happened after the move was that the television itself got stolen, the window-locks having apparently been too feeble. Geoff's first thought – making the worst of things as usual – was, 'Dammit we won't get another; they'll only do it again'. But then he thought, 'No, sod 'em, we'll get a *great big one* – one that's too big for them to carry away and too hard for the fences to dispose of. And it'll have better quality reproduction and we'll watch some operas.' This was what happened. We did watch operas, causing Geoff to get really involved in shouting (and indeed writing something) about the right way to interpret Wagner, and the awfulness of various opera productions. And the thieves did get discouraged, whether by the new locks or by the big telly, which is still working today.

He also fixed up his grand stereo system downstairs, getting much interested in the effect of the differently shaped room – not so cubical, therefore better, but still too many armchairs. He used sometimes to hanker for an acoustically correct room with only hard chairs, but I don't know whether he would have liked it if he'd got it. He continued to work at his computer much of the time on various projects and, though he had never been able to draw at all in the ordinary way, at this time he began to use computer graphics occasionally to make fascinating little pictures. The grandchildren who were now coming on the scene interested him very much and he got on well with them. (He was always a great success with babies.) Thus there was an Indian summer, as our son Tom remarked at his funeral:

> In his final years, as his physical health began at last to deteriorate, by some cosmic symmetry the inner conflicts that had caused him so much pain throughout his adult life began to resolve themselves, so that by the time his last illness began, he had achieved a marvellous tranquillity of soul and a complete acceptance of death – for he knew the end was near – which enabled me, at least, to feel, in the midst of my grief and loss on the day of his death, a moment of pure joy on his behalf. He died as he would have wished, with his life in a mysterious way complete and perfect – a man of wisdom and compassion – a truly kind man.

In fact, that owl had been able to find its way through the darkness. Or, as our long-time colleague the historian Alexander Murray put it on the same occasion, 'I hope we all agree here who knew him, Geoffrey died young. In defiance of all normal rules, he died with a mind apparently as fresh as if he had been 19, and first going up to college.'

His health began to fail towards the mid-1990s. A serious chest infection brought back the asthma from which he had occasionally suffered before, and he began to have difficulty in walking uphill. (He had already had to stop playing his oboe because of trouble with teeth.) He got one of those collapsible stools to sit down on and used it for a time when he was out walking. In 1995 he was still able to drive me over to Durham when I went to accept an honorary D.Litt., given me as part of a group of distinguished ladies – including Maya Angelou who was wonderful value – assembled to celebrate the centenary of that university's admitting women. The lunch party after this ceremony was extremely jolly and he much enjoyed it. But soon after this something else, which was never fully understood, went wrong with his legs and made all walking difficult. And in the spring of 1997 he began to get abdominal pains.

Tests suggested that he probably had cancer of the pancreas, which is usually a long and troublesome business. Thinking about this, he said, 'I really don't mind going. I'm 75 and I've had a good life. But I'd certainly like to go quickly.' And, to the surprise of the doctors, that is exactly what he did. On 15 April, only six weeks after the abdominal pains started, he suddenly died.

Since his death I have still gone on living here peacefully, looked after by my sons and friends and doing all of the various things already mentioned, one of which of course has been writing this memoir. Apart from outside matters like global warming and the Iraq war, my life has gone on quite well. My books have begun to be read rather more widely of late, as people have become less attached to the strident extremes of thought that I always opposed. Routledge has now even brought out an anthology from my writings, rather nicely entitled *The Essential Mary Midgley*. But in the life of the actual Mary Midgley there hasn't actually been anything very startling to report. So I think it is probably best to end this memoir here.

Index